MW00777739

Reality
and *Its Dreams*

Reality
and *Its Dreams*

Raymond Geuss

 Harvard University Press

Cambridge, Massachusetts
London, England   *2016*

First printing

Library of Congress Cataloging-in-Publication Data
Geuss, Raymond, author.
  Reality and its dreams / Raymond Geuss.
    pages cm
  Includes bibliographical references and index.
    ISBN 978-0-674-50495-0
    1. Political science—Philosophy.   2. Politics,
Practical.   3. Utopias.   I. Title.
  B65.G48 2016
    320.01—dc23   2015032021

Contents

Preface vii

1 Dystopia: The Elements 1

2 Realism and the Relativity of Judgment 25

3 Chaos and Ethics 51

4 Russell Brand, Lady T, *Pisher* Bob,
and Preacher John 64

5 *The Idea of a Critical Theory*, Forty Years On 79

6 István Hont (1947–2013) 85

7 The Moral Legacy of Marxism 91

8 Economies: Good, Bad, Indifferent 117

9 Can the Humanities Survive Neoliberalism? 148

10 Identification and the Politics of Envy 163

11 Identity, Property, and the Past 184

12 The Future of Evil 204

13 Satire, Who Whom? 218

14 The Radioactive Wolf, Pieing, and the
Goddess Fashion 226

15 What Time Is It? 253

16 Augustine on Love, Perspective,
and Human Nature 261

Notes 279

Index 295

Preface

THE CONTENTS OF our dreams, imaginings, hopes, fantasies, and
inventions should not be mistaken for elements of our waking world.
Nevertheless in another sense dreams, desirous projections, utopian
hopes are a part of our reality. That we have the ones we have is a
fact about us. They do not come from nowhere. As Feuerbach noted,
we imagine the god we need, and so a study of the nature of that god
will tell us a lot about us, our needs, and our situations. Without that
knowledge, we do not know ourselves fully, but part of what we need
to know is from what real source our imaginary constructions arise.
As a response to what real difficulties do we imagine that the world
ought to be other than it is? Rather than following Feuerbach, and
looking for the roots of our moral conceptions and our political
fantasies in the reality of our situation, philosophy in the English-
speaking world has since the 1970s increasingly turned to Kant. Kant
claimed that his Critical Philosophy represented a "Copernican Revolution" in that it vindicated a major shift in the way philosophy was
to proceed and how it was to conceive of what it was doing. Rather
than starting from the world and asking then how human subjects
came to know that world, one needed to reverse the order. It was necessary to begin by studying the conditions of the possibility of

experience, conditions rooted in and prescribed by the nature of the human cognitive subject. These conditions put limits to what we can know and how knowledge must be structured. Only then could one go about the task of studying how the world was constituted, and this would always mean how it was constituted in the light of "the conditions of the possibility of experience." We might say, although Kant would probably not have put it this way, that he preached a priority of epistemology (study of the conditions of the possibility of experience and hence of knowledge) over ontology. Similarly, some philosophers followed the lead of Richard Rorty in thinking there was a parallel "linguistic turn" sometime in the early twentieth century. If all knowledge had to be formulated in a language, it might be thought essential to study the nature of language before embarking on an investigation of what we could know (and a fortiori of how the world was constituted). In political philosophy, finally, one might wish to speak of a similar "normative turn" which took place in the 1970s. Instead of studying human societies, their needs, technologies, specific institutions, cultural forms, and history, as the basic starting point and continuing framework for understanding and evaluating them and for orienting potential political action, most contemporary political philosophers in the English-speaking world turned their attention to a purportedly pure normative realm that could be studied in relative isolation from the messy facts of history and the empirical study of human society. Philosophy being the kind of discipline it is, of course, there is no consensus on the exact status of this realm, how it was internally constituted, and what its relation to real human action should be. Some philosophers think we have moral intuitions and should begin by getting clear about them (although this "clarity" is not to include any knowledge of the origin of these intuitions or the actual social results of holding them); others hold that preparation for a "normative evaluation" of politics is best conducted via a thought experiment in which one imagines anonymous people trying to make decisions under various artificial conditions, such as that they are ignorant of certain facts about the world; some begin with a simple stipulation of a set of "rights" whose status is not really seriously questioned; others favor still other variants. What is common is the systematic exclusion of sociology, real politics, and history in favor of an appeal to some kind of "normativity" which is conceived as being contrasted with them.

It has often been pointed out that Kant's Copernican Revolution was really a counterrevolution. That is, Ptolemy put man in the center of the universe and had the heavenly bodies revolve around him; Copernicus displaced the human subject from this central position. With Kant, however, man (or "the finite rational agent") goes back into the middle as the first and most important object of philosophical attention. So also the "normative turn" is best understood as a counterrevolution against historically and sociologically sophisticated views about ethics and politics developed in the period of Herder and Marx (that is, roughly 1770 to 1850), which continued to represent an important strand of thinking until the normative deluge of the late 1970s and early 1980s. The followers of Herder (as one might call them for the sake of convenience) held that "normative ethical and political conceptions" did not arise from nowhere, as divine commands or ahistorical imperatives of pure reason, and that their origins in historically constituted societies were not always politically and ethically irrelevant.

The chapters in this book are held together by a certain outlook. This is the view that the normative (counter)revolution has been an unmitigated catastrophe for ethics, politics, and the humanities in general. The reasons for the success of "normative approaches" include the failure of the movements for political, social, and economic change of the 1960s, and the especial suitability of normativism as an ideology for the established economic and political structures that, after the challenge of the 1960s, were able to entrench themselves even more firmly than before. It is a constituent part of the view that I am proposing that I can assert this while also claiming that normativism is a cognitively distorting way of looking at society, and also morally and politically reprehensible. This is a consistent thing to say (which is not to say it is true) because I do not accept the sharp dichotomies between History and Normativity, Fact and Value, Ought and Is, Philosophical and Nonphilosophical, Empirical and Rational, which the normativist wishes to impose as preconditions to discussion. The chapters in this book are part of the attempt to see how the world would look if one were to undo the normativist

counterrevolution. This does not mean ignoring or denigrating
human dissatisfaction with the status quo or the human utopian impulse to demand what seems to be impossible.

The first six or seven of the chapters stay close thematically to
topics that are recognizable as central to many forms of political philosophy in the narrow sense of that term, but part of my intention is
to suggest that the traditional focus of the subject is too narrow. I
make no apology then for the fact that the last half a dozen or so
chapters treat issues that do not belong to the recognized standard
inventory of "topics in political philosophy."

Bernard Williams once said to me that the reason he could not
enter "real" politics full-time was that a politician in a democracy
needed to keep repeating himself and a person of either scrupulous
intelligence or lively imagination would find this intolerable. My experience suggests to me that the profession of teaching has some of
the same drawbacks. The prevailing "liberal" conception of democratic politics has a number of well-canvassed weaknesses—it tends
to devalue discrimination between different positions on any grounds
other than that they can muster a majority of the available votes behind themselves: it tends to focus attention of winning elections as
if that were an end in itself rather than simply a sometimes useful
means to get certain things done: it tends to favor those with the
power to control the sources of public information (which, in modern
conditions, means the wealthy, and increasingly, those who control
electronic media).[1] A further weakness is the idea that democratic
politicians should simply "reflect" the will of those who elected them
or of their constituents (assuming that not *all* their constituents voted
for them), rather than trying to shape and educate them. We all know
that politicians do not actually reflect the will of those who voted
for them, the will of their constituents, or the will of "The People"
(as a whole), but that their action is guided by a number of different,
competing, and sometimes incompatible considerations. Still, the
myth of the democratic politician who is simply articulating the existing views of his supporters or constituents, rather than trying to
enlighten them and change their beliefs and attitudes, even their
deeply held convictions, is still powerful. "Ideology" is a term sometimes used for myths of this kind which continue to have an effect,

even though they are false, and are widely half-recognized as false. If politics is to have a pedagogical dimension, then a certain amount of repetition of messages will be essential, assuming one is dealing with a real population with (potentially) other things on their minds and limited powers of concentration. If philosophy is construed as a kind of politics, one in which the educative function is especially marked, a certain amount of repetition need not necessarily be a serious deficiency. So although I have removed some of the repetitions of material and formulation that existed between the chapters of the following collection, each one of which was originally written as a separate paper for a different occasion, after some thought I have allowed some of them to stand for this reason.

Five of the chapters in this collection (1, 3, 6, 10, and 16) have not appeared in print before in any language. Chapter 2 originally appeared in *International Relations*, Vol. 29, No. 1 (March 2015), 3–22. Copyright © 2015 by Raymond Geuss. Reprinted by arrangement with SAGE Publications Ltd. Chapter 4 is an expanded and slightly revised version of an essay first published in *Radical Philosophy* 190 (March–April 2015). Copyright © 2015 by Radical Philosophy Ltd. Chapter 5 is the original English text I wrote as introduction to the translation of my 1981 book *The Idea of a Critical Theory* into Chinese and was published in *The Point*, Issue 8, Summer 2014. Copyright © 2014 by The Point. Chapter 7 was originally published in the October 2015 issue of *Analyse & Kritik: Zeitschrift für Sozialtheorie*, Verlag Lucius & Lucius, 2015 (37), Issue 2. Chapter 8 is an abbreviated, slightly modified version of my article in *Inquiry*, Vol. 55, No. 4, 331–360, August 2012. Copyright © 2012 Routledge, Taylor & Francis Group. Chapter 9 is an English translation I made of an essay I wrote in German entitled "Können die Geisteswissenschaften den Neo-Liberalismus überstehen?" that appeared in *Die Bildung der Moderne* by Michael Dreyer, Michael Forster, Kai-Uwe Hoffmann, and Klaus Vieweg, 243–256. Copyright © 2013 Narr Francke Attempto Verlag GmbH+Co. KG. Chapter 11 was first published as "Review: Identity, Property, and the Past," in *Arion: A Journal of Humanities and the Classics*, Third Series, Vol. 18, No. 2 (Fall 2010), 107–130. Copyright © 2010 Trustees of Boston University. Chapter 12 was first published in *Nietzsche's* On the Genealogy of Morality: *A*

Critical Guide, edited by Simon May, 12–23. Copyright © 2011 Cambridge University Press. Chapter 13 was first published in English as "Who may make fun of whom?" in *Cambridge Humanities Review*, Issue 9, Easter Term, 2015. It was originally written in French, but it was then solicited for publication by the German journal *360°* and translated into German by Maria-Luise Döring, who made several exceedingly helpful suggestions for addenda, all of which I adopted, adding them directly to the German text. Lorna Finlayson then translated that German text into English for *Cambridge Humanities Review*. Chapter 14 appeared in *Figuring out Figurative Art: Contemporary Philosophers on Contemporary Paintings*, edited by Damien Freeman and Derek Matravers. Copyright © 2015 Routlege, Taylor & Francis Group, 87–108. Chapter 15 was published in *Cambridge Literary Review*, Volume 3, Issue 6 (2011). Copyright © 2011 by Cambridge Literary Review.

I am extremely grateful to the members of the *Cambridger Forschungskolloquium*, Robin Celikates, Manuel Dries, Lorna Finlayson, Fabian Freyenhagen, Michael Hampe, Richard Raatzsch, Jörg Schaub, and Christian Skirke, in whose company, until my retirement in 2014, I was able to elaborate the thoughts contained in these chapters. Ian Malcolm has been a model editorial presence throughout the gestation and production of this volume, and I am very grateful for his flexibility, support, and constant good advice. The anonymous readers gave me much to think about; I hope the changes I have made in response to their comments have improved the text. My most significant debt of gratitude is to Hilary Gaskin, whose impeccable judgment has so often been exercised on my behalf and that of my texts. It has been my privilege and my pleasure that this has been so.

1

Dystopia: The Elements

—◦◦◦—

THE ACADEMIC MOVEMENT known as "analytic philosophy" had its origin in the first half of the twentieth century in Vienna and Cambridge.[1] It is also well known that this movement was originally held together by the credo of a small group of philosophers who had an explicit agenda and strongly held views about how this agenda was to be pursued. Philosophy, they thought, needed to be brought into the "modern" world, by which they meant the world of "science." The model of "science," however, was modern natural science. In "science," it was thought, theories were formulated in the language of mathematics and empirical methods were used to test them. The huge success of technology in applying scientific theories and thereby allowing us to predict and control natural processes was the best possible indication that "scientific method" held the key to understanding the world. Philosophy could stop being a children's playground where rival groups squabbled incessantly without ever being able to agree on anything and where there was no such thing as cumulative progress in cognition, only if it, too, could find its own appropriate analogue to the "scientific method." These philosophers had a number of ideas about how to proceed in developing and deploying such a method. Philosophy, they thought, was "analysis" (hence the name of the movement). The concepts we use in everyday life, in our beliefs and arguments, and that are implicit in our ways

1

of dealing with the world are mostly vague and unclear, and what is more such concepts usually occur not as sharply illuminated individuals but in obscure clumps in which (strictly) conceptual, theoretical, empirical, and often also associatively emotive elements are complexly copresent. The task of the philosopher is to cut paths through this undergrowth separating the different strands and analyzing them into their elements. So do not investigate the uses to which our concepts are generally put, the inherent plausibility or empirical well-foundedness of our convictions, or the truth of our beliefs—to do that is the job of one or another of the "special" sciences. The philosopher should take these concepts and beliefs as given and try to analyze their "meaning." This limitation is construed positively as a laudable form of modesty, or recognizing one's own limits, or as a necessary consequence of the modern principle of division of labor. It turns out that not only "everyday concepts" are in need of clarification and analysis; some more informal, or (as yet) insufficiently mathematized, kinds of science can benefit from the same treatment. After analysis of concepts, there is perhaps a further task of reconstructing the formal structure of the scientific and everyday theories which lie behind our everyday beliefs. This is mostly assumed to be a relatively simple matter of putting the newly clarified concepts in formally specified relations to one another and perhaps specifying in an equally simple way their relation to possible modes of verification. However, everything relating to the actual verification of a theory, the collection and evaluation of evidence, decisions about which sets of concepts were more insightful (as opposed to which were "clearer"), which hypotheses were more fruitful, what the implications of acting on one set of hypotheses rather than another might be—all of these were matters that were to be considered outside the purview of philosophy altogether. Seen from an external point of view and a sufficient distance, one can in retrospect discover ethical, moral, and possibly even aesthetic motives that played a role in the genesis of analytic philosophy. Some of the early supporters of the movement seem clearly to have been strongly influenced by a moral predilection for a certain kind of intellectual sobriety, or an aesthetic liking the simple, the plain, the "pure," and the unpretentious,[2] or to have had an especially highly developed psychological need for "certainty." In some cases the absolute aversion to "theology" in all its forms seemed to have political roots in a dislike of the forms of political absolutism that have sometimes been associated in the West with certain forms of theological thinking. It is one of the weaknesses of the movement that for its own internal reasons it was never able to acknowledge and hence give any coherent and articulated account of these motives. The utopia of the early analytic philosophers was a society in which "science" had completely replaced the traditional forms of humanistic culture, especially art, rhetoric, and religion, and had seen itself established as the sole guide to sensible human action. "Scientific method" was to set the terms within which any serious philosophical or political discussion could be conducted.

The word *utopia*, coined by Thomas Moore in the 16th century,[3] is ambiguous because the first letter *u* in the Latin (and then the English) form of the word can represent either one of two different possible sounds in the notional original Greek: *ou (not)* or *eu (good)*. So "Utopia" is either "Noplace" or "Goodplace." More's island, as described, is not just a nonexistent good place but an ideally good place, and this third semantic element—that "utopia" is not just good but ideally good, a place of perfect, unsurpassable goodness—has now become part of the meaning of the term.

Utopian thinking, if one means by that the imaginary construction in thought of an ideally good place, is a two-edged sword. Speculation of the kind that finds its expression in utopianism is often associated with setting free human impulses and powers that can easily escape our control. There are at least two very different ways in which utopian political projects can fail. First of all, the project can simply fail to attain the concrete goals it has clearly set itself, such as Shakespeare's "hang all the lawyers," the redistribution of land, the abolition of money, the disbanding of police forces, or what have you. However, the project can also fail because it turns out that when its concrete goals have been attained, the resulting utopian state for whatever reason no longer seems so desirable. Simply killing the king does not get you anywhere if he is succeeded by a Lord Protector who is just as unsatisfactory. In fact, of course, it is a standard liberal fear that the ability of utopian projects to muster some of the apparently

more prepossessing human sentiments in support of their goals represents a special danger. To be able to cloak a course of action in a
mantle of disinterested commitment to what is ostensibly god's command, a demand of justice, or a necessary part of the common good
is, they claim, often a way of reducing the ethical barriers that limit
human ruthlessness.

Thinking about ideally good societies naturally leads one to
wonder about societies that are particularly deficient, humanly especially unpleasant, or otherwise reprehensible. Formed by analogy
to More's coinage, the word *dystopia* (from the Greek *dus/dys:* "bad")
is now used to refer to an (imaginary) ideally bad society. It is important to keep in mind that utopia/dystopia have their origins in a
specific literary work and have remained to some extent literary
genres. They are not intended to be realistic sociological descriptions
of any given society, but rather imaginative constructs the purpose
of which is to allow us to get aspects of our world into sharper focus
in the interests of evaluating features of it that might otherwise fail
to be fully appreciated. More's *Utopia* presents a communist society
as a foil to the primitive accumulation of capital in the sixteenth century, and Orwell's dystopian *1984* now looks more realistic in our
world of virtually universal electronic surveillance than it did when
it was written in the late 1940s as a criticism of what at that time were
no more than primitive anticipations of the NSA.

Philosophical discussion can sometimes have the effect of sharp-
ening some oppositions, but if sufficiently systematically pursued, it
can also sometimes have what is something like the opposite effect
of effacing the highly distinctive profile certain positions originally
possessed. As objections are raised and responded to, distinctions
proliferate and qualifications are added, more and more revisions are
made, and as more and more epicycles are introduced, the initial motivation gets lost.

For a hundred years now "analytic philosophy" has been involved
in such a continuous and progressive process of historical abrasion.
One can have two different attitudes toward this process. Should one
admire the way in which the approach has become "more sophisticated" with the passing of time or feel that it has lost the plot and
that its practitioners are now like latter-day "Arval Brothers" going

through the motions of an archaic ritual while singing words that no longer make any sense to them? Historically, however, the more extensive and deeper the dominance of "analytic philosophy" in the established institutions (universities, journals, foundations), the less sharply outlined and more mealymouthed the originally provocative program has become, but also the less willing philosophers seem to have become to reflect on the presuppositions and the implications of doing philosophy in this way. Is anything left of the original utopian hopes of analytic philosophy? If these were connected with the use of a certain method, how do things stand with that method today?

A "method" is generally a specified sequences of steps directed at allowing someone to attain a certain end or goal. What "method" is right will depend on what the goal is, and in the case of forms of cognition, that will mean what one wants to find out and the conditions under which one is investigating. If I want to find someone's telephone number and have an old-style telephone book, a good method will be to search alphabetically for the surname of the party whose number I am looking for. If I am speaking to Information, a good method will be to pronounce the name and perhaps also the address very distinctly into the receiver. Sometimes internal evidence will make clear some of the conditions that need to be fulfilled before a method can be applied. If the first step is "count the number of buttons" and the coat does not have any buttons, the method will not apply, but there will be a limit to how far such internal evidence can lead. The more formalist the approach one takes to a "method," the less the "method" will be able to comment on itself. In general, it seems reasonable to distinguish between what we might call "the method itself," formulated in a relatively abstract way—"open the telephone book and look alphabetically at the surnames"—a single actual instance of applying that method, and the various general claims that might be made about the usefulness of the method, the conditions under which it can most usefully (or at all) be applied, and what kind of results one might expect from using it. So, for instance, in the early modern period Newton formulated a series of laws with the help of which one could explain and predict the motion of bodies. When one could explain some natural phenomenon by reference to these laws, one spoke of a "mechanical" explanation. One might then become so impressed by the beauty, simplicity, and explanatory power of such "mechanical explanations" that one might try to extend the domain of phenomena of which a mechanical explanation can be given. If one were in a particularly exalted mood, one might even claim that one could give such a mechanical explanation of (virtually) everything. How far does the realm of phenomena extend for which one can give such an explanation? The mere concept of a mechanical explanation alone tells one nothing about this, rather a theoretical statement about the extent of mechanical explanation—about what sorts of phenomena will admit this kind of explanation and what kind of phenomena will not—will be a statement of a completely different kind. Let's call that a "program."

Programs can be more or less theoretically ambitious, and they can be more or less detailed in what they purport to encompass. So a program might be minimalist: "In some cases natural phenomena can be explained 'mechanically,' so it is never a good idea to exclude from the start the possibility of giving a mechanical explanation." Or somewhat more positively one could claim: "It is always useful to start by seeing whether one can find a mechanical explanation, and only when that shows itself to be unavailable should one look for other ways of trying to make sense of whatever phenomenon it is one is investigating." Or even more positively: "As far as forms of motion in *this* domain (for example, planetary motion in our solar system) are concerned, the best explanations will turn out finally to be mechanical." The strongest version of this would, of course, be that (finally) all explanations will be "mechanical," that is, will be capable of being couched in terms of applications of the Newtonian laws to specific configurations of material elements. So "programs" are more like what Kant calls "regulative principles" than sets of descriptive or theoretical assertions. That is, their use and intention is to point researchers in a certain direction and recommend a mode of proceeding, rather than making any kind of substantive claim. Of course, one can in one sense gather "evidence" for or against a program, but the way this "evidence" bears on evaluating the program will be different from the way a simple observation might confirm or refute a theory. If I say, "In historical explanation always look for psychological explanations (or economic factors, or environmental

causes or institutional reasons)," I can marshal evidence in the form
of acknowledged good explanations that have the required form or I
can fail to be able to find such explanation. This is different from
what happens when I am trying to evaluate a specific (historical)
claim such as "the incidence of *kuru* fell in New Guinea in the 1970s
because the authorities began strictly to enforce the prohibition on
cannibalism (and *kuru* is caused by eating human brains containing
the pathogen)."

I wish to claim that a full-blown "philosophy" (in the traditional
sense) is something different from a philosophical "program." A
"program" can be more or less modest in its claims, but a "philosophy" has to make something like what Hegel would have called a
claim of "reason" not just of the "understanding," that is, a totalizing
or maximalist claim. So a "mechanistic program" might merely say
it was in general a good idea to start by looking for mechanical explanations, but a "mechanistic philosophy" would be one that was
committed to the universality, self-sufficiency, and exclusiveness of
mechanical explanations. Mechanical explanations could always be
given (for any phenomenon that was at all significant and capable of
explanation at all), they were always sufficient in themselves, and they
needed nothing else to supplement them.

So one can distinguish in principle four slightly different things:

1. An "analytical method," a relatively abstractly defined set
of procedures about what to look for and how to proceed (based
on dividing complex meaning structures into their elementary parts and specifying clearly the way those parts related to
each other and to some purported source of authority [usually,
"experience"]).

2. A specific application of that method to some concrete case,
domain, or problem.

3. The "analytic program" (in a more extensive or less extensive form).

4. "Analytic philosophy," which makes some kind of claim to
"totality" for the analytic method, that is, it asserts that the
method has (virtually) universal application and needs nothing

else to support it; it also tells you why the universal application
of the method is possible and important, why this is relevant,
and why you will not be leaving anything else of importance
out, if you simply use the method.

It does seem to be a deeply rooted feature of modern life that we
sometimes feel the need to break down complex unities into their
elements. We find that this gives us a sense of understanding and
control, and perhaps there are also various other advantages sometimes associated with this way of proceeding. And what reason could
one have to object *in principle* to the use of this method, where appropriate? However, the fact that we all do occasionally proceed by
analyzing complex cases into their element or distinguishing between
different meanings of "the same" words does not in the least indicate a commitment to "analytic *philosophy*" in any serious sense. Not,
at any rate, if "analytic philosophy" retains any commitment to some
of its earlier slogans such as "philosophy is analysis of language, or
analysis of concepts [*sotto voce:* and *nothing but* analysis of language]"
or "all philosophical problems are problems of language."
Analytic philosophy in its original form was cognitively comfortable with the way science was actually organized—it was not
fomenting anything like a revolution *in science*. Science was to be
accepted as it was, to be sure formally tarted up a bit—cleaned and
brushed, as it were—and put into the correct "logical" form, but not
questioned in any significant way. The fact that what philosophers
called the "logical form" was not formally interesting enough to at-
tract the attention of a serious mathematician for a moment did not
seem to matter, nor did the fact that empirical science had seemed
to get on perfectly well without philosophical "analysis" and showed
every sign of continuing to do so. The suspicion that despite the
perfectly honest protests of some of its earlier, especially Viennese,
devotees, analytical philosophy had a proselytizingly conformist
streak seemed more and more difficult to suppress.
To be more precise, each of the two subgroups into which the analytic movement divided had its own sacred cow. For one group
("ideal-language philosophers" or "positivists" of the stricter observance) this was "science." For the second group "ordinary language"

was not in all its particular manifestations sacred and thus to be held absolutely inviolate; still it was considered fundamentally sound and a source of healthy insight and, for some, potentially spiritual re-invigoration. "Science" (and "ordinary language") are "really" "in order" in themselves and can take care of themselves. They need philosophy only at best as a form of minor therapy and prophylaxis to protect them from being misunderstood. Philosophical "problems" characteristically arose when language was on day release from its workaday task of ensuring smooth communication or when the clear and austere structures of science were misinterpreted by being incorrectly recast in a medium that was foreign to them. The task of philosophy is to prevent these avoidable aberrations and to untangle them if they arise. Many of these misapprehensions in fact arise because people have become fixated on a historically superseded stage of philosophical inquiry. Either they continue using obsolete scientific categories that have passed into philosophical usage and become ossified there—"substances," "essences," "principles of natural teleology"—or they fail to understand something about the way ordinary language works and they try to parse it in conceptually inappropriate ways, by, for instance, construing what are in fact performatives as if they were simple descriptive statements. Very often, then, philosophy is called on to clear up problems it has itself (in a previous incarnation) generated. Beyond cleaning up its own mess, it does not seem to have much of a point apart perhaps from giving secondhand overviews or superficial syntheses of the salient results of science or of some of their more interesting procedures. Much of this might be of some aesthetic, but little cognitive, interest.

So does analytic philosophy tend to foster a naive trust with respect to and excessive solicitude for certain kinds of facts—the "facts" of established sciences and the "facts" of everyday linguistic usage? Nothing, of course, against "the facts"; as long as one can be sure they are facts and not just artifacts. And as long as one does not appeal to one set of facts to distract attention from other facts. And as long as one does not falsely insinuate forms of relevance into certain kinds of facts that they do not possess. The naive trust in question is one about the status of "facts," either the "facts" of some particular science or the "fact" of some form of ordinary linguistic usage. What we know as "the facts" are not in general irrefragable certainties that cannot ever be problematized, and they certainly do not have the determinateness that we ascribe to simple pregiven objects of perception such as tables, chairs, clouds, or cats. Rather they are more correctly defined through certain positions in the process of inquiry. When we speak of "the facts," we generally simply mean either the set of those things that are presupposed in a given inquiry or, alternatively, what we treat at some point as the detachable result of an investigation. If I want to produce a useful map, it should for most purposes conform to the "facts" such as that Edinburgh is north, and also west, of Bristol. I say "for most purposes" because, of course, there are possible purposes I might have to which the orientations north–south and east–west will be irrelevant. How these relations will be expressed will in any case be, as we say, a matter of "convention." However, the initially rather counterintuitive fact that Edinburgh is farther west than Bristol is something that can be determined only as a result of a long series of previous investigations, all of which themselves are theory driven and theory dependent; in particular they will make a very large number of assumptions. In more complicated cases than those of everyday cartography many of these assumptions will be highly fallible. In any case, "facts" are not in general anything like the contents of the perceptions of untrained observers. To call "facts" in this sense constructs in no way implies that they are to be ignored or rejected, but it focuses attention on them as possible objects of investigation themselves, rather than as simply building bricks that can be taken as given and used unreflectively.

Whatever one thinks of the plausibility of a trusting attitude toward facts in the world of science, everyday perception, and the manipulation of objects our own size in our immediate environment, it seems highly questionable that the lack of suspicion about "the facts" which is characteristic of analytic approaches is appropriate in the study of political philosophy. The reason for this is that political philosophy, at least in any of its more self-respecting and ambitious forms, will not simply accept the political world unquestioningly as it finds it and try analytically to clarify the concepts that political actors use in a given society, but will be at least open to the possibility that fundamental political changes are desirable. The political "facts," however, are clearly partly constituted by the concepts and theories political agents themselves use: A process is not an "election" unless the people who are (as they would say) "voting" have a certain conception about what it is they are doing. It is true that fundamental changes in politics can take place without the agents involved being aware of them, but if I am a theorist trying to understand a particular political configuration, *without* automatically endorsing it as "good" or "necessary," why should I be prevented from adopting a critical attitude toward the concepts the agents involved themselves use or theories they would endorse? That *they* think they are "electing a new Overseer" (and cannot imagine a society without an Overseer or a different way of installing one) is in *one* sense a "fact" I must take account of, but it does not follow from this that I ought not to keep my cognitive distance from *their* conception. I might think that it is especially important that I keep my distance for both, as it were, cognitive and for "moral" reasons. If I just use their terms and concepts, I may not actually get the best or at any rate the fullest possible understanding of what is going on, and I might not be in the best possible position for evaluating what is happening. Examples of the sort of thing I have in mind might be taken from various exclusionary practices. *They* think they are electing a new Overseer by the traditional method, and that is not wrong, but an outsider can see that the traditional method is set up so as to exclude systematically the poor, women, those without certain kinds of social connections. One might find it difficult to *see* this, if one simply adopted the concepts and point of view of the agents. It is difficult to evaluate what one cannot see.

So if political philosophy is to be even potentially "critical," it will need to find a way of getting some distance from its subject matter and that means (among other things) from the self-conceptions of the agents who are being studied. Analyzing the concepts they use will not be of no use, but it is unlikely to be enough. So where, then, might one find an appropriate kind of "distance"? One place might be a study of the historical and social origins of the concepts, theories, and arguments that partly structure the discursive space of a society. Another place would be a study of the function the holding

of certain concepts and theories might have and the effects that result from acting on these conceptions.

At this point, someone might be tempted again to appeal to the
principle of division of labor. Philosophy can and should only be analytic; it cannot and should not be or attempt to be "critical." A relatively simple observation scuppers this as a possibility. Formulating
and propounding a philosophical view is itself a way of acting. Propounding a political philosophy is itself in fact intervening politically,
one way or another, into the realm of politics, and as such it expresses
a tacit evaluative judgment and can itself be evaluated politically. To
fail to take account of this, when it has once been pointed out, is to
adopt an attitude of willful ignorance about an important aspect of
one's own theoretical activity. Some confusion can be avoided here
if one keeps in mind that "critical" does not mean "negative." A "critical" attitude or theory is one that evaluates what it is studying,
whether that "evaluation" turns out finally to be negative or positive
(or, for that matter "neither negative nor positive, but indifferent,"
if that turns out to be one of the evaluative positions available in a
given case).

To the extent to which it aspires to give a correct representation
of the way in which politics in a given society is constituted, a political philosophy must of necessity be "realistic." How is "realism"
to be understood if one holds that "facts" are constructed, and if
every representation of the sphere of politics is a potential intervention? If new knowledge (and new concepts) do not leave the domain
they purport to describe unchanged, but potentially constitute new
political facts? This is a real process that anyone who has studied
human societies historically will be likely to have come to recognize.
Only by acknowledging this does it become possible to formulate
certain kinds of criticisms. So "critical" and "realistic" are not in any
obvious sense incompatible.

The idea that critical intervention is a part of political philosophy
is something which makes many philosophers find uncomfortable. I
suspect there is an element of this underlying the very thoughtful
attempt by Richard Raatzsch to turn some of my own arguments
against me.[4] My position, he thinks, is not "realist" at all. I try to
criticize various "analytic" political philosophers by pointing out

ways in which their theories are connected with various interests, or ways in which these theories fit in to existing structures of power, for instance, Rawlsianism and a certain relatively well-off stratum of people, especially in the United States, who had an interest in legitimizing their own privileged position against a variety of possible objections that could be raised against it. However, as Raatzsch no doubt completely correctly points out, it is not as if the pursuit of one's own interests were a kind of perverted and outrageous aberration. It is the very stuff of human life and part of the normal texture of politics. To criticize political philosophy, then, for being enmeshed in relations of power or contributing to fostering the interests of some group is like criticizing fish for swimming in the water; that is what they do. Any purported *objection* to this could only be based on applying completely unreasonable standards in judging a political philosophy. To put the same objection another way: I first criticize "analytic" political philosophy for *not* recognizing its own political dimension—for ignoring its potential connection with power relations—*then* I *criticize* it for being "political," for being enmeshed in the nexus of agents pursuing their interests. It does not seem to be very coherent to do both of these things. If I criticize political philosophy for being interest bound, then that can only be against the background of a possible political philosophy that was *not* thus interest bound, and that is just what I seem to be denying.

This line of argument depends, though, it seems to me, on a misunderstanding of the concept of "criticism." "Criticism" can be used to mean "reject, deny, negate," but it can also be used to mean "subject to evaluation (*whatever* the result of that investigation is)," as in "critique of practical reason," which presumably does not mean that practical reason does not exist or is to be rejected. So it seems to me eminently coherent to start by "criticizing" political philosophy, meaning by that to subject it to investigation, and especially investigation with respect to its own relation to political interests. If the form of political philosophy in question itself explicitly or tacitly denies that it *has* any such connection to interests, then the investigation will reveal, I claim, that *that* assertion (even if it is only one made implicitly) is false. So a form of political philosophy is "criticized" (in the sense of "evaluated") and then also "criticized" in the sense

that an objection is raised against it: that it acts as if it had no relation to political power and the pursuits of interests, whereas it actually does. So the "negative" criticism is not that a form of political
philosophy is political—connected to power and interests—but that
it *presents itself as if it were not* political. One can *deny* these claims,
but they do not seem to me to be obviously internally incoherent,
or, for that matter, in any way incompatible with a nondogmatic
"realism."

Raatzsch, however, has another fundamental reservation about my
approach. There is an unresolved tension in it between two different
attitudes or points of view. There is on the one side the standpoint
of the "anthropologist" or "ethnologist" who is a (theoretically inclined) observer trying to give good descriptions of the concepts, beliefs, convictions, and the characteristic theoretical views of an odd
tribe, the members of contemporary "liberal" societies. As such an
ethnologist I have special interest in the views of the medicine men,
warlocks, archimandrites, faith healers, and shamans of this tribe,
among them the "analytic philosophers." These philosophers, however, are both an object of study and also, to some extent, a pool of
informants—for who would know better than they how the natives
think? So if one can avoid being deafened by the rattling of their
bottles of different kinds of snake oils, one can learn something from
Rawls, Nozick, Dworkin, Nagel, Gauthier, Waldron, and all the
other more minor *doctores miraculosi.* These people are both participants in certain performances that are interesting objects of study
for me—many of them vote like anyone else, they sign petitions (or
not, as the case may be), they demonstrate (or do not), they complain
about certain policies pursued by the authorities, they use terms like
iniquitous, injurious, progressive, decent, rights, unfair (or their equivalents in the local language)—*and* they have articulated views about
what they and their fellows are doing when they are engaged in these
performances. Because political philosophers are likely to have especially articulated views, they may be particularly good at explaining
what the people involved in these practices think is going on in them
and why they engage in them. It is not unlike the case of any ethnologist who observes the natives engaging in various ritual activities,
including some that may have very extensive verbal components

(chanting, formulaic recitation, and so on). Some of the native participants may, however, serve as informants to the ethnologist, trying to explain to him (or her) what is going on in the rituals.

Raatzsch, however, I believe, thinks it both inherently more appropriate and also more consistent with my own deepest intentions for me to adopt the purportedly strictly detached stance of the traditional "pure observer" of the bizarre goings-on of the members of this outlandish tribe, but he sees me slipping from this position into one in which I actually take what they say seriously as a potential contribution to an understanding of society (or a serious proposal about how humans should act) rather than just a symptom. So I should really and consistently treat "democratic theory," or the purported "theory of human rights," as they occur in the existing philosophical literature like nymphs in Hesiod's *Theogony*, but I do not always do that. It sometimes looks as if I were arguing with/against theorists of democracy, justice, rights, and so on, rather than just observing and explaining their behavior.

It is true that my attitude toward witch doctors like Rawls and Nozick is characterized by the same ambiguity that sometimes infects the ethnologist's relation to an informant. On the one hand, Rawls was clearly an active member of and participant in the social formation I am trying to study, an important producer of an ideologically highly useful product, and in every sense an "insider," just as the native witch doctor who conducts some ceremony is an absolute "insider." On the other hand, to the extent to which I treat him not as a *mere* object to be described, classified, but use him as a source of information, I am treating him not just as an object but in some sense as a coworker, co-discussant, and collaborator, but also theoretical competitor. The witch doctor has his "theory" of what is going on, just as Rawls has his, but also just as I have mine. Considered as an object of study who is going through certain motions, including bits of verbal behavior, it does not make much sense of say that his verbalization is "wrong": "*Gubujubuh; Gesundheit; Sorry; Justice is fairness; Hosannah; Whambojambo* is just what they *say* in this context" (and the task is first to figure out what it could mean). However, as an informant the witch doctor will not generally simply repeat the ritual performance, but will give some further account of it. This further account might not be at all like anything I would accept as a "theory"—it might contain and depend on mythic elements, merely associative narrations, wordplays—but one can also consider it as a kind of competitor to the account I shall finally give. In treating the informant's account in this way I am not just treating it as an object to be studied, but as an account of the social practice which I am trying to evaluate and perhaps correct, as I might try to evaluate the account of a colleague engaged in the same normatively structured practice of inquiry as mine: trying to get the fullest and most accurate description and the best explanations of what is going on, that is, the best cognitive grasp on the society or practice in question.

To be more exact, then, analytic philosophers have in my account not just two, but three slightly different standings: first as objects of study, second as "native informants," and third as potential theoretical competitors (because they usually have their own theories about what is going on which will not be identical to the theories I will propound). If my own view is correct, that theorization is always intervention, then one might also add to this a fourth: they are practical competitors peddling *different courses of action* from those I favor.

There should not be any doubt but that these positions can be distinguished only analytically, however it is not absolutely straightforward to juggle them in a single inquiry, and it also seems clear that they are in fact always copresent in our everyday life to the extent to which that life involves interactions with others (that is, virtually always). It has been a commonplace of the ethological literature for a long time that there is no "pure observation" of a society with the members of which we are even minimally interacting. Even asking a simple question of an informant is a kind of minimal interaction—no matter how neutrally the question is phrased, one cannot be sure it will not, by virtue even of being asked, bring about a change in the informant's attitudes and thus potentially a change in the society, perhaps a minimal change but a change nonetheless. For this reason ethnologists have come increasingly to describe themselves in their traditional role as "participant observers." So what Raatzsch takes as a "tension" between observation–description and argumentative–practical engagement is a basic feature of all human social interaction and constitutive for it. In dealing with other people we are always at the same time observers, inquirers, consulting informants, theorists, partners in quasi-theoretical argumentation and in action-oriented discussion. That my own work has this property is not something I can consider a deficiency.

Raatzsch sees correctly that I am committed to defending two theses, a negative one and a positive one. The negative one, crudely speaking, is that there is no pure, and certainly no purely philosophical, ethics in the traditional sense. That is, there are lots of things we "ought" to do. *Ceteris paribus*, we ought to brush our teeth every morning, we ought to be grateful to benefactors, we ought to try to help the weak, we ought to like to cook (because it is a necessity of human life), we ought not to promise to do what we expect not to be able to do, we ought to resist the further monopolization of the flow of information by Google, and so on. But are the *cetera* ever *paria?* These "imperatives" have a wide variety of different senses, sources, and strengths, or, to put it in a different idiom, there are different forms of "normativity." However, the different "oughts" do not form a single rational system of the traditional type, and there is no interesting *general* concept of "normativity" from which any substantive conclusions about human action could be drawn. In particular, there is no fully autonomous, closed, fully rationally grounded doctrine that prescribes for us in all important cases how we ought to act. If one likes to put it this way, one could say that a certain "normative dimension" runs through all of human life, or that all human life has a (number of) normative aspect(s), but that you cannot isolate it (or them) and make it (or them) the object(s) of a coherent, unitary, separate rational study. This means, among other things, that the "normative turn" in political philosophy which started with Rawls is a mistake. It is a turn toward something that does not exist, the purely normative.

The positive thesis I favor states that it does not matter that there is no unitary and separate "normative ethics" because political philosophy is always in itself already praxis-orienting and potentially interventive. Even political philosophy that takes itself to be simply descriptive and enjoins abstention from action is already intervening, because taking any position at all is intervening. There are, to be sure, situations in which not doing anything concrete or refusing

to take sides or act is the best course, but it is a course of action. A
political philosopher cannot, however, appeal to this fact to justify
a general disinterest in the effects of his or her own theoretical
activity.

Raatzsch is surely right to point out that the negative thesis is
actually much less clear than it might at first glance appear to be.
"Traditional ethics" is an ideal type referring to a number of complex entities, each composed of a number of different elements. But
which specific *parts* of this ideal type does one object to? Should one
object to the claim made by such forms of ethics about themselves
that they are "autonomous"? that they are "rational"? against the very
conception of "reason" they presuppose? Against some notion of
"completeness" that could purportedly be instantiated by ethics, or
could be an object of possible aspiration? Against the claim that
ethics can be formulated as a doctrine, rather than, for instance,
being a practical skill, a method, a form of critical or reflective activity, or what have you? An open-ended collection of different kinds
of activities? Against the whole idea of "guidance for life"? So, for
instance, if the criticism was directed against "autonomy," this would
be compatible with the existence of an "ethics" that were simply a
part or and dependent on a larger political philosophy. Such an ethics
might enjoin me always to act as a good member of a political community of *this* kind should act—or a philosophy of history—always
act so as to foster historical progress.

Raatzsch focuses his objections to my view on the concept of "justification" or "grounding" *(Begründung)* and, more precisely on the
concept of a specifically philosophical "grounding" of ethical concepts, norms, or value-judgments. If I understand him correctly, he
wishes to follow the late Wittgenstein and deny that there can be
any such thing as a "final" justification in ethics. Equally there can
be no justification that has a "specifically philosophical" character.
Raatzsch writes: "der Punkt auf den es ankommt [ist der] dass die
Philosophie Begründungen oder Rechtfertigungen dessen, wie man
zusammenleben soll und was eine ideale Form des Zusammenlebens
ist, nicht geben kann" (S. 14). Since I, too, have no use for the kan-
tianizing concept of final justification, and also have no interest at
all in distinguishing sharply between what is a part of "philosophy"

and what is not, I do not feel myself at all affected by this line of criticism. "Philosophy is always finally oriented toward *praxis*" does not mean that there is a single well-defined area of human experience ("praxis") which has an invariant structure and can serve as a source of definitive ethical arguments that it is philosophy's task to find and elaborate.

There is no reason to assume that unless one has an acceptable universal philosophical theory of ethics, there can be no nonarbitrary use of simple first-order "ethical statements" (such as "do not lie") considered as crude rules of thumb, or for that matter that rational discussion about how to evaluate forms of human action is impossible. Even without an overarching theory, one can bring forward arguments for and against an assertion, an attitude, a particular value-judgment, or an action, and sometimes one of these arguments will show itself to be superior to the others that can be marshaled. There is also no reason why someone who rejected universal theories giving a "philosophical justification" of ethical claims could not at any given time try to get an overview of the dialectically better supported positions, and even might try to articulate and systematize them for the purposes of easier surveyability. As long as one remained aware of the limitations of such a project, there could be no objection in principle to doing this. Of course, this would not yield anything like what the traditional kind of a philosophical ethics in the emphatic sense aspired to. A clarified overview is not a philosophical "final justification."

Since there is not anything like a pure philosophical final justification, the traditional dichotomies between describing and giving a theory, "justifying" and giving a systematic overview, "everyday use" and "philosophical interpretation," even perhaps persuasion/ preaching and arguing are not as sharp and as categorical as they are sometimes made out to be. They seem better understood as defined contextually. So one can, contrary to what Raatzsch suggests, easily envisage a philosophy that would be oriented toward guiding praxis *without* needing to presuppose the whole traditional apparatus of "final justification" that the Wittgensteinean rightly rejects.

Political philosophy is not a pure "normative science," and it is always at least potentially a form of intervention. To put the view I am propounding in an especially unsympathetic way, the members of the ruling party in Orwell's *1984* were right that thoughts and attitudes were already forms of action. Forms of action *of a certain kind.* Thinking murder is not the same as plotting murder, which is in turn not the same thing as actually attempting murder; none of these is the same as committing murder, but that does not mean they are not all actions in some sense. Entertaining a theory of murder is also an action, as is propounding that theory in speech or writing. There are reasons, and some good reasons, not to sanction certain forms of thought, and the literature of liberalism is so full of these that it would be tedious in the extreme to rehearse them, but none of these reasons seems to me a good reason for denying that thinking and imagining is acting, and that means acting politically.

If all forms of political theorizing, including political philosophy, are at least potentially forms of intervention, then why not try to reflect on this fact? Why not try to become aware of what kind of intervention one is engaged in? This is my response to Raatzsch's suggestion that I would do better to construe what I am doing as *mere* ethnology of a set of peculiar practices and outré conceptual constructs. Even attempting to give a "pure" description would be acting in a certain way: if my views about Rawls are correct, it is virtually impossible even to describe this position correctly without in fact discrediting it because if nonmystifyingly presented, its deficiencies become unmistakably obvious. Is Raatzsch suggesting I should *ignore* this, or try to mitigate it? Why? To say that this is "not part of *philosophy* proper" seems to return to exactly the idea of "philosophy" as something with an inherent essence that it was, I thought, one of the great glories of late Wittgenstein to have seen through.

This brings me to another objection raised by Jörg Schaub,[5] which is to the effect that my own positive theoretical contribution to the understanding of politics and to providing some kind of orientation for political action is not really very large. So he writes: "Eine Ausführung seiner realistischen Alternative, die recht vage und abstrakt ausfällt, bleibt RG weitgehend schuldig." My question is about what *schuldig* means in this statement. I have the strong suspicion that Schaub is applying to my texts a set of standards that I am precisely denying, that is, assuming that what is required is a kind of full-blown "realist" political philosophy which has the kind of ambition and structure of traditional political philosophies. I am not just claiming that existing theories (like those of Rawls and his successors) are inadequate—although I am claiming that, too. Rather, I hold in addition that their kind of political philosophy, a purportedly ahistorical, sociologically uninformed, "rational" theory of politics that gives the kind of justification and guidance *they* claim for it, is not possible. The properties of closedness, universality, and invariability they seek are not attainable; the concepts of "reason," "justification," and so on, they presuppose are not tenable. Rejecting this model and thus the idea of a "realistic alternative (political philosophy)" does not, in my view, imply that (variant, modified, or augmented forms of) some of the sorts of thinking that have traditionally been associated with philosophy might not be fruitful in helping us think about action (and hence also in guiding our action). They will not, however, have the form of an "alternative theory." Neither Socrates, nor Marx, nor Nietzsche, nor the late Wittgenstein, nor Adorno, nor Foucault had a "political philosophy" of the prescribed form, although retrospectively attempts have occasionally been made to torture their views into a form that mimicked (more or less) currently acceptable models.[6] Their importance is none the less for their failure to conform.

I do appreciate Schaub's dissatisfaction. In the past it was usual for philosophy to aspire to some kind of totality or even some kind of transcendence. To express this aspiration in a slightly more sober form, philosophy aspired to give precisely what the original program of "analytic philosophy" wanted to eradicate, namely, the generation of a kind of surplus meaning. Although traditional philosophers usually understood themselves as people who discovered, described, and brought out meaningful structures that preexisted in the world: god was out there and made a world full of meaning; it was man's task to recognize and express these meaning-structures, and "philosophy" was the place where that occurred. In an odd way one can see this traditional understanding of philosophy as having some similarity to what later came to be called "analytic" philosophy. In contrast to both traditional and analytic forms of philosophy, some have suggested that the philosopher should be seen not as a discoverer of what is already there but as someone who constructs, invents, or produces new forms of meaning or significance.[7] "Invent" does not, of course, mean create from nothing, but rather to put together into a new conceptual unity some existing semantic elements. As when physicists were supposed to postulate the existence of a new particle on the basis of a series of observed effects. The effects have been observed before, but attributing them to the particle gives them a unity they did not have before, and, as the extensive discussion of the failure of various forms of "reductionism" from the 1930s through the late 1960s seems to have shown rather conclusively, saying, "Particle X is present" is not *just* saying, "Effects A, B, and C have been observed." By postulating particle X something is added. Something similar happened when Hobbes put together various observations about institutional developments in the realm of politics, some existing views about what it was rational to think, how it was rational to act, biblical reminiscences, projections about what might or could happen under what certain circumstances, and invented the concept of the "state."[8] Philosophical conceptualization is like this type of theoretical postulation but on steroids. The concepts philosophers used never "merely described what is there" nor were they ever intended to do that; this is where there human significance and indispensability lies. A final echo of this is to be found in Adorno's thesis that exaggeration was an essential part of philosophy. In political philosophy the element of exaggeration and excess of meaning often takes a utopian form. To be sure, an ethos of criticism is also an essential constituent of philosophy, and much of its history is devoted to developing techniques that will allow one to prune back any given set of theoretical excrescences and to destroy the surplus value in the realm of meaning that philosophy also, and necessarily, produces. Philosophy is a continual and unending sequence of production and destruction, breathing in and breathing out. It does not exist except where both of these processes—exaggerating creation of surplus meaning and ascetic pruning/criticism exist in tandem. The idea that it can escape this cycle by getting rid of one of the two constituents is illusory. The full realization of the positivist ideal is impossible in itself, but even if *per impossibile* it were to be effected, it would simply prevent us from saying anything interesting and informative about whole domains of the human world, and one can be rather sure that even more unreasonable theoretical offerings than traditional forms of philosophy—theosophy, Mormonism, speculative aroma therapy,

Rosicrucianism—will cue up to fill the available void and will find lots of takers. On the other hand, generation of "meaning" without some associated critical activity will also just result in nonsense or at best warmed-over versions of particularly dogmatic forms of theology. Negativism, the need for mental hygiene, an inclination toward skeptical suspension of belief can all themselves take a hyperbolic form, as they do in different ways in Adorno, ancient and modern skepticism, and among some analytic philosophers. The process of positing and then canceling "excess" meaning in philosophy is not one that leaves us at the end exactly back where we started from, which is to say that the whole thing constitutes a "history." Going through the whole process from beginning to end leaves a residue, which cannot be removed without cognitive loss. Post-monotheist agnosticism is not the same as pre-monotheist agnosticism; the history of Occidental theology has left a trace even on those who work their way through to the other side of the monotheistic systems. There is no discernible state of "equilibrium."

Anyone who tries to stop the cycle of production and destruction of sense or to step outside it, either quickly exits from the discussion or makes simply one more contribution to the turning of the great wheel. I have no intention of trying to stop this process, which is in any case probably impossible, but merely of diagnosing its mechanism and trying to begin to think about how one might locate it in its historical and sociological context.

The kind of criticism I have been trying to develop is always uncomfortably settled between different attitudes and perspectives and different kinds of linguistic usage. This is partly because I need to use the language available to make myself understood and yet part of my point is to reject exactly that existing language and the forms of conceptualization embedded, in my view, in it. So I constantly surprise myself just on the verge of using terms like *essence/essential, a priori, foundations, natural, final justification*, although I think that these terms make little sense and point in the wrong direction. Partly this is just a matter almost of style or aesthetics. It is tedious in the extreme to have to keep repeating that if I mention "rights," I do not think they have anything like the standing attributed to "natural human rights" or that "justice" is a perfectly respectable concept describing a limited and subordinate virtue even if not, as now usually assumed, the "basic virtue" of a political system, or that *fair* is a useful term in local discussions among natives who have been socialized in the same way. It is as if the critic had continuously to be putting on and taking off quotation marks, and once one starts to do that, it is easy to make mistakes of mere inadvertence that then seem to give rise to contradictions. Nevertheless, Raatzsch seems to me, as usual, to be on to something exceedingly important. If humans have a "natural" tendency to absolutize their local environment, and to form and use purportedly "fundamental" concepts that presuppose that that environment is the only one possible (or the only one that can be "finally justified"), then this, too, is a fact that must be taken seriously and not simply ignored (on the general grounds that their local situation is merely local). Analysis that reveals vagueness, unclarity, or ambiguities in everyday usage, contradictions between different beliefs, and other deficiencies can have an important critical function, but "criticism" cannot be limited to "analysis," or even a combination of analysis and empirical evaluation. Historical, functional, genealogical, and ideological forms of criticism are not merely forms of "analysis," and without them we are more at the mercy of the particular local form of life we lead than we need be.

The illusions propagated by the likes of Rawls, Dworkin, and others about the world we live in are not simply their own inventions. They arise as a natural response to the world of capitalism and liberal democracy in which we live. They do, in some sense "describe" that world correctly. What is more important, they "suit" it. That is the problem. Simply leaving it at that—that, despite their differences, they share deep-seated features that seem plausible to us as ways of dealing cognitively with our society—is just what will reinforce the power that our local form of life exerts over us. Whatever its potential liberating effect might have been in the 1930s, analytic philosophy has become dystopian in its effects in that it now encourages us to make ourselves at home in our social world, imagining ourselves to be secure in the knowledge that analysis and "empirical evaluation" are sufficient forms of criticism.

2

Realism and the Relativity of Judgment

—◦◦◦—

EDWARD HALLETT CARR (1892–1982) has always struck me as one of the most interesting and imaginative thinkers about politics Britain produced in the twentieth century, but he also seems to me rather underappreciated nowadays.[1] One of the aspects of his work that is most fruitful is his attempt to make the study of politics and history "realistic." I think that Carr was on to something of the utmost importance in his theory of realism, although I also think that some parts of this theory would benefit from being refocused. I am not a scholar of Carr or of the history or theory of international relations, but rather a philosopher, so I do not intend to try to give a close exegetical account of Carr's views, something I would not be competent to do in any case, but rather to use them opportunistically. I make no apology for this because while close textual study is a perfectly legitimate intellectual pursuit, so is the attempt at productive appropriation. So I would like to try to isolate and develop one strand in Carr's work, which seems to me important, and which is at least a close relative of his "realism."[2]

I start by describing the two central theses I shall try to defend. First, the term *realism*—like *democracy, liberalism, freedom, reason,* and a number of others—is used in such a variety of different ways that one might be forgiven for thinking that it was as useless as they are in giving any sharp contours to our understanding of politics. So it might be useful to adopt one of the strategies philosophers often use to get some initial clarity about the terms under discussion, namely, trying to get increased conceptual definition by contrast. Carr in his perhaps most influential work, *The Twenty Years Crisis,*[3] sets out his theory of "realism" by contrasting it with what he calls "utopianism."[4] One of my theses is that by appealing to this distinction, Carr actually makes it more difficult to see what he is really getting at and actively encourages potential objections that are finally not telling, but that do succeed in muddying the waters.

"Realism" is not, I wish to claim, best understood in contrast to "utopianism," as in Carr's construction, but in contrast to what I shall call "moralism." I should make it clear to start that I mean by "moralism" something very specific, and something I wish to distinguish very clearly from the simple employment of moral judgments. Moralism means, roughly speaking, a kind of moralized preaching and an associated assumption about the causal efficacy and cognitive significance of making moral judgments. One can, however, make moral judgments without thereby being committed to what I call "moralism." "Moralism" as I use it, is, however, also something like a Weberian ideal type. That is an artificial construct of a number of elements chosen partly to illustrate a possible internal consistency or affinity these elements have. The construct will be useful if the elements of which it is composed are widely distributed in society and do have the affinities the model tries to exhibit, even if no individual ever held precisely *all* the views and attitudes I attribute to the moralist.

I further wish to distinguish sharply, following Nietzsche and Bernard Williams,[5] between making a (specifically) moral judgment and making a value-judgment. Not all value-judgments are *moral* judgments. So this part of my chapter is structured around a threefold distinction. The most general and all-encompassing category is that of assessment or value-judgment, which includes things like judging that the point of this pen is too broad, or that some given proposed policy is too dangerous or a bad strategy. It is a universal phenomenon of human life that people make value-judgments like this and act on them, and we would not know what a human society would look like in which that was not the case. Within this very broad category of value-assessments there is a much smaller one of specifically "moral" judgments. Our contemporary conception of a "moral judgment" and of the existence of specifically "moral" values is obviously deeply influenced by Christianity, but by a Christianity that was already construed within a basically Platonic conceptual framework. This general framework finds what is perhaps its clearest and most coherent articulation in the works of Kant. For Plato politics is essentially a matter of knowing the ethical truth about the world—or of failing to know it—and to have this knowledge is to have a grasp of eternal verities, which, in order to be understood and appreciated at all, need to be stripped of their connection with the accidents of empirical existence and of history. Politics is action directed at, for instance, ideal "justice," formulated in as general and abstract a way as possible. The main danger for the politician is to be so dazzled by the minutiae of the historical situation that he loses sight of this ideal. One must, in a sense, learn to ignore the context in order to focus on what is essential (and that is the realization of some very abstractly defined structural good). So if this peace treaty satisfies the ideal demands of abstractly formulated "justice"—and these are always and everywhere the same—that is all the politician really needs to know and is the end of the matter; further considerations about context or possible effects are strictly irrelevant. Kant takes over this basic framework and adds to it a strong dose of the Christian "absolute ought." For Plato the "philosopher-king" does what he knows is ideally just; if he fails to bring the good into existence, that is regrettable, but no more. For Kant the political actor is the individual anxiety-ridden Christian citizen whose conscience is burdened by the terrible weight of what Kant calls "the categorical imperative." In politics this requires him to act with absolute consistency and in the spirit of a kind of universal republicanism, treating all others as autonomous potential citizens of the same cosmopolitan structure. If he fails to act as that imperative demands, he shows himself not merely to have fallen short of what is best in a regrettable way, but to be "evil," a concept unknown to Plato and the ancients.[6] The third and even narrower category is that of "moralism." "Moralism" in the sense in which I use the term refers to a specific set of theses and attitudes that give particular practical prominence and explanatory power to moral judgment.

My second thesis is that the contrast between "realism" and "moralism" is best understood as a difference in the understanding of the nature of human judgment and the possibilities we have to form, evaluate, revise, and apply the judgment we make. The "moralist" thinks it is possible to attain a kind of absoluteness, apodicticity, and definite determinateness of judgment that the "realist" denies is possible. In particular, "realism" ought to be committed to a certain kind of open-endedness, indeterminacy, and context-dependence of judgment, or at any rate to agnosticism about absolute and categorical claims. Some versions of realism might properly be said to emphasize the "relativity" of judgment, but even this "relativity" is not at all like the "relativism" that traditional philosophers since Plato have analyzed and criticized. The specter of a toxic "relativism" is a bugbear created artificially by philosophers, and it depends on making a large number of assumptions, many of which were first formulated by Plato but nowadays are otiose or, to put it more sharply, visibly outdated.[7] "Moralism" depends on making these Platonic assumptions, and so part of my intention here is to show how much obscure, eccentric, complex, and, frankly, highly dubious philosophical speculation one has to accept in order to make anything like moralism at all coherent and plausible. Thus, in addition to its more strictly argumentative function, I hope that my treatment here may also have the rhetorical effect of shifting the *onus probandi* from realism to moralism. If moralism is, on reflection, really as prima facie implausible as I claim it is, then realism should in the interim at any rate become at the very least the default position. One consequence of this, I think, is that realism and a certain kind of utopianism are in principle compatible in ways that Carr did not envisage.

Moralism

I shall start the actual discussion with an attempt to approach realism *ex negativo* by describing the position with which it is to be most strongly contrasted, "moralism" or the "moralizing" approach.

Moralism is a quasi-technical term describing in the first instance a complex consisting of a conception of morality, and a particular set of assumptions about the motivational force and the explanatory value of appeals to (this) morality. There are, I will claim, two slightly different but related dimensions to moralism, or contexts within which moralism needs to be located. First, it must be seen as a set of attitudes and views in a "practical" context, in a very general sense of "practical" that is one of exhortation, advice, and the justification or legitimation of action. But second it is associated with a set of beliefs and attitudes in the theoretical context of understanding and explaining our human world. A lot of what makes this whole domain problematic is connected with our tendency to flip back and forth between the "practical" context of exhortation and the justification of action, on the one hand, and the "theoretical" context of trying to understand and explain, on the other, and this discussion will unfortunately have to instantiate this complexity. To start, let us try to understand what moralizing as an approach is by looking first at its "practical" dimension, at a specific social practice in which its nature emerges particularly clearly.

Consider the phenomenon of popular Christian preaching in settled European societies. The Christian preacher operates in a particular, highly structured social context which is governed by a number of shared expectations. The context is an asymmetrical one: the preacher speaks in a quasi-public space, addressing a potentially varied crowd of people that anyone in principle can join: all the rest of us constitute an audience and are silent. We simply listen without interrupting, or contributing to the discussion, or indeed even applauding at the end. If the situation is *not* asymmetrical, if anyone can contribute *ad libitum*, it can quickly stop being one in which "preaching" takes place and become a general discussion. Applause would be inappropriate because it would indicate that what the preacher said (or how he or she said it) had pleased us, but the point of the exercise is not to please us. Furthermore, to permit even expressions of approval might give rise to the idea that we were competent judges of what we heard and entitled to make independent evaluation of it. Thus, only in certain highly demotic forms of religious observance is it even permitted for the audience to encourage the preacher by shouting out, "Hallelujah" (or "Hear! Hear!"). This is the format of preaching in societies that are already Christian. There is, to be sure, a special category of "missionary preaching" that does not fit this ideal type because it is to peoples who have not yet been socialized into the standard forms of behavior and hence may depart from the ideal script, for instance, by stoning the preacher, but one would need a different ideal type for them.[8]

It is, of course, true that some deviant (or at any rate "minority") Christians did in fact have doubts about the practice of preaching. There could be two distinct reasons for these doubts. First of all, there were moral reasons. Christianity was partly founded on an opposition to "pharisaism,"[9] which meant a form of self-satisfaction with one's own moral state, and preaching could be seen as encouraging this state, at any rate, in the preacher himself. It also seems that a certain (minority) strand of Egyptian monasticism took Christ's words "judge not that ye may not be judged" to heart, and consequently refrained from preaching and proselytizing.[10] To be sure, what seems to have troubled them most was the moral and spiritual danger that preaching posed for the soul of the preacher, who by virtue of presenting himself as a kind of judge should himself expect to be judged, but views about the inefficacy of moral exhortation (as opposed to exemplary action) seem also to have played a role, and this is the second reason for having reservations about the institution of preaching.[11] Some of these minority views may seem to us to have humanly attractive features, and we might even go so far as to consider them more in keeping with the original theological message of Christianity than what later became the Christian mainstream, but the point here is that they did not themselves for whatever historical reason become the dominant view, rather preaching became an accepted and recognized institution.

In settled Christian societies, then, the preacher has over the ages had a variety of tasks including the enunciation, explanation, and advocacy of a variety of supernatural and spiritual truths, the inculcation of approved modes of piety, consolation in time of trouble, and so forth. One important task, however, has often been moral exhortation. This practice can be thought to have two relevant preconditions. First it seems incontrovertible that traditional Christian preachers held that they had access to absolute, universally valid, and universally applicable moral truths; their task was to formulate and transmit them clearly and authoritatively, and not, for instance, to submit them for consideration and discussion, analysis, or argumentation. Again, if the "preacher" is not in some sense dogmatic, we have what may quickly turn into a seminar discussion. Second, it seems to be a pragmatically integral assumption of actual practice that the preacher believes that *verbal* exhortation, of the kind he is engaged in when preaching, can change both people's beliefs and their behavior. If he does not think that preaching would change people's attitudes and beliefs, why is he doing it? In the traditional dominant Christian configuration, absolute moral truth stands on its own two feet, and presenting it in a clear and competent way will have a tendency to bring it about that people believe and act on it. If this does not happen, either the presentation has not been competent or the audience is at fault. The failure of the audience to be persuaded is a form of resistance; the members of the audience, then, are perverse, benighted, backsliding, weak-willed, "carnal," or what have you.

"Moralizing," then, is basically a set of views and attitudes about the *importance*, centrality, and efficacy of expressing judgments of morality. What, however, is this "morality" or "moral truth" which is the main content of preaching?

The term *morality* and its associates are used in two distinct ways. First of all, recall that humans are capable of assessing or grading the objects in the world in a wide variety of different ways and of making a variety of different kinds of evaluative judgments. So we categorize apples as larger or smaller, more or less crisp in taste, green in color or red in color, or we can judge an international trade agreement to be more or less conducive to fostering further peaceful relations between the signatories, more or less "just" (by one or another conception of "justice"), more or less "transparent" in the operations it permits and prohibits, more or less likely to increase trade. We can sometimes give an abbreviated, cumulative judgment by describing them as "better" or "worse." We do this overall assessment in a variety of different ways for different purposes: an apple good for cooking will not necessarily be good for eating; good weather for the ducks, or for the fields, is not necessarily good weather for us if we are on holiday and looking to swim outdoors. Just as we can class books as good reads or bad reads or the weather as good or bad, so we can classify humans, their intentions, or their characters, or their actions, or the habitual results of their actions. This is done relative to certain purposes of functions: a good military leader, a bad administrator, an indifferent negotiator. We can then abstract that form of classification from any highly specific form of function and speak of a person as "good" without adding any particular further qualification. We might say "a good egg." This means "good" in general, that is, in a broad-gauged sense for a wide variety of the purposes for which we evaluate humans, whichever they may happen to be.[12] So "morality" may be used in an extremely broad and general way to refer to any even minimally organized and systematic way of evaluating or assessing individual people as "good" or "bad," "better" or "worse," on the understanding that that evaluation is taken to have the property of being a final or overall or definitive judgment. I merely note that the objects of "moral" evaluation are generally individual humans and it will be an open question whether or not "good" and "less good" are used to refer to societies as a whole, social institutions or political decisions or actions, in the same sense in which they are used to classify individual humans and their actions, intentions, and personality traits.[13]

Christians generally use the term *morality* not in the broad sense outlined above but in a very much narrower sense. To say that a person is "a good citizen" or "a good egg" is not necessarily the same as saying he or she is a *"morally good"* person in the highly specific Christian sense of "moral." "Morality," that is, in the specific Christian sense, is not here a mere gesture at some vague distinction between good and bad, but has a much narrower and more specific meaning that is centered around a way of assigning value to individuals based on the quality of the exercise they make of their "free will," where this exercise is construed on the model of a set of choices individuals make between the clear, but exhaustive, alternatives of "good" and "evil."

With this notion of morality and of a "(specifically) moral" truth about the potential choice between that which is absolutely good and that which is absolutely evil, there comes a particular epistemology.

Knowledge of the absolutely good (and the absolutely evil) must in some sense be potentially context-free and relatively easy to acquire. Of course, one can reject the good and choose evil, but the absoluteness of the good means that *recognizing* what it is—once it has been minimally pointed out—is not difficult. It is not like learning to distinguish antecedently boys who will make good football players from those who will not, or a good scientific experiment from a poor one, or a good historical account of some series of events from a bad one. All of these require contextually based experience, perhaps complicated theoretical training, and nice judgment, but once you have understood what lying is, you know it is absolutely wrong, and will be wrong in *all* contexts, so you do not need to take account of the particular context. Judgment in any case is, in principle, simple— even a child can do it—and absolute.

Furthermore, the moral knowledge which Christian preachers transmit is construed as in some sense (potentially) self-realizing. This does not mean that people always do what is good, but it does mean that the knowledge of good and evil in itself should be a sufficient motivation for acting so as to realize the good. To be more exact, traditional full-blown Christianity had a doctrine of "divine grace" to which appeal was made to explain human choice of the good: if you choose the good, it is because you have accepted or are ready to cooperate with divine grace, although the nature of this "acceptance" and in general the relation between divine grace and human free will was a sore spot and breeding ground for infectious and insalubrious theories for centuries. In any case, the story about divine grace and human free choice ended any interesting further discussion of reasons why someone might have chosen the good. If, on the other hand, I choose evil, there was a similarly simple theological story about the sinfulness of the human will, original sin, and thus about intentional human resistance to the moral truth.

Moralism, Judgment, and Explanation

Up to now I have spoken of "moralism" in practical contexts like those of preaching, namely, as an attitude which exhibits a particular optimism about the possible effects of enunciating moral truths (of a certain kind). Now let me shift to the second aspect of "moralism": moralism not in an exhortatory but in a theoretical or explanatory context. We turn now from the preacher to the theoretician trying to understand and explain what happens in the world. The first difficulty in applying the moralizing paradigm is that moralism is focused on *individual* decision making, and it seems completely unclear how it can be used to understand and explain some large and important domains of politics, social action, and international relations, given that these are collective phenomena in sometimes highly institutional settings. Note, too, and this is a second difficulty, even if one does have something that can be made to seem like an individual decision, such as Saddam Hussein's decision to invade Kuwait or to use chemical weapons against his own people, or Tony Blair's decision to invade Iraq, a moralizing approach will not be explanatorily useful and will not give one much real understanding. If the most important thing to say about Saddam's gassing of the Kurds is that his doing it was an evil act, that does not tell us much. Similarly if Blair claims that the proper explanation for what he did was that, as he would put it, it was "the right thing to do"—as we might say it was an act of absolute goodness opposing absolute evil and thus self-transparent and self-motivating—even if you accept that it was a good thing to do, this is no explanation and gives no understanding. So moralism makes for a cognitively lazy approach to the world. Once you get the moral reading on some event, you have what is most important. The question of how they came to see "what is good" and "what is evil" is simple to answer, because this distinction is really elementary and drawing it context-independent, so you do not need much further knowledge, and the question of why they acted as they did—doing good or evil—is also easy. If they did what was good, that was only what was to be expected, given that good is naturally attractive and (potentially) self-realizing, in that it requires no further external incentive to move someone to do it (although, depending on your theology, it may require god's grace) and if they did evil, that is just sinfulness, perversity.

Just to draw out this point and make it unmistakable, if one thinks it is a difficult task requiring much cognitive effort, and therefore a potential object for study to understand *why* people thought it was good to do Z, that is, what factors made it possible for them to see that Z was a good thing to do, then one has already placed oneself outside the framework of moralism, and this is true even if one agrees that it was right to do Z. Similarly, if one thinks there are complex factors that explain why one did in fact act on Z, even after one saw that Z was the moral thing to do, one has also already positioned oneself outside the paradigm of moralism. So, one initial specification of "realism" is just that there is always a nontheological explanation for why people come to hold that X is the right thing to do that is worth investigating and discovering, and further that there is always a nontheological explanation for why people do even what we or they take to be the morally right thing to do, and it is always worthwhile discovering this. If "moralism" is correctly understood in this way, it is easy to see that one can reject it most vigorously without denying that some moral valuations might be true while others are false, without denying that moral judgments play an important part in our lives and need to be taken seriously.

Moralism in Politics

Moralism then skews and biases the landscape in which real explanation has to take place and thus blocks understanding that might otherwise be accessible, and it short-circuits the political decision process. Thus, before the invasion of Iraq in 2003, a group of experts on the Middle East met with Tony Blair to urge caution because, as they told him, the situation in Iraq was very complex. Blair is said to have listened with evident lack of interest and increasing annoyance, and to have repeatedly interrupted the experts with the rhetorical question: "But Saddam is evil, isn't he?"[14] This was obviously intended as a knockdown argument that would close discussion and also serve as an adequate justification for the policy of military intervention.

This does *not* mean, of course, that the true explanation or a full understanding of Blair's decision would run: he decided on this foolish and disastrous policy simply *because* he thought that Saddam was evil. The distinction made above between theoretical contexts (in which one is looking for good explanations) and practical contexts (where one is concerned with justification of action, exhortation and the like) is highly relevant here. Blair's assertion about Saddam belongs to the context of justifying action, and he thought he could use it effectively to close discussion and if not convince, at least disable his opponents. Moralistic forms of discourse were sufficiently well established in the society to permit him, correctly, to think he could appeal to them to silence critics; he might *also* himself have believed some version of some of the things he said, but that is a separate point. Saying that the function of the assertion in this context is to put an end to further inquiry and putting an end to discussion is compatible with thinking that a full and correct explanation of what he did would require reference to all sorts of other factors.

The very notion of a "full" explanation of a large-scale event like the invasion of Iraq might be problematic, and it might be better to work with a notion like "an explanation adequate for the purposes at hand." This would make it clear that "purposes at hand" was an important variable that could not be simply factored out or ignored. Taking this into account, a contextually more adequate explanation would refer to geopolitical, structural, historical, conjunctural, strategic, and institutional factors: the presence of oil in Iraq, the history of UK (and U.S.) relations with that country and the region, the powers and interests of the major actors, the institutional forms decision making takes in the various state-structures of the countries involved, and so on. Then within that framework one could move on trying to understand how the UK decision came about (and was implemented). In that process various decisions by Blair as prime minister would be seen to have played a role, and one could study as part of that process the factors that may have weighed in his decision. Some of these will have been considerations he consciously entertained and took account of. I do not myself think that I know exactly what those factors were, but I would submit that they were things such as an analysis of the configuration of power in the House of Commons—the certainty that the Conservative Party would support intervention and the correct calculation that the Labour Party would fail to mobilize itself against intervention—calculations about the expected electoral advantage to be gained from certain courses of action—the expected "Baghdad bounce," a set of assumptions about the advisability of cultivating a positive, long-term relationship between the UK and the United States. Other factors may have been explanatorily relevant, but not because they were objects of his conscious attention. For instance, one might think that his desire to be in the spotlight was important for understanding what happened because it meant that courses of action that would allow him to think he would be seen as central to what was happening would have special salience for him in making his decisions. He may have calculated that the Conservative Party could not resist a military adventure in the Near East, but it is unlikely that he sat down and consciously considered what he could do to put himself in the spotlight, or at any rate, he will not have considered this question in exactly these terms. Finally, part of the explanation of his decision might be his belief that Saddam Hussein was evil (and belief that that in itself was reason enough), or part of the explanation might be that he thought he could appeal to this moralistic attitude and use this vocabulary to make his point publicly in an easily comprehensible way and silence possible critics.

The point here is not that Blair's moral judgment would be irrelevant in *all* contexts, or whether or not it is rhetorically effective. Blair's moral judgment might be all-important if one were to suppose that politics is essentially an eschatological exercise in the moral evaluation of leaders, but it presents itself as *also* something more than that, namely, as a contribution to what most of the rest of the people who live in Britain take politics to be: the attempt to make a reasoned choice of policies based on as full an understanding of the existing situation as possible. It is not a useful contribution to that discussion, if only because it actively devalues the pursuit of "*full* understanding," if that phrase is taken to refer to *any* nonmoral aspect of a situation. Blair's moralizing intervention arbitrarily limited political vision and cut short inquiry in several respects. First of all, it actively derailed discussion of the real situation in Iraq in all its complexity. Second, it diverted attention from, and was almost certainly intended to divert attention from, a discussion of what Blair's real motives might have been in adopting and pressing for a policy of military intervention. Finally, by focusing on the individual moral attributes of the leaders in question—the "evil" purportedly represented by Saddam Hussein and the moral rectitude purportedly exhibited by Blair—it strongly discouraged potential discussion of such further things as, for instance, the institutional arrangements and the international context that constrained British foreign policy decisions at that time.

Bismarck gives a good instance of a position that is the opposite of moralization, which I have tentatively identified as "realism." He replies in a letter (1857) to a correspondent about policy toward France: "I too accept as my own the principle that one must struggle against the revolution but . . . I do not think it possible to apply this principle in politics in such a way as to allow something which is only a potential further consequence one might draw from this principle through an arbitrarily large number of further steps to override every other consideration. One should not, that is, allow this principle to constitute the only trump in the game, so that the weakest card of this suit simply trumps even the highest card of every other."[15]

Bismarck had his "principles." One might argue about whether the principle he articulates here is a "moral" or a "political" principle, but I do not think that matters much. In any case his political judgment here is contextual: whether or not to act on the principle of opposing revolution, and if one is to act, how exactly, are matters that can be determined only in the concrete case, and one will get varying answers depending on the context in which the question is asked.

If one takes this passage from Bismarck as the expression of an archetypically "realist" position, as Blair's reply to the experts was an archetypical expression of an antirealist position, or what I have called "moralism," then it seems clear that Bismarck at any rate sees no connection between rejecting moralism and rejecting the content of our post-Christian morality, although he does reject the absolutist framework within which this is usually presented. Bismarck, that is, can be construed as rejecting "morality" tout court *only* if one assumes that "morality" must be a set of absolute, contextless principles that automatically legitimate acting on them no matter what. I call this "Plato's assumption": if morality is not absolute and contextless, it does not really exist. Why, however, should one assume this?

Realism, Relativity, and Relativism

Realism can be said to have a negative and a positive aspect. It is constituted by a rejection of moralism—that is, its negative aspect. Since "moralism," as I have described it, is a complex conjunction of a number of positions, one can reject one component of it without necessarily rejecting the others. This will give rise to a spectrum of views, all of which have some claim to being called forms of "realism." So I construe "moralism" as a narrow, if very powerful, sect, but "realism" is a very broad church indeed, encompassing a very wide swath of nonmoralizing positions.

I do not at all think that even if realism was just an inherently critical or negative doctrine, this would be any serious objection to it, provided that the configuration of which it was critical was sufficiently well entrenched and sufficiently significant. Still, Carr does propose a positive view about the importance of couching satisfactory explanations in terms of powers and interests, and the practical analogue would be advice in terms of powers and interests. The simplest formula one finds in Carr is that moral views and conceptions do not come from nowhere, but arise from specific constellations of powers and interests and always retain the property of being a reflection of such powers and interests.[16] Even moral claims are to be analyzed in this way. You do not explain why X did Y by simply claiming that Y *was* "morally the right thing to do," although you might explain why X did Y by showing that X *believed* Y to be morally right, and then explaining the origin of that belief in a nexus of powers and interests.

The first thing to note here is that the term *relativism* can be used in two quite distinct ways. There is common or garden-variety relativism—which is not in any way a toxic doctrine, but just a form of common sense. Reasonable answers to the question "Should I take an umbrella?" will depend on (that is, be "relative to") the present visible conditions, whether it is raining, looks menacing, or is set fair, and on the prognosis (if any is available). This is what I have been calling "contextualism." When philosophers, and other theorists who stand under the influence of philosophers, however, use "relativism" as a term of opprobrium or abuse, they have in mind not this commonsense use of the term but a special philosophical sense.

In cases of garden-variety relativism—my contextualism—I can take away the *appearance* of some deep-seated "relativity" and decontextualize the statement by simple rephrasing that gives it a categorical syntactic form. Thus instead of saying, "Whether or not you should take the umbrella depends on—that is, 'is relative to'—the circumstances," I can bring the "circumstances" into the formulation of what then will look like a categorical statement:

> "In *all cases* categorically, take your umbrella when the weather is predicted to be rainy; otherwise not."

Nonphilosophers might suspect that this is some kind of trick. If such a simple device can work, there cannot have been much of a problem there to start with. I have great sympathy with this intuition that in the final accounting "the problem of relativism" is a made-up one. Something, though, can be learned, I think, by seeing what is wrong with this simple maneuver. The sloughing off of the appearance of relativity depends on being able to locate the relative system in a wider system that is taken to be closed. To say that a system is "closed" means to assert that nothing else outside it is relevant to judging it. What is and what is not relevant will depend on the purpose we have in making the judgment. Once you know that this action would be an instance of lying, the Kantian will claim, the situation can be considered a closed system—that is, this information *in itself* is enough to allow you to make a definitive judgment about it. No further information, such as that the lie is told in order to save a human life, is relevant, and so using this maneuver allows one to preserve this misleading structure.

The traditional view that goes back (at least to Plato) has it that if you cannot at least "in principle" "resolve" a relative or contextual statement into an absolute and categorical one, then the original statement *could not be* a reliable guide to action. So the existence of some final absolutist framework is necessary for there to be any form of valid knowledge or of practical orientation in life at all. This is what philosophers mean by "relativism" and why they take it to be sure a danger. "Relativism" for these philosophers is the denial that there is an absolute final framework for theoretical practical knowledge, the failure to provide such a framework, or simply agnosticism—the view that the existence of such a framework is an open question. They take such "relativism" to be tantamount to the undermining and destruction of all of our ability to orient ourselves in the world.

Perhaps it would be a good thing for us to have such a final framework into which all our contextually specific statements could be univocally slotted—although if this very idea is incoherent, it would be neither a "good" nor a "bad" thing to lack such a framework—but to claim that the validity and usefulness of *any* contextual claim *depends* on the existence of such a final framework seems to be a non sequitur. Suppose I am in the desert and suffering from thirst. You tell me that if I go to my left one hundred meters I shall find two liters of water. Does the usefulness and "validity" of this information actually depend on your or my or anyone's ability to provide a categorical framework? I can go left even if I cannot locate myself on any kind of Cartesian grid that would give me an absolute position.[17] Similarly, even if I now get the water and drink it, I know that I shall get thirsty again tomorrow. The water's ability to quench my thirst is limited because there are only two liters. To say that *this* piece of advice or guidance is not *real* guidance because it is only relative to my situation is to miss the point, which is that I am *in this situation* and all I need is guidance in it. If the guidance is sufficient for my context, one might think. It is sufficient, *period.* To say that this directive does not give me (valid) knowledge and an orientation *at all* is like saying that because two liters of water will not quench my thirst *forever*, it will not quench my thirst now. But unless one has a very peculiar and highly dubious quasi-religious view, to the effect that when I *seem* to want a drink of water now, I really want "the waters of eternal life" or a kind of water that will not quench my thirst for two days but forever, this is utterly implausible, although it has a kind of tempting plausibility that is especially important to resist. Plato's own example is that the pilot does not *really* have knowledge or skill because although he can get me from one side of the river to the other, he does not know whether it is *(finally)* better for me to cross the river or not.[18] But this is to make the same mistake of assuming that unless you have *everything* you might want—water that quenches thirst forever or knowledge both of how to cross the river and whether that would (in the final analysis) be good for you, you have *nothing*. To fear the toxic effects of "relativism" you need to make this implausible assumption.

The traditional absolutist model of thinking about morality that is common to Plato, (most forms of) Christianity, and Kant is that we do not simply *treat* certain contexts as closed, or even that we are sometimes virtually forced to treat them as closed, but that there really is a context, or a god's-eye view as it comes to be in Christianity, in which or from which or for which everything *is* really closed. The realist denies that such a god's-eye view, even if it exists, is accessible to us and fears for the consequences of pretending that it is.[19] To claim that *if* morality is contextually embedded in configurations of power and interests, then this *must* imply some kind of toxic moral relativism, or even must imply that there can be no guidance for action at all, is to make a highly controversial theoretical claim. This claim would seem plausible only if one also thought that there was no way to evaluate complexes of powers and interests *apart* from reference to some absolute standards of the Platonic kind. How inherently plausible is that? After all, it is a restatement of Plato's claim rather than a defense of it, and to appeal to it in the context of a discussion about "contextualism" would seem to be a case of petitio principii.

Utopianism and the "Impossible"

One might say in conclusion that the concept of "realism" which I have been discussing in this chapter deviates rather noticeably from one of the things people sometimes mean by "realism." When the students of Paris in 1968 wrote on the walls "Soyez réaliste; demandez l'impossible,"[20] this slogan got its point from the assumption that there is an apparent or prima facie contradiction between the first demand and the second, which the person who invented the slogan and who stenciled it on the wall recognizes, but is exhorting the reader to struggle to overcome. The assumption is that being realistic means *not* asking for what is impossible. This is a position like the one Carr suggests when he contrasts realism with utopianism. The utopian asks for that which is impossible.

"Realism" as the theoretical position I favor, and "being realistic" in the sense in which this expression is being used above are two different things. The second is not a theoretical position, but a policy, attitude, or disposition to behave in a certain way. The realist is someone who denies that a certain kind of morality has a special status. The person who "is realistic" accepts the existing framework for defining what is possible and impossible, and tries to cut his desires to fit the cloth that his particular society has made available. Rejection of the special status of morality, however, is a theoretical position which is compatible with being realistic or unrealistic in one's particular demands. Indeed on some accounts one might think that theoretical realism should start with a recognition that the process by which a society sorts certain potential courses of action and certain outcomes into two groups—"possible" and "impossible"—is itself highly variable, and that it to some extent always reflects the given distribution of powers and interests. The distinction between what is possible and what is impossible is itself in most political contexts to some extent a social construct. A realist who understands this will refuse to take this distinction as it is socially defined at any given moment to be the final and unquestioned framework for thought or action.

When we are told that it is pointless to strive for what is impossible, this is often associated with the assumption that "impossible" is used here in something like the sense in which we speak of "physical impossibility"—that is, something that is incompatible with basic laws of physics, or rather with our everyday conceptions of how the physics of large-scale objects in our world operates, namely, according to strictly exceptionless laws. So "a body cannot really be in two places at once" might be one such law. Most of the things we call "impossible" in politics do not have a standing that is anything like that. They are context-dependent in at least two senses. First of all, the sorts of things we say are possible or impossible are generally things that depend on "laws" that are themselves descriptions of the ways in which highly changeable social configurations operate. Thus, in the modern world many people have tried to claim that it is a law that democracies do not go to war with each other, so trying to get Ireland to go to war with Iceland over any issue or sequence of issues is out of the question.[21] Regardless of the plausibility of this particular example, the purported general law would not seem to be of much use until one gave some further content to the concept of "democracy," and that means providing much more information about the concrete context. The second kind of context-dependence results from the fact that in politics most of the discussion about what is (practically) possible or impossible partly depends on what price the people involved are and will continue to be willing to pay to attain various ends, and this is a variable. What counts as "impossible" is defined by society, and what "society" means in the relevant sense is also something that must be contextually determined. Sometimes it can mean a local community, sometimes a large institutionally structured sector, sometimes something like a nation or nation-state, and sometimes one or another of the systems of states that have existed from time to time. Here, too, choosing the right context is of great importance, and there are probably no hard-and-fast rules that will remove from us the need to exercise our judgment. While we must take this construct—"the (socially) impossible"—in some sense as given in that we must recognize it and start from it, we can learn to treat it as a construct, not as a simple fact of nature, and we need not limit ourselves aspirationally to what it prescribes. After all, in the human world much of what we might desire is not antecedently given as possible or impossible. Many options are not available until someone has made a play for them, perhaps an unconditioned and cognitively thinly grounded play. Wishing does not make things so, but there are things that can become possible only if enough people want them (and pursue them) in the right way, and that otherwise are "impossible." This set of facts about the human situation is the continuing soil in which utopianism rightly flourishes.

Carr tends to assume, and I think this is an assumption that has often been made, that utopianism must be absolutist, in the sense that the values that are instantiated in a utopian society are held to have a status like that of the traditional Christian, Platonic, or Kantian "moral" values, and there are plenty of examples of this. Certainly in their descriptions of the ideal societies Plato himself and Thomas More do seem to be appealing to what they take to be absolute values. Carr himself, after all, had written a book on Dostoyevsky, whom he interpreted as a utopian author.[22] However, there are also instances of utopianism that do not seem obviously to have this structure, such as the description of the Abbey of Thélème in Rabelais.[23] It is in any case unclear why the attempt to demand what is "impossible" under the circumstances in which we *happen* to find ourselves need imply any kind of context-free absolutism. If it is impossible to provide all the members of our population with adequate medical care *because of* certain existing social institutions, I can demand the impossible—health care for all—without being committed to the view that health care has any kind of absolute, categorical, or transcendental value. I just think it, on balance and in the situation that now exists, *more* important than the maintenance of the social institutions which now make its universal provision impossible.

Why did Carr identify "utopianism" as the thing with which realism was to be contrasted, rather than, as I wish to claim, seeing that the appropriate contrasting configuration is what I call "moralism"? I suspect that he was influenced by Marx's criticism of "utopian thinking." There are any number of different ways in which a particular utopian project can be criticized. I can say that even as explicitly presented, the utopian society or state of affairs is not really attractive, or that although the way it is presented makes it seem attractive, it would have other consequences that are not mentioned but are inevitable and that would make it on the whole significantly less attractive than it initially seems to be. I can also criticize utopian constructions to the extent to which I assume they *must* be images of closed societies that are construed to be perfect and thus immune to further historical change;[24] I might, in contrast to this, think that any such thing as "the human good" has no possible closed and "perfect" realization, that the human good is something historically open and always developing. By far, though, the most usual criticism concerns the lack of specification of any mechanism for attaining the utopia starting from where we are, from our present.

The main focus of Marx's objection to utopianism is on this final point.[25] The utopians thought that presenting their suggestions and showing why they were attractive was *enough*. But to think that presenting a state of affairs as attractive is "*enough*" in *politics* means tacitly to make a very substantial further assumption, namely, that it

is "enough" for a certain state of affairs to be *seen to be good*, for people
to aspire to realize it, and then that this was enough to expect that
it would eventually be realized. This, though, looks very much like
one of the basic structures I analyzed earlier in this chapter when
discussing "moralism." It looks, that is, as if the utopian thinks his or
her utopia is (to some extent) "self-realizing," just as the moralist
thinks that showing that something is morally right or wrong is self-
motivating; it is "enough" to point out clearly what the "(morally)
right" thing to do is. Further thought about why and how one then
does "the right thing" is not terribly important.

Although Marx's criticism of what he calls "utopianism" is focused
on the lack of specification of a mechanism for realizing the utopian
state, there is a further strand in his work that would cause him also
to object to another aspect of one kind of utopianism. This is the
utopian idea that the human good could potentially be exhaustively
embodied in any kind of steady state or closed and perfect social
form. Many utopian thinkers have subscribed to this "done-and-
dusted" ideal of a perfect society not subject to further change, and
we are familiar with the criticisms of this by thinkers who point to
the potentially totalitarian uses to which such utopian conceptions
can be put. However, not all utopians were committed to some positive image of unchanging perfection. Thus, for instance, Gustav
Landauer construed the task of utopian speculation as *not* to construct of the image of a possible perfect world, but as a focused study
of those human desires and needs that continue to torment us, but are
incapable of being satisfied under present social circumstances. These
desires, needs, and aspirations are not "absolute" but historically constituted and changing, and so this view is perfectly compatible with
the idea that there can be no complete and final state of absolute perfect in which any change could only be a falling-off from the ideal.
For a variety of reasons, low-level and relatively unsophisticated
simple empirical methods will not be sufficient for studying "impossible" aspirations and needs—you cannot perhaps "directly observe"
them or read them off from responses to questionnaires—rather determining what they are and how in changed circumstances it might
become possible to satisfy them will require using a variety of interpretative techniques and perhaps a complex theoretical apparatus of

assumptions. It is probably also the case that making any headway in coming to see what these desires are will require a form of "experimentation" that will have a rather different relation to political action than that envisaged in simpler kinds of social inquiry. That need not imply that there is nothing cognitive about the attempts to discover what these unsatisfiable "utopian" needs and desires are. There is no reason to assume that we can find and circumscribe a definitive set of them that we can satisfy once and for all in an imagined "ideal" state; we may rather assume that they change over time and trying to find and satisfy them is a historically open-ended task.[26] For a number of reasons, it seems a good idea to shift the focus of utopian thinking from images of purported future unchanging perfection to a more historically informed analysis of existing, but changing, dissatisfactions and needs, and possible (contextually and historically specific) ways of satisfying them.[27]

"Utopianism" is used in (at least) two ways, with reference to "content" and with reference to "form." The content-based usage refers to the fact that the utopian project is outside the bounds of what is conventionally thought to be politically or morally possible, or that it focuses on human needs and desires that cannot be satisfied in the basic structure of society as it now exists. The more form-based use describes utopian thinking as presenting the advantages of a final state to be attained *without* giving an account of how we are to get there. It is this second form-based usage that bring "utopianism" close to "moralism" (as I have described it) and that is the main object of Marx's criticism. Note that Marx's own suggestions come close to having a "utopian" *content* if you think that he focused on desires (for a decent life on the part of the proletariat) that were, he thought, "impossible to satisfy" under the then-prevailing socioeconomic conditions.

This distinction between utopianism with regard to content and with regard to form is not the same as the other important distinction between the Platonic variant of utopianism, realization of absolute values in an ideally unchanging, and Landauer-style utopianism, focused on articulating deeply rooted, but historically constituted human desires and aspirations that are in fact impossible of realization in current society, with no commitment to any kind of "closure."

While my main aim is to defend "realism" and aspiration to the impossible (and the conjunction of the two), I wish to propose that the distinction between Plato and Landauer may throw some light on things Carr says that might otherwise seem peculiar. Carr sometimes seems to think of "realism" and "utopianism" as opposite and incompatible[28]—as if one had to choose between the two—but sometimes as if they were opposite but complementary, so that it was not only possible but desirable to combine the two.[29] I suggest that this is a result of a slight shift between two senses of "utopianism" or, perhaps one might prefer to say, two different major accents one can place differentially on different parts of the utopian tradition. The "utopianism" that is incompatible with realism is Plato's absolutist version, and, I have already suggested, what is wrong with this is its commitment to something structurally very similar to what I called "moralism." The "utopianism" that should be a part of a sensible realist project is one of "wishful vision"[30] (rather than "wish-dreams").[31]

Judgment and the Importance of Context

Realism then is about the importance and centrality to politics of a form of judgment that is context-dependent, although not "relativistic" in the traditional philosopher's sense. Avoiding moralism is perfectly compatible with making evaluations of a more contextually specific kind. In fact international relations cannot be any more value-free than most other parts of the human sciences, but it can be, as Nietzsche puts it, *moralinfrei*—free of that highly idealized, colorless, odorless "value" of "pure morality" so prized by traditional philosophers.[32] The moralist wishes to construe politics as basically a way of taking a rather primitive and limited absolutist scheme for judging the "morality" of individual actions and applying this scheme to complex social phenomena. The realist rejects this, partly because of the various important differences that exist between individual humans and social institutions. Politics is not applied individual morality, although there is a politics of individual moral behavior and judgment.

One misses something in Carr if one does not see that he himself had some strongly held value-judgments, and consistency with his own theoretical reflections in no way required him to deny this. He did think, I assume, that these views were not absolute but were founded in hard empirical study and the exercise of context-dependent judgments. He also perhaps had a disinclination to trumpet them magisterially in what he thought were inappropriate contexts, such as that in which his primary task was to understand as clearly as possible what had happened in history and politics. To say that moral systems arise from and have to be understood in the context of conjunctions of power and interests is not to say that local might is always right,[33] and what we mean by "local" is capable of indefinite extension. To say it is capable of "indefinite" extension is not to say that it is capable of arbitrary or infinite extension or that the question of its extension, of how far it can appropriately be extended, is rationally unanswerable; it is just that there will be different answers depending on the context in question and that one cannot antecedently say what the reasonable limits will be. So Carr's realism neither condemns him to silence when the practical question "what is to be done?" is asked, nor does it force him (even tacitly) to endorse the status quo or prevent him from speaking the truth to *local* power. He thought the Treaty of Versailles was a very bad idea, although the Allies did have the power to impose it—they had the might, if one wants to put it that way—and expressed his opposition unmistakably enough. It is important to get as clear an account as one can of the grounds and reasons for his opposition to the treaty, but the idea that these will fall out into neat, separate boxes, labeled "moral reasons" and "nonmoral reasons," or into a set of pigeonholes labeled "moral reasons," "political reasons," "other reasons," is highly implausible, and the insistence that they *must* conform to one or another of such system of categories is a sign of an obstinate temperament, not of special insight or a particularly high level of human moral or political development. Judgment has to be more flexible than this. Systems of categories are invented for a variety of different reasons, and it is unlikely that the categories in any system (apart perhaps from mathematical ones) will be absolutely clearly definable, or that the system will be able to accommodate neatly everything in a changeable human world. Judgment requires us not merely to use given categories but to modify and amend them as circumstances change, as they are doing continually, and that the categories themselves are subject to historical change is an insight that is one of Hegel's abiding contributions to our understanding of politics, society, and history.

Anyone who studies Carr's life carefully will see that it conformed to this pattern of engaged, theoretically reflective commitment that was no respecter of persons or institutions.[34] Such a commitment, which should be considered an integral part of the wider realist project, can still serve as a model to us all.

The rejection of the narrow sect of moralism in favor of one of the many variants within the broad church of realism will not, of course, in itself ensure that the political judgments any one person or group of people makes at any given time will be wise, humane, and enlightened. Indeed it will not even guarantee that judgment will be careful, informed, and well grounded, and how could it? The fact that "realism" does not offer a simple formula or recipe for success and the fact that it is not and is not intended to be a panacea are both strengths of it as an approach rather than weaknesses. Part of the point is precisely that judgment is a kind of contextual activity for which any *such* guarantees are lacking, and that nothing is gained by pretending they could exist when they patently do not.

So I would like to leave you with three thoughts: First of all, one can make evaluative judgments, even, if one wishes to use this terminology, "moral" or "ethical" judgments, without engaging in what I have called "moralism." Second, realism is not incompatible with all forms of utopianism. In particular, it is difficult, but not obviously impossible, to envisage a "realistic" engagement with forms of human desire that cannot be satisfied by present society. Finally, human judgment is context-dependent, and thus, if one wishes to call it that, "relative" but from that it does not follow that it has the toxic form of the philosopher's bête noire: "relativism."

3

Chaos and Ethics

—⁓—

I WOULD LIKE to start by describing a deeply rooted human dream or aspiration that lies, I think, behind much traditional philosophizing. We find ourselves as human beings in an uncertain, potentially dangerous, and confusing world. Even in the highly regulated and artificial environments provided by modern urban spaces, we do not know what to expect around the next corner, and are often surprised in ways that are potentially unpleasant. So it is perfectly comprehensible that we would like to find some means of reducing unpleasant surprises, and some way of dealing with those that remain. Some way, in short, of attaining peace, tranquility, composure, placidity, and quietude in a world that does not seem set up to foster, or even permit, these attitudes.[1] This is a recurrent human ambition.

A first question arises because "we" in the above statements can be read in two distinct ways. In the first way, "we" refers *singillatim* to each individual in some notional group. "We need water" means "I need water, you need water, he needs water, and the same is true of each member of the group to whom the 'we' refers." A second way of reading "we" takes it to apply *cunctim*, that is, to a collective subject of some kind. "We won the election" does not mean in a sense that is at all parallel to the first case: "I won the election, you won the election, he won the election, and the same is true of each of the members of the group to whom 'we' refers," just as "we (the members of this orchestra) make a better overall sound than they (the members of that orchestra) do" does not mean "I make a better sound, you make a better sound, he makes a better sound," and so on or "we, the members of this collective, owe them, the members of that collective £100,000" does not mean "I owe them £100,000, you owe them £100,000," and so on. If we *each* need water, I can in principle get it without your also getting it, whereas if we win in a collective enterprise as a kind of team, group, or collective subject, I cannot be part of a winning configuration without it also being the case that you are part of that winning configuration. The use of "we *(cunctim)*" is characteristic of politics; "we *(singillatim)*" of ethics. The exact understanding of each and the relation between them is unclear and highly controversial.

Much of human life can be seen as devoted to a kind of compulsive ordering activity that is our response to the perceived conjunction of disorder, surprise, and danger in our world.[2] Order, we assume, will make it easier to orient ourselves and cope with the world and will thus contribute to allow us to attain the peace and tranquility which we seek. Since human life is constituted by an almost inextricable complex of collective and individual projects, and disorder threatens both kinds of undertaking, it is not surprising that there is an important place both for the "we *(cunctim)*" and the "we *(singillatim)*." The terms I have used in describing this human aspiration—knowing how to "deal with"/"cope with"/"orient oneself," and so on—are both vague and ambiguous, and, as we shall, I hope, see, a certain amount of enlightenment can be generated simply by coming to a clearer and fuller understanding of the various different things they can mean.

In the 1920s John Dewey suggested that the various ways in which we attempt to cope with the uncertainties of our environment can be construed as lying on a spectrum between two poles.[3] At the one end are the "arts of control," that is, we have collectively developed the various techniques for changing our surroundings so as to make them more predictable, less threatening, and more conformable to our interests and preferences. Dewey thinks that the modern natural sciences are archetypical arts of control, but it seems to me to make sense to include in this group not just rules and principles for acting vis-à-vis nature, but also ways for controlling our modes of interacting with each other, and to some extent also with ourselves. What to do when faced not with rising water but with aggressive neighbors, unruly children, depressed partners, the need for a cellist to play a string quartet, or when each of us tries to deal with his or her own apathy, deviant impulses, unwanted obsessions, failures, or unwelcome successes.

A society, that is to say, can be seen as a kind of "we" that does various things such as organizing production and controlling nature, but also setting up rules for interaction among its members. All societies have codes referring to who can eat what with whom, who can sleep with whom, how people are to greet each other, how much and what kind of help those in need can expect. You can see the sets of such codes in any society as a way in which the "we" constituted by the members of that society are trying to introduce some regularity into the world by making their interactions with each other more predictable. These include things like rules of politeness: if I am invited to meet you for dinner, I let you know whether or not I accept the invitation, and I also make some attempt to arrive "on time" (although what counts as "on time" will vary in different places, and how important following this rule is will also vary).

As Trotsky pointed out, some of these rules will be highly particular and variable. Not all societies hold that one ought not to lie or one ought not to kill other humans. The ancient Greek notoriously admired skillful liars like Odysseus and his grandfather, and a duty to blood vengeance is still recognized in many places. Even when some of these rules are capable of being given a form that looks "universal," this appearance may be attained only at the price of depleting them of so much of their *specific* content that they will have exceedingly limited value as potential guides to action. "Thou shalt not kill" may look universal, but in fact it becomes a real guide for action only if one also formulates the (tacit) addenda that accompany it, and these will be very different in different societies: in some action in a just war or as part of a legally mandated execution does not count as "killing" (in the relevant sense); in many societies wide discretion in allowed in cases of visible and immediate emergency;

societies differ in their views about the relation between "killing" and "letting die"; and so on. Anthropological studies are full of discussions of situations in various societies in which, for instance, the rule about trying to tell the truth conflicts with a rule never to tell a person directly something unpleasant.

Social rules may be seen as ways of introducing order, but they will not help me as an individual to attain tranquility unless I have mastered them; otherwise they may actually contribute to my uncertainty. If I an invited to dinner, I will not wish to come at an unintended or inconvenient hour, so we may regulate that by having the host specifically name an hour, for example "8 PM." This rule is presumably intended to contribute to preventing misunderstanding, embarrassment, and confusion. However the existence of this rule can make that contribution only if I know "8 PM" means "8 PM" (as it does in some places); "8:10 PM" as it does in other places, "anytime between 8:05 and 8:20 PM" as it does in yet others; "anytime between 7:55 and 8:15" as it does in yet others. If this convention is not clear and not "mastered" by both the host and guest, the existence of the rule instead of contributing to reducing unexpected surprises, making social interaction more predictable and reducing fear, can have the opposite effect.

That, then, is one end of Dewey's spectrum—the end in which we try to mold our world, control it, or at least predict what will happen so as actively to prepare what measures to take. At the other end of the spectrum, there are systematic ways of coming to terms with our world that consist not of trying to change it, but of learning to conform ourselves, our desires, and our expectations to the way things are—that is, learning to accept what is unavoidable, and tolerate pain and uncertainty. Traditionally it has been one of the tasks of religions to preach this kind of acceptance. Dewey also thought that for most of human history it made sense to give priority to learning to tolerate what is disturbing, but that with the growth of modern science, the arts of control have come to loom larger in our lives. Since "control" and "acceptance" represent extreme poles, most of our efforts to deal with the world will lie between these extremes or represent a kind of mixture with elements of both approaches. The situation is made more complicated by the fact that the mix of control and acceptance must be attained in concrete cases by individuals who are acting either on their own or as parts of a number of different groups and groups who are composed of different, sometimes overlapping, sometimes mutually exclusive groups. Which groups are the relevant ones to pick out? Who are the relevant "we"? And is the "we" who try to control (and/or try to accept) the disorder of the world to be taken *singillatim* or *cunctim?*

To illustrate the mixture of control and acceptance, consider a case that is clearly one of an individual, not a group, trying to learn to deal with or cope with a confusing and potentially unpleasant world: Freud famously says that the point of psychoanalysis is not to allow us to attain happiness, which is an inherently unattainable goal, but merely to help the patient overcome neurotic conflicts, and come to be able to face the true misery and horror of normal human existence.[4] Freud's statement is in two parts. The first, "to help the patient overcome neurotic conflicts," seems to refer to something like a program of control, and Freud certainly took his psychoanalysis to be a "scientific," or at any rate a *wissenschaftlich*, project—although the "control" which the analyst and patient jointly learn to exercise is in its internal structure perhaps very different from the control an engineer has over a natural process. The second phrase in Freud's formulation of the goal of psychoanalysis, about facing the misery of life, presumably means something like helping the patient learn how to tolerate the necessary remaining insecurity, pain, and disappointment. This second part, then, seems to be closer to an "art of acceptance." The full program would seem to be, then, "Control what we can; learn to bear what we must. As our control increases, we shall have less uncertainty to bear and so come closer to composure and tranquility." That seems commonsensical enough—provided, of course, that our actual state of distress at the unpredictability of the world automatically decreased with our increasing control over natural processes. There seems reason, however, to doubt that this is universally the case. What if the human condition is more like that of the princess and the pea: the thicker the mattress, the more irritating the remaining pea-size irregularity in the surface?

In any given case, then, should we (or I) try to control our (or my) environment, and if so how and to what extent, or should we (or should I) try to accept it? How is one to know which to do? Can this be decided case by case, or is a general policy needed? Might we need not merely a general policy, which is something that could be adapted, modified, or even given up over time, but a set of once-and-for-all, fixed life-plans to give us guidance?

Where, however, could we get guidance for life? There have been a number of different ways of trying to answer this question, and I will mention just a few of the historically more important answers. First of all, we can try to get guidance from appeals to existing (or invented) custom/tradition. Or we can try simply to follow what the local authorities—political, legal, religious—tell us to do. Finally we can have recourse to a variety of what are sometimes called "charismatic" sources. These may include forms of faith or inspiration, or what philosophers sometimes call "intuitions," or the attempt to follow the example of particular people who have no formal standing but whose action is considered paradigmatic. There are difficulties with each of these forms of orientation. Traditions and customs are usually too indeterminate to give guidance in unpredictable situations; local authorities are potentially too arbitrary and may be idiosyncratic; and charismatic sources are too contradictory. These deficiencies are too well known to require detailed review.

Most philosophers have tried to elaborate what they take to be a more reliable way of obtaining guidance for life than any of the ones just mentioned. They did this through appeal to reason, that is, to some kind of ratiocination, discursive argument, or rational inquiry. Originally "reason" seems to have been a method, a form of organized and self-reflective public discussion of the kind one finds in Plato's dialogues. It then gradually developed into the internalized analogue of this discussion that could take place as a psychological process in the mind of an individual. The question is whether such ratiocination is even a single unified thing—whether there is actually anything one could call a "single" method here—or whether it does not on closer inspection dissolve into a mere collection of diverse and rather ad hoc techniques and procedures. It is certainly unclear whether it constitutes a single "method" that could be formulated definitively once and for all. In addition, even assuming it is some one coherent, specifiable thing, why assume, as most traditional philosophers did, that reasoning can be completely freestanding or "autonomous," that is, that it follows only its own rules, or even gives itself its own rules? Perhaps it eventually needs to appeal in a substantive way to observation about the way the world is, to tradition, or to one or another of the charismatic sources of authority mentioned above. Finally, one can wonder whether rational discussion will ever actually result in any determinate outcome, rather than simply running on forever, or as many of the early Platonic dialogues do, ending in even more helpless confusion than one started with.

The search of the historical Socrates was open-ended, but the traditional ethics that started with Plato's development of Socratic themes ideally took the form, not so much of a method but of what I shall call a "doctrine"—that is, an elaborate, interconnected set of theoretical propositions that was supposed to give one complete guidance for action and that was legitimized by virtue of being the uniquely specified outcome of a correctly conducted process of ratiocination. To put that another way, traditional ethics holds that the world has a discernible structure—there is a way in which it predictably is; it is not chaos. It further assumes that if we discuss or reflect rationally on how we should act in view of the way the world is, the result will be a "doctrine," a kind of ethical knowledge that can be formulated in a set of interconnected propositions and that will be a guide to appropriate action in the world. The "knowledge" which traditional forms of ethics claim to provide, since it is supposed to be a form of "true knowledge," is also supposed to have the property of being "certain." The final purported upshot of all of this is that we have no real reason to fear the unpredictability of the world— that is in some deep sense a mere illusion—and our ethical doctrine, it is claimed, will always enable us to cope while remaining unperturbed.

Traditional ethics in this form would be the realization of the Platonist's dream: we can know the good through rational investigation, and formulate the results of these investigations in a definitive "doctrine."[5] Anyone who knows this doctrine will always know how to act and will have no reason to lose composure. Originally, in the work of Plato and Aristotle, ethics, the theory about the good life for each individual, was developed in tandem with politics, the theory of the good life for social groups; however, by the latest in the Hellenistic period this connection tended to be broken, and "ethics" tended increasingly to establish itself independently as a theory of how individuals should act, and the focus on individual action came even to be projected back onto on earlier figures. Christianity helped to break the connection of individual ethics with politics. If the world was about to end anyway—as most early Christians firmly believed—what was the point of politics?

If one follows for the sake of discussion this development of a free-standing "ethics" as theory of the good life for "us" (*singillatim*), that is, for each of us considered individually, it comes to be basically a view about how *I* can cope. Being able to cope does not mean that the world is fully amenable to my will—to think that is to be seriously deluded—but it does require that there be at least a minimal degree of predictability. If the point of the whole exercise is to put me in a position to manage my fear of uncertainty by making me able to know in every situation what to do, then an "ethical doctrine" will be doing its job only if it can convincingly demonstrate to me that acting on it will at least not lead me into visible catastrophe. An ethical doctrine will need then to rest very firmly on assumptions about how the world is constituted.

There is, to be sure, one highly popular version of an ethical doctrine that does *not* depend very obviously on a set of assumptions about the way the world is constituted, although it does depend very heavily on a full set of assumptions about "rationality" and its motivational power. Kant thought that *because* you could not know everything about the world—there was no divine viewpoint—you could not ever know what the final consequences of your action would be. The only way to get the certainty we crave in ethics, he argued, is by adopting a form of ethics that detaches it completely from what actually happens. In fact, Kant not only thinks that we cannot know *everything;* he thinks we cannot "know"—in the strict sense of "know"—*anything* about the relation of our own decisions to what happens in the world. I have no secure knowledge that when I decide to raise my hand, my hand will rise. This does not just mean trivially that I may find that I lack the power to make my hand rise or that my action has unintended consequences at a great causal distance. Rather it means that I may decide to raise my hand and that decision may have a perfectly random immediate effect, that is, something that seems completely unconnected with my decision may occur. My deciding to raise my hand, for instance, may cause an increase in sunspots, or a decrease in the number of fleas on dogs in Budapest. But for Kant this is not supposed to matter, because the *actual effects* of my action are for him completely irrelevant to its ethical status. In fact even the *intended* effects of any decision I might make to act are beside the point. So it is true to say that the Kantian *has* a "doctrine" that is a rationally based mechanism for always getting a decision about what to do. However, he or she pays a high price for this: the complete detachment of his or her mechanism of decision from what will actually happen. What I originally wanted, though, was freedom from fear about what will happen. At this point Kant moves his ethics very much in the direction of the arts of acceptance. He offers the agent not guidance for action but what he himself calls "consolation." The consolation is supposed to reside in the fact that I can derive an enhanced sense of self from the fact that I have done my duty. This is supposed to serve as a replacement for my desire not to be unpleasantly surprised by the world and the randomness of the distribution of pleasure and pain in human life.

Plato's Socrates, a model of philosophical honesty, admits that he cannot *prove* one of the propositions that formulate what ultimately motivates him. He is driven on, he says repeatedly, by the "hope" that no evil can befall a good man, and that means a man who knows and acts on the correct ethical doctrine.[6] Anything like traditional ethics seems to rest on such a "hope" that the world is structured so as to be amenable to our rationality and thus that acting on our rational doctrine will not lead us anywhere genuinely dangerous or fearsome. This "hope" might in the short run be self-validating. If I hold on to the hope firmly enough, that will perhaps calm my fears. However, this is a trick, and it shares the property of all such tricks that they work only if you do not see through them, and this one is particularly easy to see through. To put it slightly differently, if Plato's Socrates tells us to question *everything* and look for the final reasons one could give for any belief or any action, he cannot expect his own "hope" to escape that scrutiny, and any kind of at all close scrutiny will reveal that its calming effect is based on a violation of the basic Socratic demand that one clearly know oneself and what one is doing. Any post-Socratic should be able easily to diagnose simple forms of self-validating beliefs and should be intensely suspicious of them.

Platonists have one further card up their very ample sleeves. I spoke above of their dream of a form of ethical knowledge that would be certain and universally orienting; now one must add to their arsenal of arguments what I will call "the Platonist's Blackmail": if you do not have a guide to action that is absolute certain and absolute universal, you have nothing at all. If you do not have Platonic-style ethical knowledge, you have no alternative but to live "at random," meaning doing whatever you please, pursuing what happens to seem best at the time, and following your momentary impulse, without trying to make systematic sense of the world at all.[7] If this were the case, Plato's dream would not merely be a hope, but it would be, as it were, the only hope we could have. That still would not demonstrate that an ethical doctrine is possible, but it would present us with a clear alternative: either Plato or chaos. I need not expatiate at any great length about the obvious authoritarian overtones of this.

Why should Plato think that this is the choice? His own example is that of a person trying to cross a body of water. How ought I to proceed? I might think that I can orient myself by asking a pilot. The pilot does have the knowledge and skill to get me safely from one side of the river to the other. Plato, however, denies that this means that the pilot can give me proper guidance for action in the sense in which I am looking for guidance, and the reason, he claims, is that the pilot does not know whether it is better for me to cross the river or not.[8] Suppose, however, I am looking for my cat and you tell me you saw her go upstairs half an hour ago. Is this information completely useless because it is not absolutely certain and because it refers only to my present situation, and does not give me universal orientation? To say that *this* piece of advice or guidance is not *real* guidance because it is relative only to my situation is to miss the point, which is that I am *in this situation* and all I need is guidance in it. If the guidance is sufficient for my context, one might think it is sufficient, *period*. To say that this directive does not give me (valid) knowledge and an orientation *at all* is like saying that because the

cat is not *always* upstairs, sometimes she is in the garden, your observation of her going upstairs half an hour ago is useless as a guide
to action. If I act on this observation, though, I am not acting "at
random."

There is, I suggest, no reason to assume that "orientation in life"
or "guidance" need necessarily mean having a single systematic
theory that provides us, either individually or collectively, with a certain way of proceeding in *all* situations. Even if such a theory is unavailable to us, or even incoherent, we need not live at random, and
there is no reason to believe that observation, theorization, and rational argumentation may not well satisfy our need for orientation,
especially if this need is construed as something that arises piece-
meal and thus can be adequately satisfied in each case in its given
context.

Traditional, post-Hellenistic ethics tried to put together three
things that simply will not fit. First the idea of having a guide to
acting in all possible situations, second the idea of complete and thor-
oughgoing rationality, and third the idea of the rational calming of
the anxiety of existence in a chaotic world. It is not difficult to get
the first and third of these *in isolation*. If all you really want is a universal guide to action, then just adopt one and stick to it. Become a
Kantian or Utilitarian, a Mormon or a "libertarian," dig in your
heels, be bloody-minded, and do not let yourself be talked out of your
chosen position by even the most convincing arguments. Similarly
it is also not difficult to get a calming of the feelings of anxiety and
fear of the unknown and the unpredictable: alcohol used to be used
here, but modern pharmacology has given us even more effective
forms of sedation that will generally do the trick. But philosophical
ethics was not supposed to be a sedative or a form of obsessive
clinging to a pregiven set of formulae. The further and the more consistently, though, that one follows the call of "rationality," the less it
will give one reason to think it can in itself provide satisfaction of
our need for composure in the face of uncertainty. The philosopher
Antisthenes is reported to have said that virtue was sufficient for
happiness, *provided* one added to it (προσδεῖται) "the strength of
Socrates."[9] Interpreting this wildly, one might take this as saying that
ethical inquiry could yield an appropriate tranquility, but not by

itself alone, *only if you had the strength of Socrates*, something that, unfortunately, not everyone has and that cannot be attained by ratiocination alone.

I started this by saying that I would discuss a dream or aspiration, but now I must revise that and admit that there are at least four different versions of that dream. First is a fantasy of omnipotence or complete control over the external world, of being able to bend it fully to our own will and interests. In its most extreme form, this is a pathological god-fantasy, but one can also see it at work residually even in relatively sophisticated philosophical positions like certain forms of positivism. The second dream is that of complete and utter acceptance of what is, which, in the paradoxical way of such things, often seems to turn into its opposite: the Nirvana promised by Buddhism, which is a full acceptance of *everything*, is not a form of human life but a state of nonbeing. A third dream that obsesses humanity is that of a completely well-oiled society, or rather a society so without inherent friction that it needs no oil, in which the social rules would cover everything and work without conflict; everyone would know their place and act as prescribed, so that serious individual initiative would have no place. In this dreamworld anything like ethical thought would be superfluous. The fourth dream is only slightly less fantastic. It is the illusion that any human could come to have a rationally well-grounded, fully fledged ethical doctrine in the traditional sense, that is, one that will give universal guidance for action and guarantee tranquility of soul.

None of these dreams is realizable, but that does not mean there is no place for ethical inquiry in human life, only that ethical "doctrines," in the sense I have defined, must be treated with extreme caution and not taken on the terms they prescribe for themselves, as absolutes.

Now you might all be disappointed by the results of this set of comments, because you might feel that the results are wholly negative. I understand this reaction but I do not actually share it, because I think that getting rid of pernicious illusions is not nothing, and also that it is particularly important in the world we live in to resist the pressure simply to sign up to one or another of the prefabricated views on offer, just because one had, it was claimed, to subscribe to *some* global view. Humans have some powers of suspension of commitment, and these are not always to be despised.

Finally, then, I would like to leave you with three thoughts:

First, there is no such thing as a *doctrine* of ethics in the sense traditional philosophers thought there could be, something like a theory or a structured method for telling you authoritatively what to do in most circumstances.

Second, one should resist "Plato's Blackmail," the idea that if you do not have such a "doctrine," you can have no orientation in life at all, you are forced to act simply on impulse, and the use of intelligence is pointless.

Third, if you still feel what you take to be a deep-seated desire or even a need for a traditional-style ethical doctrine, ask yourself why—that is, ask yourself what the origin of this perceived desire is and why you think it even conceivable that it be satisfied.

We are left, then with the Socratic method but without the Socratic "hope." That is not a completely comfortable situation to be in, but no one is born with the promise of a comfortable life.

4

Russell Brand, Lady T, *Pisher* Bob, and Preacher John

───⟨∞⟩───

RUSSELL BRAND's new book *Revolution* is an impressive contribution to political philosophy, a field that during the past thirty years or so has not been overly populated with interesting work.[1] Brand's argument can be summarized in ten steps:

1. Our lives are to a large extent given structure by a set of economic practices and institutions that have enough determinacy and continuity to be singled out as an object of systematic study. Call these collectively "C."

2. The operation of C has brought about a state of affairs in which the richest eighty-five persons (of a world population of more than three billion) control more economic assets than the poorest billion and a half (p. 13).

3. The continued normal operation of C will in a very short time render the Earth completely uninhabitable for humans (pp. 14–17, 86ff., 316).

4. Therefore (by 2 and 3), C must be radically changed, that is, "revolution" is necessary (for example, p. 97); we have no choice (p. 250).

5. If 4 is impossible, then excessive drug use is as understand-able a way to live one's life as many others (pp. 9, 10, 34) (and the same is true of "apolitical" rioting [p. 88]).

6. "Drug use" in 5 above includes both the ingestion of chemical substances and such things as consumerism (pp. 7–9), celebrity obsession, sports (pp. 39–43, 96–97), or religious beliefs and rituals (pp. 45–60).

7. Brand has tried most of the drugs and can reliably report that consumerism (p. 29) and celebrity obsession (p. 51, 113) are not satisfying even in the short term to persons of relatively unde-manding and indiscriminate taste, and that, notwithstanding 5 above, ingestion of chemical substances is fraught with its own dangers and has highly unpleasant associated effects (pp. 35, 51).

8. What are left as possible ways of structuring a meaningful life are revolution, certain forms of collective experience (like that of the ardent sports fan at a football match), and religion.

9. The revolutionary abolition of C is not only compatible with but is a necessary precondition of a full revival of the spiritual dimension of human life; this dimension is so important that the need to reconstitute it is a third powerful reason (pp. 170–180), in addition to 2 and 3 above, to abolish C. In addition, *some* form of at least incipient spiritual renewal must also be an integral part of the process of revolutionary change (pp. 259–260).

10. Serious further philosophical discussion, to which Brand's book is a kind of *Prolegomena*, should *begin* from 8 and go on to discuss the three modes of meaningful life, and their relations to each other, and to other features of our human and natural world.

Whatever one might finally think of this argument, it is hard to deny that it deserves to be taken seriously. It raises a number of is-sues of pressing human concern; it attempts to be clear in what it assumes; it marshals some (purported), personal experiences, obser-vations, theories, and other considerations and brings them to bear in support of a conclusion. Now what might a philosopher say about the argument, as outlined above? Let me now introduce three inter-locutors whom I shall call "Lady T," "*Pisher* Bob,"[2] and "Preacher John."

Lady T would, I think, find Brand's observations *à propos*, and would, refreshingly, try to meet them head-on. She would fully admit that 3, if true, would be of great importance, but since she would hate to have to confront the implications of this, she would have to deny that it was true. She might try to do this by denying straightfor-wardly the seriousness of the degradation of our environment, or she might appeal to the species of hope that is actively cultivated in our society by claiming that further technical and scientific advances will in ways now unimaginable provide a solution to these problems within the framework of C. Or finally she might try to deny that C was in any way causally responsible for them. Perhaps the true cause, she might argue, is not in any interesting sense our socioeco-nomic system itself, but a form of individual moral irresponsibility having nothing inherently to do with C, which caused people to re-produce at too high a rate. Having disposed of 3 to her own satisfac-tion, Lady T would be able to consider 2. Here, she could embrace the empirical finding wholeheartedly, but instead of seeing 2 as in any sense something that ought to give us pause, she would encourage us to "glory in it." Think of it this way: I do not "find" "value," cer-tainly not "a valuable life" or "value in my life," in the way I might discover gold or oil, or even something like a cure for a certain kind of viral infection. Value is not found; it is created. My life is valuable if I can make it valuable, and I do that by, as we say, "making some-thing" of myself. This, Lady T might argue, is mostly a matter of self-discipline, focus of will, and determination; exercise of will is meritorious. This, of course, in itself will not give one reason to value inequality positively because perhaps we are *all* gifted, disciplined, meritorious agents, collectively engaged in creating ourselves.

So where does the positive valuation of inequality per se, or of eco-nomic inequality (to the exclusion of virtually everything else) come from? Why should there be something good, or even especially good, about comparative, or even specifically competitive, achievement? There are two kinds of reasons one can give for this emphasis on dif-ferential rewards and unequal valuation. The first is that this is part of a highly individualist view. Value must always be located in human individuals: human individuals are the ones who experience value and their experiences must be the final valued objects. "Value" must be finally connected with giving me an enhanced sense of myself *as opposed* to others. Collective achievement is to be denigrated, because it dilutes this sense of individual accomplishment. One could in principle ask why one should make this assumption, but since everyone in this discussion does make it and a proper discussion would be a very lengthy matter, I will pass over it in silence for the moment. However, I merely point out how genuinely weird this view is if you think about it in a sustained way. The solo playing of a pianist is more valuable than a string quartet; the achievement of an individual sprinter more valuable than that of a football team. I also point out that this assumption is not obviously compatible with the hypernationalism Lady T also preached. The second kind of reason would be to think that differential "rewards" were not just good in themselves—they mapped individual merit attained through achievement—but they had good effects for everyone, for "society." But who could actually believe that everyone in the United States (or even the world) was better off because the half a dozen heirs to the Walmart fortune owned more than the poorest 30 percent of the inhabitants of the United States (Brand, pp. 13–14). This claim is so palpably false that to preserve any plausibility at all it is necessary to shift ground completely and move from the realm of actual outcomes to that of motivation or what is sometimes called "incentives." The argument would be that this concentration of wealth and economic control does not actually improve the life of the large majority of the population, but that it is important to defend the possibility of accumulating so much wealth and power, because the continued existence of this possibility has overall positive motivational effects on the members of the society.

Seeing the success of the successful does not, however, automatically improve the quality of my life and is not necessarily a positive experience—whether or not it is will depend on the context.[3] Watching one set of neighbors successfully subdue another set may not please me or make my own life more valuable at all. Equally the claim that seeing the success of the successful *always* increases my motivation to work harder is unfounded. The very idea that people work (or "work harder") because of any kind of independently identifiable external "incentives" is itself highly problematic and the tacit assumption that recognized success, or at any rate great success, in the economic world is connected in any but a random way to "effort" is hard to sustain (Brand, p. 242). Lots of perfectly hardworking people fail and any number of layabouts who happen to be at the right place at the right time succeed. One might speculate that the popularity of gambling has something to do with a realization on the part of a large section of the population of the essentially aleatory nature of the connection between endowments, hard work, and economic success. What sort of person would I have to be to be motivated to work harder by seeing the prosperity of six individuals whose claim to merit is that they are the children of one particular person rather than another? For that matter, why should the knowledge that the founder of Walmart was able to accumulate a huge fortune motivate me to work harder? Is it rational for me to work to acquire more money than I could possibly spend and would have no use for? To be sure there are social pressures to admire those who through a combination of luck, happy accident, fortunate conjunction, craftiness, and ruthless self-assertion ended up at the top of the economic hierarchy, but these social pressures do not always work—they have not succeeded in getting me to admire someone who was, in Russell Brand's phrase, "good at supermarkets" (p. 14). What is supposed to be so great about building a lot of supermarkets, even if they were places where the workers were treated well? In particular, what is so great about building an empire of supermarkets where the workforce is treated badly? In addition, I know, as I suppose every reflective persons also knows, that different societies have put pressure on their members to admire and, if possible, emulate, very different types: "fine gentlemen" in the nineteenth century, ladies who were the presiding presences in fancy *salons* in the eighteenth century, self-abnegating ascetics in fourth-century Egypt. Sometimes these models are more individualist, such as the Egyptian ascetics, sometimes, more collectivist, like unflinching hoplites in ancient Greece whose overwhelming virtue consisted not in heroic individual exploits, but simply in staying in a line that, if unbroken, was difficult to defeat.

Where there are discernible "incentives," however, these derive their specific shape and power from social pressure and are not necessarily the direct results of any inherent, acontextual tendency to admire this particular kind of person, life, or form of achievement. The particular configuration of motives and incentives that is said to be most dominant in our society is first of all not nearly as universally shared here as "common sense" would have us believe, and second, to the extent to which is it present, it is produced at least in large part by C itself and hence is part of C. It does not give one any kind of independent standpoint to evaluate C. Note that saying this incentive structure is "in part" produced by our society need not imply that it is made up whole cloth and implanted on passive subjects from the outside. Any reasonable social formation will take material that is in some sense preexistent—highly malleable drives, impulses, fancies (pp. 32–33, 54–55)—and form them into something socially specific and concrete.

Although Lady T was not keen on the very idea of "society," probably not even she could, with any consistency, deny the importance of the question of the possible effect on society of great economic inequality. She presumably thinks that *on the whole* the effect is positive. Still, *someone* has to have lost the race, even if only a small group of what François Hollande calls *"les sans-dents."*[4] It is in principle possible, like the economist Hajek, to take a radically nonmoralizing view about the economy, but this is difficult for a politician really to maintain and there can be little doubt but that Lady T's attitude did take a deeply moralizing turn. Not only *should* people be inspired, rather than being left cold or even revolted, by the Walmart example, but it is always up to them to work hard, because social circumstances play no role in endowing them with this ability or allowing them to cultivate it; this is a matter of their "individual responsibility," and hard work will always be (more or less) appropriately rewarded, because a society structured around C rewards people (more or less) according to their real worth. So, if you look at the Walmart example and fail to be inspired, you are obtuse or perverse and "deserve" what you get.

Notions like "individual responsibility," "external incentive," "the need for individual hard work," and "merit" may well be present and play some role or other in a very wide range of human societies. Brand, as a recovered drug addict from a modest background, instantiates the qualities of determination and focus that those who have views like those of Lady T say they value most highly, so his testimony ought not to be completely without moral force for them. Yet the specific theoretical construction of incentive, merit, and economic success and failure described in the last two paragraphs, if considered as a *general* theory or a good description of our society and our politics, is just preposterous. Still it is rooted in deep ideological needs our society has and in prejudices without which our economy could not so easily operate, so it is not surprising that few can free themselves of these conceptions completely. Lady T does not even try.

Compared with the refreshingly robust and engaged, albeit callous, ignorant, and vindictive, approach of Lady T, both *Pisher* Bob and Preacher John cut very poor figures indeed. They have in common that they would reject most of Brand's argument not as false, but as irrelevant; for them he is addressing completely the wrong question. Political philosophy for *Pisher* Bob and Preacher John has a clear central focus: distributional justice. "Justice" is the basic virtue of a society, so that is what a proper philosopher must focus on. Brand, however, has nothing to say about "justice."

In fact, Brand does not ever use the term *justice.*[5] It could, however, be claimed, that although he does not use the word, he clearly is appealing to the concept, because the only way in which 2 could in fact be a relevant contribution to discussion would be if one assumed that it was supposed to have an addendum:

> 2*. The operation of C has brought about a state of affairs in which the richest eighty-five persons (of a world population of more than three billion) control more economic assets than the poorest billion and a half *and this is unjust.*

Although Brand does not say this, he *"must"* (actually) mean it, because he is obviously citing this as a reason for distancing oneself from C. But if he did not think it "unjust," what he says would hang free, utterly unconnected to our structures of argumentation,

BRAND, LADY T, *PISHER* BOB, AND PREACHER JOHN 71

motivation, and the justification for action. This philosophical use of "must" in highly suspicious—you *must* use the concept we prefer, or you *must* tell us why not—and the claim as a whole seems implausible; I shall return to it, but for the moment let us suspend disbelief and follow where *Pisher* Bob and Preacher John wish to lead us.

Pisher Bob points out that in a complex society there is a constant recirculation of goods, assets, and resources, so that if one ever once attained perfect equality, that point would be perpetually lost, or at any rate threatened, by various free transactions between the members (voluntary gifts, temporary loans, or pooling of resources). Either one would have to ban such transactions altogether on the grounds that they disturbed equality, or one would need to have an all-powerful, but also utterly unwieldy, centralized apparatus of redistribution of resources and assets that would operate constantly. This would have manifold inconveniences, and, if you thought about it hard, might even be thought to constitute some kind of logical refutation of absolute egalitarianism about resources. Resources, it might be argued, are inherently things to be used, but things that were *continually* being redistributed would never actually be used.

This is a good, interesting, and relevant argument, but *Pisher* Bob thinks it cuts against both Marx and Brand. It is not at all relevant to Marx because Marx was not an egalitarian. He did not think a good society was an equal one, but one that was, in contrast to our society, so satisfactory in so many ways to its members that existing inequalities did not *matter* at all.[6] *Pisher* Bob's argument cuts against Brand only if one makes two further assumptions. First, that Brand accepts *Pisher* Bob's and Preacher John's addendum to his 2—that the state of the world in which eighty-five people own more than the poorest half of the world population is unjust—*and* second, that this state of affairs is "unjust" *because* it violates absolute equality. There is, however, no reason to make either of these assumptions. Brand might think that equality was neither here nor there, but that having eighty-five people control all these resources was imprudent, ruinous, dysfunctional, visibly deleterious to the well-being of humans and of the natural environment, contrary to Christ's commandments (pp. 66–69), a contribution to human alienation (pp. 167–169, 242), an affront to decency, contrary to what most humans would want

(p. 154), and so forth. Several of these seem very good reasons, and none of them has anything much directly to do with equality or justice. Are none of these in any sense relevant considerations? In short, then, there may be any number of possible ways in which 2 might be connected with guiding rational action. To say that Brand "must" be appealing to a concept of justice in this context is like arguing for god's existence by pointing to a star and claiming that this is proof because god put it there.

For that matter, why could Brand not just appeal to an "intuition," for instance, an intuition that ruining one's environment is bad? *Pisher* appeals to an "intuition" when he says that I can acquire "ownership rights" over objects, places, even some sentient beings (horses, cows) by satisfying various conditions, and that if I have satisfied those conditions, I can use or abuse these objects as I see fit and you can do nothing about it (without violating my rights). These "rights" are also called "entitlements." This is rather complex for an "intuition," because an "intuition" was supposed to be a punchy immediate emotional and normative reaction. *Pisher*'s little trick is to insist that all genuinely philosophical questions have to be couched in terms of "entitlements." So, *Pisher* might continue, to cite 2 does not begin to constitute part of a philosophic discussion until one specifies what kinds of "entitlements" the eighty-five people mentioned in 2 have to the assets they control. This ownership distribution is "just" if, but only if, one can trace their entitlements back through a series of voluntary and legitimate transfers to an initial act of legitimate acquisition. Taking this seriously means that virtually no one now has any legitimate title to anything, because historically the chain of legitimate voluntary transferences is bound to have been broken at some point, and so almost all ownership fails to be just. One might think this is a *reductio ad absurdum* of the initial set of assumptions about rights, ownership, and entitlements, and thus that that particular set of conceptions is useless for any significant political purpose. *Pisher*'s "entitlements" are as "self-contradictory" as his argument showed the concept of "resources in a society devoted to absolute equality" was. It is *Pisher* who is asking completely the wrong questions.

Preacher John, too, thinks that 2 is underspecified. His pet view is that in order for 2 to be politically informative and significant, we need to know not about the historically accumulated entitlements the eighty-five people actually have, but whether if there had been other economic arrangements in place, the welfare of the worst off would have been enhanced. Furthermore, Preacher John holds, roughly, that in evaluating societies (and thus in thinking about politics) ignorance is bliss. The right way, in his view, to get a really profound insight into the most important issue in politics (in his view "justice") is to imagine a situation in which a large swathe of our knowledge is blotted out as irrelevant. Imagining that you do not know what your particular position in society is will nullify the cognitive and evaluational effects that standing in that position might have on your mode of judgment. If you grow up a slaveholder, then just imagine a social state in which you do not know whether you will be a master or a slave, and any cognitive prejudices you might have will drop away and your judgment will be unclouded. Only if we imagine what we would think under conditions of controlled but extensive ignorance, will we get genuinely valuable insight into politics. Preacher John has no account of how we might nonarbitrarily control the appropriate "ignorance" in question.

Brand represents the opposite trajectory: advocacy of increasing awareness of and sensitivity to oneself and one's environment (pp. 40, 254–259). There are dangers associated with this: if one lives in a society like ours, it is easy to find one's surroundings objectively intolerable and to try to deal with the pain of this by escape into the world of intoxicating or narcotizing chemical substances, which (as we have seen above in 7) is a self-destructive cul-de-sac. Still he thinks it better to see and try to deal with our world rather than close one's eyes and admire the beautiful internal spectacle of a congress of the ignorant.

Followers of the Preacher sometimes claim he changed his mind in his later years and realized he was producing not a universal theory of politics and society but only a set of suggestions directed to the members of pacified, highly organized, liberal societies in nonemergency situations. Unlike Plato, Saint Paul, or Kant, he was preaching only to the members of his own tribe and then only telling them how to proceed in "normal" times. It is a theory of routinized politics-as-usual in states of a certain kind, where there is an established state structure, there are regular elections the results of which are not contested, an effective judiciary, and so on. So not even intended to be relevant to Eritrea, Yemen, Saudi Arabia, Southern Sudan, Ukraine(?), Crimea(?). If Ukraine were more like France, Britain, or the United States, it would not have the problems it does, but could direct its attention to the "serious" issue of the "just" distribution of goods and services. Well, thanks for that information. How exactly are we to change the situation in the Ukraine so that it becomes more like the Netherlands or Sweden? (And who is "we" here?) Is this not a political question? If Preacher John recognizes this as part of the proper domain of political philosophy, he gives no sign of that. Maybe he thinks that listening to his preaching, that is, reading his books, will do the trick. If so, that would not be much of a theory but would at least be a gesture in the direction of politics, but not even that much is made the object of a theoretical reflection.

If John's preaching is not addressed to situations of urgent emergency either, then it does not apply in the Czech Republic when the river Moldau floods, in France if there is an accident at a nuclear power plant, or in London if there is a strike of paramedics or a demonstration so big that it overwhelms the available security services. This would also mean that if there was any chance that 3 above, or anything remotely like 3, were true, the Preacher would have nothing to say (*tacet praedicator*). Given that 3 describes a *global* state of affairs, if the diagnosis is correct, Preacher John has no message for political thought or action at all.

One might reasonably wonder about the exact meaning of "revolution" for Brand. Revolutions come in different forms: the revolution as extension of popular riot (the Bastille), as coup d'état (the Bolsheviks in Petrograd), as saturnalia (the Anabaptists in Münster), as call for abolition of debt (*tabulae novae*, pp. 92–98). There are some apocalyptic conceptions that demand the complete destruction of the present as a preliminary (Bakunin in some of his moods) and utopian views that require the building up of a completely new set of institutions *ab ovo*.

There is, however, also in Marx the metaphor of revolution as a process in which a "new society" that is already present and growing within the current state emerges fully. It is like a fruit or embryo surrounded by a membrane, shell, or chrysalis. This is behind forms of speech such as "the industrial revolution" (Brand, p. 204), which was not like a riot or saturnalia at all. When the time is ripe, the shell pops open to reveal the new form that was within. This society waiting to emerge is being held back by some obstruction. Revolution, for Brand, then, can be like a removal of obstructions.[7] We do not have to construct a whole new society *from nothing.* We already have the infrastructure: state schools, an NHS, functioning harbors, a system of rail-tracks; we do not have to create a completely new alternative kind of rail transport. So it is not a huge task to abolish C; all the structures that would be needed for a proper and decent human life without it are *already there in place.* All we need to do is get rid of the shell, the formal set of entitlements and structures that siphon off benefits to the very rich. Since the continued existence of this shell is in the interests of no one but the tiny elite of owners of the world—although some have been deluded into "aspiring" to identify with this group or even dream of becoming one of these, an aspiration that does not have the slightest chance of ever being fulfilled—what exactly is stopping us? Each must answer that question him- or herself with as much clarity and introspective honesty as Brand shows in this book.

Even if the new social structures are in some sense already there under the membrane, it does not follow that some pushing or cutting might not be required to allow them fully to emerge. Forceful intervention to facilitate the birth of a fully formed infant is not the same kind of thing as using violence indiscriminately, and it is also clearly less difficult to envisage than creating a whole new human *ab ovo* from basic components. On the question of violence, Brand seems to have the greatest admiration for and feel the greatest affinity to the views of Gandhi and of certain anarchists (pp. 91, 271, 322).[8] All political movements, Brand holds, must begin as they intend to go on; the process of acting must prefigure the outcome. If the goal really is a society without organized violence, this must be mirrored in a nonviolent approach: "violence as a means [to a more humane society] is always unsuccessful" (p. 90).

This, however, is not the end of the story, because Brand also wishes to make three further points. First the issue of violence–nonviolence is of subordinate importance compared with the overwhelming necessity (in view of 3) of getting rid of C. Some might think that this is in a certain tension with the Gandhian claims above, but there is nothing inconsistent about holding that nonviolence is always better than violence, but that if C really is ruining the Earth as a possible human habitation, the goal of preserving the viability of our planet should reasonably take priority over the avoidance of violence. Second, one must also recognize different kinds of violence. Organized, systemic forms of violence—armies shooting phosphorus shells that have been produced with great care in order to inflict maximal damage and targeting refugees—should be distinguished from spontaneous, momentary reactions of outrage. Third, as has been repeated continually since Sartre wrote his preface to Fanon's *Les damnées de la terre* in 1965,[9] the only reasonable way of judging the violence associated with the abolition of C is not absolutely or in isolation, but in the context of, that is, in comparison with, the violence that is needed to maintain C, much of which is indirect and hard to see or intentionally hidden from us, and much of which we have become so used to that we no longer register it. This does not mean that it is a foregone conclusion that every act of violence that *actually* leads to the abolition of C is "justified"—what exactly is "justified" supposed to mean here?—and it certainly does not mean that every act of violence that an agent *claims* will advance the abolition of C is "justified," but it does mean that when discussing violence one cannot, as it were, reckon up with exactitude every rock thrown through the window of a bank, while *failing* to note at all every act of violence or destruction that is a systemic result of the normal operations of the banking system. This does not in itself settle the question of violence but does set out the terms on which it ought to be discussed.

Lady T had, if not exactly theories, at any rate contoured and differentiated attitudes toward these issues about violence. These were more or less the exact opposite of those attributed to Brand in the previous paragraph: the organized and official "forces of order" (primarily police, prison guards, military) should be assumed, as the default position, to be acting in a legitimate and justified way, unless there is really overwhelming evidence to the contrary. Demonstrators, obstreperous individuals, informal groups, and especially combinations of workers (that is, unions) who act in ways that are to any degree disruptive have only themselves to blame for any violence visited upon them. She did have some views about a "common good" that was to be protected and about the use of force in foreign affairs and in the pursuit of collective goals. Whatever one might think of her attitudes and views, she did at least make an attempt to engage with a wide range of political issues, including the possible use of violence in a serious way.

Pisher Bob is concerned about self-defense and, of course, defense of my own property, but the possible use of force for collective goals or ideals plays no role for him, because the very idea of collective goals or ideals has little meaning for him. Apart from some platitudes of his time and place, Preacher John has little to say on any of these subjects. What views he does express about the structure of meaningful work, gender relations, history, issues of war and peace, and international relations are so excruciatingly ill considered that even many of his most devoted followers are embarrassed and wish he had held his peace completely about them.

Religion is a topic of extensive discussion in this book, and Brand's own religious views are very prominently on display (pp. 45–75, 137–158, 175–189). These are doctrinally eclectic, but held together by a single great emphasis on the sense of a feeling of oneness with nature and all other sentient beings. Brand presents them as the natural concomitants of his rejection of the individualism and materialism of contemporary society (p. 69). We can get access to this sense of oneness through certain techniques of meditation that can have a calming effect on the individual, give access to a complex inner landscape, and even have some political effects in the form of moving us toward the possibility of harmonious living with others. Acts of individual kindness to others play an important role in the overall process of spiritual development (pp. 146–147). Some of the possible effects (pp. 127–128) of meditation seem to be overstated, but Brand also seems aware of this (pp. 148, 151–152), and this honesty of perception is one of the most striking and attractive features of the book.

In contrast to most books about political philosophy, Brand's actually engages with facts that we can recognize as part of our everyday lives, and in that it resembles the most interesting other book on political philosophy of the past two decades or so, *L'insurrection qui vient*,[10] although the latter has a slightly more apocalyptic tone and gives slightly more hard-edged advice. Brand gives a remarkable number of concrete political suggestions, such as dismantling any corporation with a revenue larger than the GNP of the smallest state in the world (p. 81), limiting the life spans of corporations (pp. 225–239), relocalizing food production (p. 86), prohibiting private security arrangements (pp. 113–116), canceling private debt (pp. 92–97, 171–173), creating co-ops (pp. 240–250), decriminalizing drug use, and so on.

I must confess that I do not find Brand or his book at all funny, amusing, droll, or entertaining, but there is no accounting for differences in sense of humor; mine runs rather to something coarser, more obscene, and more fantastic than Brand—like Aristophanes or Rabelais—so I find *Revolution* a bit too genteel, restrained, and decorous, but this is, I know, an idiosyncratic taste. But then I do not find *Leviathan*, *Le contrat social*, or *de legibus* that droll either. I had not really registered Brand's existence until his book came out, but when I read it, I was surprised to find it an absolute treasure trove of keen observations and good sense: "We know . . . that the dismantling and privatisation of the NHS is not for the benefit of us, the people who use it. It benefits the government that proposed it and the companies that are purchasing it. Nobody voted for it because nobody would be stupid enough to give us the option" (p. 124).

5

The Idea of a Critical Theory, Forty Years On

—◦◦◦—

IN THE MIDDLE OF the nineteenth century Hegel wrote that every philosopher is a child of his time and none can jump over his own shadow: every philosophy, then, is "its time grasped in a concept." In the twentieth century Adorno took up this idea again when he spoke of the irreducible "kernel of time" embedded in the center of any philosophical view, and of the "temporal index" of truth. Whatever these rather difficult doctrines mean, they clearly are not intended to imply that at any given time all opinions are equally true.

I started this small book in Heidelberg, Germany, in 1973 and finally finished it in 1980 at the University of Chicago; it appeared with Cambridge University Press in late 1981. Looking back at the text from the present—from 2013 and my home on this small island off the northwest coast of Europe—I think I can begin to see rather more clearly than I could then some of the relevant features of the historical context within which it was conceived and executed. To return for a moment to Hegel, who is the major spiritual presence hovering over this book—and whose work is the more important for understanding what I was trying to do for not being mentioned at all in the main text—the reader will recall that he also holds that philosophy is essentially retrospective, a reflection of a historical

79

moment or movement that when it finally takes philosophical form is essentially already over. This doctrine marks a distinction between what is "really" happening in the political, social, and economic world and the subsequent reflection of this in philosophy (religion, art, law, and so on). As far as what was "really" happening is concerned, we can now see that the period of unprecedented economic growth and political and social progress that took place in the West after the end of the Second World War began to plateau in the 1970s, when productivity began to stagnate.[1] By the early 1970s, though, the assumption that economic growth would continue, levels of prosperity continue to rise, and the social and political structures continue to evolve in the direction of greater flexibility, realism, and humanity had become very firmly entrenched in Western populations. The period during which anything like that assumption was at all reasonable was ending just as I was beginning work on my book, although, I, of course, did not know that at the time, any more than anyone else did. It would have been political suicide for any major figure in the West to face up to this situation courageously and to try to make it clear to the population that the possibilities of relatively easy real growth were exhausted, and the era of ever-increasing prosperity was gone for good; this would have raised intolerable questions about the very foundations of the existing socioeconomic and political order. What the 1980s and 1990s had in store for us, then, was the successive implementation of a series of financial gimmicks that created financial bubbles and allowed the illusion of increasing growth for a significant minority of the population to be maintained for a while; this was accompanied by a massive change in our socioeconomic system and culture that made possible and in fact actively encouraged individuals and institutions to incur increasingly significant amounts of debt. This in turn was attended by a massive shift in resources and economic power away from the population, further concentration of wealth in the hands of a very few superlatively rich individuals and families, and a great increase in social inequality. Needless to say, the proliferation of debt *ad libitum* could not under existing conditions continue for long, and the system began to collapse in 2007–2008. Catastrophe was averted only by a bizarre, not to say perverse, set of political interventions in the Western economies—interventions that have correctly been described as "so-cialism for the rich": defaulting banks and failing industries were propped up by huge public subsidies; private debts were taken over by the state, while any profits continued to be allowed to flow to pri-vate investors. This structure certainly bears no similarity whatever to the ways in which proponents of "capitalism" have described their favored arrangements.

At the latest by the end of the 1970s it was visible that a huge coun-termovement was in progress that it would be incorrect exactly to call a counterrevolution (because the immediately antecedent period, although one of a certain relative progress, was hardly a revolution). The forms of economic regulation that had been introduced during the Great Depression of the 1930s and had stood the West in good stead for more than forty years were gradually relaxed or abol-ished during the 1980s, systems for providing social welfare that had gradually been developed came under pressure and began to be dismantled, public services were reduced or "privatized," the infra-structure began to crumble, and inequality increased, as did pov-erty and homelessness.

The academic reflection of the massive social and economic changes that took place between 1970 and 1981 could be seen in the gradual marginalization of serious social theory and political philos-ophy, and particularly of "leftist" thought. The usual story that is told about the history of "political philosophy" since World War II holds that political philosophy was "dead" until it was revived by Rawls, whose *Theory of Justice* appeared in 1971. This seems to me seriously misleading. Rather than the publication of *Theory of Justice* being a renewal of political philosophy, it seems to me more fruitful to see it as part of a failure of nerve, and a turning away from the real world of institutions, politics and history toward the never-never land of purely normative theory. The 1940s, 1950s, and 1960s, after all, were not lacking in political philosophy. They saw the elabora-tion of major work by the Frankfurt School (including Marcuse's *One-Dimensional Man*); a rediscovery of Gramsci; various essays and books by Sartre, Camus, de Beauvoir, Fanon, and Merleau-Ponty; Guy Debord's *La société du spectacle;* early pieces by Foucault—all works roughly speaking "on the left." All of these were works of political philosophy that tried to take some account of real history, the real state of Western societies, and real politics. If Anglophones took no notice of this material, that was not because serious work in political philosophy failed to exist, but for some other reason. Similarly, on the "right" Popper, Hayek, Leo Strauss, and Oakeshott (to name only a few) were active. Rawls's *Theory of Justice* seemed an irrelevance to those engaged (in 1971) in the various and diverse forms of intense political activity that now collectively go under the title of "the 1960s." I completed and defended my doctoral dissertation in the spring of 1971, and recall my doctoral supervisor, who was a man of the left, but also an established figure and full professor at Columbia University in New York, mentioning to me that there was a new book out by Rawls, but telling me that no one would need to read it because it was of merely academic interest, an exercise in trying to mobilize some half-understood fragments of Kant to give a better foundation to American ideology than utilitarianism had been able to provide. Many people will perhaps think that that was a misjudgment, but I think it was prescient. I cite it in any case to give contemporary readers a sense of the tenor of the 1970s. Rawls in fact eventually, in the 1980s, the era of Thatcher and Reagan, established a very well-functioning academic industry that was quickly routinized and which preempted much of the space that might have been used for original political thinking. He was one of the forerunners of the great countermovement, outlining proleptically a philosophical version of what came to be known as the "trickle-down" theory. Crudely speaking, this theory eventually takes this form: "value" is overwhelmingly produced by especially gifted individuals, and the creation of such value benefits society as a whole. Those who are now rich are well-off because they have contributed to the creation of "value" in the past. For the well-off to continue to benefit society, however, they need to be motivated, to be given an incentive, to create. Full egalitarianism will destroy the necessary incentive structure and thus turn off the taps from which prosperity flows. So inequality can actually be in the interest of the poor because only if the rich are differentially better off than others will they create value at all, some of which will "trickle down to" or be redistributed to the less well-off. Rawls allows people who observe great inequality in their societies to continue to feel good about themselves, provided that they support some cosmetic forms of redistribution of the crumbs that fall from the tables of the rich and powerful. The Rawlsian system is argumentatively extremely highly elaborated, but the intense focus on specific details of argumentation that is, justifiably, considered one of the glories of analytic philosophy can have the effect of allowing one to lose sight of the larger context. The apparent gap many people think exists between the views of Rawls and, say, Ayn Rand is less important than the deep similarity in their basic views and the similarity of the social niches into which they fit. The warden of a prison may put on a benevolent smile (Rawls) or a grim scowl (Rand), but that is a mere result of temperament, mood, calculation, and the demands of the immediate situation, and will have only marginal effect; the prison may have a resident chaplain who will console the inmates with comforting words (Rawls) or a fire-breathing pulpit-thumper (Rand); there may be an associated staff of social workers or not. The fact remains that the warden is the warden of a prison, the chaplain the chaplain of a prison, and, more importantly, that the prison is a prison. To shift attention from the reality the prison to the morality, the ideals, and the beliefs of the warden, the nature of the rations provided to the inmates, or the exact nature of the comforting doctrine preached by the prison chaplain is an archetypical instance of an ideological effect.

In counterpoint to Hegel's view about the philosopher as a child of his time, one might note the views of some other nineteenth-century German thinkers; Nietzsche, for example, held that philosophy is not "its time grasped in concept," but is by its very nature *"unzeitgemäß"* ("out of synch with the present time"). The ideal is to be not behind the time but ahead of it, to write a work that would be a philosophy of the future (as Feuerbach tried to do). It is the great hope of many philosophers, particularly political philosophers, to accomplish something like this. If I am right, Rawls did succeed in this aspiration. His project of 1971 came to fruition really only after Reagan, Thatcher, and their neoliberal allies had destroyed much of the existing legal, cultural, social, political, and economic framework that patient struggle had built up for several generations in the interests of at least minimally regulating the worst excesses of capitalism. The *tabula rasa* they aspired to create, a prefiguration of the totally "flat" world of later neo-liberal thought,[2] would be a field on which the cognitive activity of agents behind a Rawlsian "veil of ignorance" could appropriately be deployed.

For the reasons I cited above, *The Idea of a Critical Theory* was *"un-zeitgemäß"* when it appeared in 1981, espousing views that were about to lose philosophical and political traction in a very serious way. With the current visible collapse of the neoliberal order, though, perhaps it has a chance that was denied it on its original publication. That, of course, does not depend on me.

6

István Hont (1947–2013)

—◁◦◦◦▷—

IstVÁN HONT was born in Budapest in 1947, emigrated to the UK in 1974, and was from 1978 to his death in 2013 a fellow at Kings College, Cambridge (with the exception of a very brief stint at Columbia University in the 1980s). He was one of the leading intellectual historians of his generation with a special interest in Adam Smith as a figure who contributed to forming one of the dominant ideologies of incipient capitalism. Hont's combination of overwhelming erudition, extreme intellectual fertility, originality, sharpness of perception, and argumentative rigor had to be experienced in the flesh to be appreciated fully. His book *Jealousy of Trade* (Harvard, 2005) is a recognized masterpiece, but gives only a pale reflection of the monumental intelligence that lay behind it. And so in a way the "real" István was the one encountered in supervisions and seminars, especially in the so-called "Monday Seminar" on intellectual history and political thought. In an ideal world any discussion of his intellectual significance would be most appropriately centered on his interpretation of the period he made his own, the Scottish Enlightenment. Since I do not have the competence to do this, my remarks will focus, even at the risk of a certain eccentricity of treatment, on some more general features of his approach that are visible even to those of us who are not trained historians.

In a relatively little known early remark Nietzsche describes his own project as that of trying to look at the world with the eyes of a "cold angel" who "sees through the whole miserable spectacle" *(Lumperei)*, yet neither bears reality any ill will nor finds the world in the least bit "cozy" *(ohne böse zu sein aber auch ohne Gemüth)*.[1] This, of course, is a modern variant of Tacitus's famous declaration of nonpartisanship when he asserts that he decided to write the history of the recent past *"sine ira et studio"*—without anger or favoritism.[2] It would be perfectly understandable if a member of the Senatorial aristocracy like Tacitus were to write a history that was motivated by hatred or resentment of those emperors who took over prestigious functions previously exercised by the Senate. Or his account might be deformed because he was keen to glorify the achievements of his particular faction, to present their motives in the best possible light, to promote their cause. *Ira* and *studium* stand for negative and positive forms of bias, actively favoring or discriminating against one side or the other in the struggle for dominance. Tacitus clearly saw both of these as pitfalls to avoided.[3]

Nietzsche's view is an existential and metaphysical intensification of this basic Tacitean tack.[4] If members of the Roman Senate tended to resent the emperor because he thwarted their plans and reduced their dignity, and they allowed this to bleed into their account of politics, this was as nothing compared to the deep-seated general human resentment against reality itself, which continually frustrates us and imposes limits on our action and against the course of human history and which can disrupt us in ways even an emperor might impotently envy. If an individual senator sought a sense of security and moral comfort in an exaggerated view of the power, the accomplishments, and the virtue of his own faction, how much stronger is the temptation for humans in general to believe that the world is basically a benign place, or, at any rate, that history is on one's side? This impulse can take a very wide variety of forms covering a broad spectrum of attitudes. At one end of this spectrum lies a grudging resignation to participation in what is recognized as being the only game on offer, and at the other end one finds active triumphalism or the "warm" embracing of the status quo as a place in which one can feel completely at home.[5] Finally, if history gives one a nasty surprise, what would be stronger than the temptation to become bitter and go sour on reality itself?

Nietzsche's image of the "cold angel" is, I wish to suggest, a good foil to use in thinking about István's work. István was impervious to the siren songs of coziness, to the *studium* of explicit or tacit theodicies, to naive belief in progress, and to the self-congratulatory forms of wishful thinking about itself and its own institutions that are particularly characteristic of modern liberal democracies. Equally, and perhaps more surprisingly, he seemed theoretically remarkably resistant to the *ira* that can be one of the usual effects of the historical disappointment of deeply rooted hopes, although, given his background and the events of the historical period in which he lived, he had immediate experience of more than his share of these.

Although this discussion is couched in a vocabulary of individual psychology—Tacitus's *ira*, Nietzsche's *böse sein*, my use of "resentment" and "going sour on reality" above—this is actually a distortion because what is at issue are *structural* features of the interaction between concepts, theories, forms of action, and human agents. If we fall back on what look very much like simple psychological terms, it is because we lack an appropriate and distinctive idiom for speaking about this whole domain. To look at the world through the lens of a theory that has the structure of a theodicy is *not* necessarily to be of a cheerful disposition, but rather to be theoretically committed to a number of assumptions about the world that will affect what else one will be likely to notice, how one will be likely to process what one perceives, and what courses of action one finds it easy—or particularly difficult—to envisage.

This reflection might help to dispel part of the air of paradox that surrounds the application of the image of a "cold angel" to István. "Cold" is certainly not the adjective one would think of using about István as a person, about his attitude toward his subject matter or about his treatment of it. He was as personally enthusiastic about his interests as anyone could be and as capable as anyone of being vexed by those who proposed or perpetuated what he took to be untenable views. Personal passion, though, just to repeat, is not the same as structural affirmation of—or metaphysical resentment against—the course of history itself. Equally resistance to the temptation of

coziness is not a form of "skepticism," if one construes "skepticism"
as a strictly epistemological category. Of course, a healthy tendency
toward suspension of belief, argumentative counter-suggestibility,
and bloody-minded insistence of seeing "evidence" is just part of
the ethos of the scholarly life, but István did not really think he was
justified in claiming to know (for certain) *fewer things* than most
people did (as would be the case for a classic skeptic). If anything, the
reverse. To return to the quotation from Nietzsche, he wanted to
"see through" things. Seeing through comforting or resentment-
based illusions does not mean *limiting* knowledge claims. To use an
example that is mine rather than István's. I do not think I know *less*
about the contemporary liberal ideology of rights and democracy
than its confused and naive advocates do, but *more*.

A second difficulty one might have with the idea of István as a cold
angel is that angels are primarily observers—*not* participants—in the
messy human process of acting.[6] One of the most characteristic features of István's thought, however, was the view that human praxis
had its own dignity, its own standpoint on the world, and its own
logic, and was not a mere weak sister of "theory." The world confronting a political actor is not really much like that confronting an
engineer trying to use a pregiven theory to build a bridge, a judge
attempting to apply the law in judging a defendant, or a scientist
testing a hypothesis. One salient difference is surely that engineering,
law, and science are limited and rule-governed activities directed at
well-defined situations in a way in which politics need not be. I can
argue with the engineer about which is the best way to calculate
stress, and that can be a question within the competence of engineering. If, however, I begin to ask whether we should build the
bridge over this river at all—maybe we do not have the money or do
not actually wish to encourage fraternization with our obnoxious
neighbors—we may quickly exit from the realm of engineering altogether. Politics is not internally bounded in this way or so strictly
rule-bound. There is the phenomenon of "routine politics"—
electoral strategy in times of peace and stability—but it is also clear
that this routine politics can at any time turn into something else.
At some point the Cossacks may turn their weapons not on the peasants in the square but on their own officers. The political actor

must always take this possibility into account in a way in which the engineer qua engineer need not take account of the possibility that people might decide they do not want a bridge at all. From this idea that there is a distinctive standpoint of practical agents, it is but a step to the further claim that the study of political thought ought to be *from the standpoint* of the relevant agents who are facing uncertain and antecedently *ill-defined* situations that call for action, and thus are not like lawyers or engineers.[7] From this one may move to the even further thought that the study of the history of political thought must somehow take account of this specific viewpoint of the political actor, the viewpoint of "praxis." The "angel" as archetypical nonagent seems out of place here.

István's view was praxis centered, but the argument given in the previous paragraph can and must also be run the other way around. Although to understand past political thought, we must understand *their* politics, it is also the case that our relation to *past* politics cannot be the deeply practical relation we have to contemporary politics.[8] My relation to the expansion of the Roman Republic in the second century BC *cannot* be the same kind of thing as my opposition to the creeping—and not so creeping—privatization of the NHS that is being implemented by the current government. We have no alternative but to have something more like an "angelic" relation to the Roman Republic than we do to the coalition government. This does not mean we cannot in some sense change the past by what we do now. What we do now does affect, no matter how infinitesimally, how *relevant* certain features of the past will be and *in what way* they will be effectively available to us. Appeals to "relevance" are potentially subject to serious misuse, most often because they can foster highly disagreeable and often ideologically motivated forms of myopia, but the possibility of such misuse should not blind us to the fact that "relevance" is not a mere epiphenomenon but is rather a constitutive characteristic of history. Past thought is *differentially* close to us for a number of different reasons.

Of course, István thought, one studied the history of political thought in order to understand, and thus presumably improve, our own politics. "Why else would you do it?" he once remarked to me. He did not have a theoretically elaborated *general* view on the relation of present and past praxis—no one has, and it is possible that it is even a mistake to think that one should or could have a *theory* of this. Perhaps contemporary political action, contemporary theories, and historical reflection form something like a singular and shifting force field within which we must move. If so, István moved in it with great skill.

To be asked to speak here today is to be thrust into a formalized situation that I find extremely uncomfortable because I must act as if I am the recording angel about my dear friend, summing him up. There is nothing I can do about this apart from pointing out that it is an artifact of the situation of grievous loss in which we find ourselves. It is customary in such cases to reflect that we have István's works. That is true but no consolation, because no replacement for the presence of his living voice.

7

The Moral Legacy of Marxism

A Legacy?

To speak of the "legacy" of something is to consider it as being dead, although, of course, one can do this proleptically. A theory is dead if it is no longer entertained and discussed, no longer thought about, and no longer moves anyone to action. To speak of the legacy of Marxism, then, is to consider it as in this sense dead. By calling Marxism a "theory" I do not mean that it can be summed up in a single general statement, such as that peptic ulcers are caused by a bacterial infection (not by stress), that the earth moves about the sun (rather than vice versa), or that bad money drives out good. Individual "theories" in this sense are, of course, of extreme importance in guiding our action, but they are not the only kinds of structures that are important in our cognitive and practical life. We also use and are dependent on more complicated sets of interconnected concepts, assumptions, methods, directives about how to go about trying to come to an understanding of the world, claims about which things are important and which less important, and so on. Examples of "large-scale theories" in this sense might be Christianity, liberalism, positivism, *tiers-mondisme*, "the economic approach to human behavior,"[1] or Marxism. None of these can be easily reduced to a single claim. If one wished one might also call them "programs," "approaches," "frameworks," or even (if sufficiently general and all-encompassing) "worldviews." In any case, "theories" in this wider sense do not usually stand and fall with the confirmation or refutation of any of the individual theoretical items with which they are associated at any particular time. They usually have a sufficiently open texture and are sufficiently robust to be able to accommodate significant changes, even the refutation of some of their original component parts, while maintaining their identity. At one point in time a geocentric view of the universe was an important component of Christianity, but, contrary to the fears and expectations of many thinking Christians of the early modern period, adopting heliocentrism did not actually make that much difference to the hold Christianity continued to exercise on large numbers of people in Europe and its dependencies.[2] Large-scale theories, or worldviews, then, are often surprisingly robust.

How, then, does such a "large-scale theory" die? Putting aside what one might call accidental and exiguous factors, for example, an epidemic wiping out the population in all the towns where Monophysitism was strong, "death" can happen for, roughly speaking, two kinds of reasons. First, powerful groups who have vested interests in preventing people from acting on a given large-scale theory may engage in specific acts or adopt policies that attempt to censor, marginalize, suppress, or discredit it, using whatever means the society provides for doing that. Thus, the Catholic Church was able to have Giordano Bruno burned at the stake for holding and propagating views it thought seditious, and many societies have had official governmental censors who decide what may be published, what plays may be produced, and what visual material circulated and displayed. The attempt at marginalization may, however, be more subtle. Thus, during the Cold War the CIA massively subsidized abstract art, hoping that this would have the effect of making the Soviet doctrine of "Socialist Realism" seem culturally irrelevant, and thus of reducing the appeal of Marxism. The variety of ploys and strategies that can be adopted along these lines is very large,[3] and not all strategies will work equally well, or indeed at all. Thus, it is sometimes claimed that the Nazi exhibition of "Degenerate Art" in Munich in the 1930s, which was intended to generate massive public disgust, backfired because many who saw it came away *liking* what they saw.

The ability of large organizations with fixed interests to direct public attention and influence public attitudes and beliefs by specific interventions is considerable, but probably not unlimited. If one wishes to understand the death of a large-scale theoretical approach, such intervention will not usually be the whole story. A second factor will be more important. A theory in this sense dies when its general view of the world or some important constituent of it comes to seem deeply implausible or irrelevant to a sufficiently large number of members of the society. Why discuss or even entertain a view that does not at all seem to ring true to our experiences of the world in which we live? Thus, in a society in which public authorities are few, inefficient, deeply corrupt, or simply "far away" (Небо высоко, Цар далеко), claims that all disputes should (or even could) be settled by "appeals to the constituted authorities" will seem significantly less plausible than they will to inhabitants of the densely policed and administered societies of contemporary Western Europe.

The different factors cited above are not mutually exclusive. Part (however, in general only a part) of the reason why certain ways of looking at the world seem natural and commonsensical to people is that institutions operate to reinforce that belief. However, even in that case, it is not always anything like a conscious *policy* that is at work. The really effective reinforcement takes place through action that people and institutions may well engage in "in good faith." People believe that "in society it is dog eat dog" partly because it is something they are told is true—as the existence of the saying itself shows—but partly because in our society this observation seems correct.[4] The operation of our institutions reinforces the view that the world is a place where every man is for himself and the only values are financial values. It is not that the bankers at Chase or Barclays sit down and intentionally plan to reinforce these beliefs. That would mean that they in some sense really knew that they were false or fragile and needed conscious support, but that, I think, is not always the case: many of the relevant people *actually hold them*. So this is the opposite of a "conspiracy" theory.

I further note that a legacy is something of continuing relevance, importance, or value, but not necessarily of positive value. In many societies I can inherit not only assets but also debts or obligations, just as I can be said to inherit a genetic malformation, or the legacy of a badly spent youth can be a chronic disease or a vicious disposition. The negative elements of the legacy of Marxism have been canvassed ad nauseam and no one is in danger of overlooking them. In the context of this essay, I shall be interested mainly in what we can consider "positive" elements in a legacy. So to speak of the legacy of Marxism is to consider it as a complex movement which is in some sense over, past, superseded, or dead, but which contained elements which deserve to be carried forward and cultivated.

A *Moral* Legacy?

But what is a "moral legacy"? It is particularly tricky to discuss this partly because "moral" and its derivatives are in general used in such a variety of ways, most of which are not very clear or well defined even by the standards of terms that apply to human phenomena. In addition, what "morality" is and how it is to be understood is exactly what is at issue between Marxism and various of its competitors.

I should like to begin by making three distinctions which seem to me useful in discussing the possible moral legacy of Marxism.[5] First, there is a difference between "morality" considered as a potential quality of certain human *actions*, practices, institutions, and this is to be distinguished from "morality" as a kind of *thinking* about or theorizing about these actions, practices, forms of individual and collective activity, and institutions. So, on the one hand, there are things we recognize as on the whole and usually good practices or good ways of conducting ourselves and structuring our practices (for example, diversifying our agricultural production, training doctors and nurses to a high standard, making sure the systems of sewers and drains in our towns and cities are kept in good repair, regulating the flow of heavy vehicular traffic by formulating clear rules, and so on), and things we recognize as on the whole and usually bad practices or bad ways of behaving (dueling, public executions, female genital mutilation, filling offices of real public power with people whose only

qualification is heredity). "Recognize" here is related to actual behavior. We "recognize it as good" means we tend to promote and
cultivate it, praise it, express concern when the practice seems to be
threatened, and so forth, and analogously for what we "recognize as
bad." However, in addition to holding that certain practices may be
good or bad as it were "in themselves," we often also recognize that
there are particularly good and particularly bad ways of organizing
and conducting these practices, participating in them, and inte-
grating them into one another. Even if there is wide agreement in
our societies about these practices and about which ways of organizing them are better and which worse, there may be significant
theoretical disagreement about how to understand the practices,
forms of action, or institutions in question, and about *why* structuring
them in one way rather than another is especially good or bad. So
there is "actually existing" morality as embodied in recognized
practices and ways in which practices are cultivated, and then there
is "morality" as a theorization of practice. For obvious reasons these
two will not be completely separate, because, for instance, there is
usually *some* connection between how people think in general terms
they should act, and how they actually do behave in valuing, pursuing, and avoiding types of activities in their lives. On the other
hand, they will not simply be the same, because people very often
do not actually avoid or work to abolish practices that in some sense
their theoretical views suggest ought better not to exist, they are
often deluded about what they actually value, they often systematically do things they think they ought not to, and they very often do
not hold themselves to very high standards of self-awareness or consistency, and so on.[6]

The second distinction is that between "morality" in a broad sense
and "morality" in a narrow sense. In the broad sense "morality" en-
compasses any kind of systematic distinction between better and
worse in the human world, particularly if "better and worse" can be
connected to human action, that is, it concerns morality if it is possible to say (in the widest sense) that you should or ought to do it, or
act in a certain way. Brushing one's teeth in the morning is a question of morality in the widest sense of that term in that we all "should"
do so; it is better to do so than not because if we do not, we run the

risk of allowing our teeth to decay. So in this broad sense "moral" can be thought to contrast with "(merely) descriptive" (such as the accounts in dental textbooks about the progress of tooth decay and gum disease).[7] The narrower sense of "morality" is, in the West, one that stands very much more firmly and strongly under the influence of residual Christian or post-Christian conceptions. Here "moral" is construed as definitely distinct from (if not actually opposed to) the merely prudential, instrumental, or tactical; it is assumed that there is a special "moral ought" different from the prudential "ought" of "You ought not to antagonize that mastiff" (because he is free to attack you) or the instrumental "ought" one finds in statements like "You ought to go to the right here" (rather than to the left, because the place you want to get to lies in that direction). "Morally good" is often construed as meaning something like "good in itself" (in purported contrast to "good relative to some assumed contingent purposes," such as avoiding a struggle with a dog in order to avoid injury or to get to a certain place quickly). The archetypical case of "morality" for some is one in which the Christian or Kantian would give advice like the following: "Although it would be convenient for you, do no harm to others, and even benefit others, still you 'ought' not to lie in this situation." This narrow sense of "morality," in turn, is sometimes connected with a whole further apparatus of ideas about human motivation, choice, intention, guilt, perhaps also conscience, and (sometimes) the virtual irrelevance of real consequences to the evaluation of action.

The third distinction is that between making a moral judgment and "moralizing." To make a moral judgment is to judge that some institution, practice, or course of action is morally valuable and good, or acceptable, or unacceptable (in the wider sense of "moral"), or that it is permitted or absolutely prohibited by morality (in the more limited sense). To engage in "moralizing" is to make a moral judgment in an inappropriate context, that is, to propound it in a context or in a way which seems to ascribe to it too much or the wrong kind of weight or effectiveness. So I am making a moral judgment (in the wider sense) if I say that you ought to brush your teeth in the morning, making a moral judgment in the narrow sense if I say that you ought never, never to tell a lie (regardless of the consequences); I am moralizing if I am a criminologist who, when asked to explain the rise of a certain kind of crime in a certain area, replies, "It is because the people who live there are wicked," because even if this were to be true, it is not an appropriate or relevant answer to the question. The headmaster of a school who believes that by preaching to the students that smoking, drinking, taking drugs, and adolescent sexual activity are "evil in themselves" he will actually effectively prevent the pupils from engaging in any of these activities is "moralizing." Marx himself gives the example when discussing the views of a certain "Herr Heinzen," who *"glaubt das* Fürstentum *zu erklären, indem er sich für seinen Gegner erklärt . . . [er hat] die* Entstehung *des Fürstentums vermittelst moralischer Gemeinplätze begründet."*[8] However, you do not give an explanation of the origin (and function) of an institution by declaring that you disapprove of it on moral grounds. Similarly to state that the Jacobins were *"Unmenschen,"* to use another one of Marx's examples, is not to make a contribution to the understanding of the French Revolution. This is "moralizing" because moral judgments are inappropriate/irrelevant/pointless in the context of looking for an explanation.

Obviously there are any number of different kinds of "moralizing behavior" depending on the various different ways in which something can be inappropriate, or irrelevant, or the various different ways in which a person might, tacitly or explicitly, give "too much" weight to the enunciation of a statement about the morality or immorality of some institution, action, or person. Obviously, too, to say that I am giving "too much" weight to making statements with a moral content is not to say that making such statements has *no weight or influence at all*, much less to say that such statements would not have any weight at all in any context.

So clearly, I can reject "moralizing" without in any way being committed to, for instance, the falsity or vacuousness of all moral theories, and without thinking that moral judgments are always useless or "ungrounded." Similarly, I can reject "morality" in the narrow sense in that I can think there is no separate and distinctive moral "ought" and yet still engage in a wide range of everyday discussions about what it would be good, better, bad, or worse to do; how the government "should" address certain problems; how you "ought" to behave toward your colleagues, your cat, your children; and so on. Finally I may continue to behave as most people do, evaluating things in my environment, including using what may look to be morally loaded terms, without actually endorsing any of the various theories that have been proposed about the status of such terms.

Thus one might say that the following was part of the moral legacy of Marxism: as a result of participating in various activities that took the specific form they did only because those who organized and participated in them were committed to some of the characteristic theses of Marxism, certain social classes acquired habits of solidarity that they had not had before and would otherwise not have been likely to acquire in such a highly developed form; this solidarity, one might argue, deserves to continue to be cultivated and perhaps expanded. This development was a legacy in the form of a change in actual recognition of some ways of acting *as being* good, and perhaps also of others (scabbing) as being bad. Furthermore, one might think that a healthy suspicion of moralizing was one of the positive legacies of Marxism. Since, however, the focus of this essay is academic I concentrate on ways in which Marxism conceptualized "morality" (in the widest sense).

Marxism is thought to have died because it seemed to have been given a quasi-experimental run (the Soviet Union, the People's Republic of China, and Eastern Europe) and to have failed.[9] "Failure" for "large-scale theories" of the type to which Marxism belongs is itself an interpretative category. Sometimes when experiments fail there is simply a general sense of disorientation and confusion, but given theoretical positions, as has already been suggested, need not be completely abandoned just because they fail in one of their concrete incarnations. The perceived failure of Soviet-style economies to provide what they promised (greater economic growth than capitalist economies) and the way in which vested interests in capitalist countries played up these failures in Soviet-style systems were important factors in the demise of Marxism. However, it is usually easier for people to give something up if they think they have some potentially viable alternative they can adopt, and at the end of the 1980s there was an alternative that had come to seem more plausible than

Marxism. This is the Western combination of political liberalism with a capitalist economy that is just sufficiently controlled to avoid, at least up to the present, an utterly lethal crisis (although not to avoid crises altogether). Was there then a way of presenting a political philosophy appropriate to Western forms of capitalist democracy, ideally one that would easily integrate the political and the ethical? Best of all, because people were not so stupid as to believe that these Western societies were flawless, would be a view that encouraged minor reformist activity while overwhelmingly endorsing the basic socioeconomic framework. This would allow its adherents to bask in a warm and comforting glow of self-righteousness while remaining firmly within the limits set for the self-reproduction of the basic economic framework, and indeed strengthening this framework.

One Popular Liberal Alternative

Toward the end of the 1970s, John Rawls's *Theory of Justice* began to establish itself as a point of reference for political philosophy. The reasons for this were many and varied, some of them having to do with the content of the theory he presented, others with his way of going about presenting and arguing for his views.[10] Thus, although his original view is a position on political philosophy, its connection with a (certain kind of) Kantianism in ethics is also clear. Also many of the assumptions Rawls made were ones that were widely shared by members of his target audience in the United States, assumptions such as those about the centrality of the individual moral subject in thinking about politics and society. As the theory was developed over the years, revised, reformulated, and extended,[11] this Kantian perspective with its focus on the moral powers of individuals became even more prominent. These "powers" were considered to be not historical acquisitions whose form and activities were shaped by the particular historically specific society in which they occurred and which possessed varying degrees of importance in different contexts and different societies, but as historically invariant and fundamental; their exercise was tacitly assumed to be always more important than all else.

Many of the conclusions Rawls came to were also familiar and unthreatening to the inhabitants of Western-style "liberal democracies": society needed to be reformed in various ways, primarily some ways having to do with the distribution of goods, services, and other benefits, but fundamentally it could be considered to be in order. "Reform," of course, has always been with us, and even those who wish things to stay the same can be intelligent enough to see that they can only remain the same if they change.[12] So calls for reform, as I mentioned above, can be comforting. There is little point in trying to "reform" something one thinks is fundamentally hopeless, like, for instance, systems of slavery; we think they need to be abolished. Rawls fits into the reassuring "reformist" mode: no revolution was needed to install a godly elite who would subject a recalcitrant population to divine discipline, no abolition of all forms of government, no prohibition on extraction of surplus-value through wage-labor, no reintroduction of slavery or child labor, no compulsory military mobilization for all eighteen-year-olds, male and female, in the interests of the higher purposes of the state or religious or ethnic group.

In addition to this, Rawls's highly abstract way of going about political philosophy was deeply reassuring. The message was clear: no need to engage in complicated, sticky, ambiguous interpretations of historical institutions (for example, slavery) or events (the extermination of indigenous populations), no need to know anything about *other* societies, cultures, polities, and their values, beliefs, practices—just see if they are "reasonable" by our standards, and that can be done in a decontextualized way. No need to think about the actual social origins, function, or consequences of concepts, theories, or belief systems: that is irrelevant to evaluating them. So the historian, the anthropologist, and the sociologist have nothing to say in political philosophy; it is a matter just for the philosopher (and perhaps, because of the centrality of claims about "distribution," for the economist). The philosopher is to look for a form of "reasonableness" (and a corresponding "unreasonableness") in a set of basic principles that govern institutions and these principles are to be easily detachable from all the mess of real history and real politics. When they are thus detached, they are to be evaluated by our "ethical intuitions," as normalized, perhaps, by the application of some simple universal principles of reason and empirical experience. No wonder academic economists loved Rawls from the start.

For present purposes the most important aspect of the kind of political philosophy that Rawls made popular is the role played by antecedent normative evaluation of institutional principles: because of the centrality assigned to our moral evaluations, it has come to be called the "normative turn." Methodologically Rawls's work and that of those who followed him represented a counterrevolution, jumping backward over about a century of political and social thought to reconnect with the late eighteenth century, and particularly with Kant. Crudely speaking, during the period between Kant and Rawls, social and political philosophers were not as obsessed with the purity and distinctiveness of the "normative," and keen on separating it as clearly as possible from the empirical, historical, sociological, the useful, and so on, as Kantians would have them be. Furthermore, they did not in general make a point of proceeding by *starting* with a normative theory of a "good," praiseworthy, "reasonable," ideal, or "just" society and then in a second step moving on to try to "apply" this theory to the world as it is. The questions of where and how one starts and of the order in which one proceeds are not irrelevant in political and social philosophy any more than they are in actual politics.

Marx represents in a particularly striking way a completely different approach to defining the issues and proceeding. He was deeply committed to a way of seeing which is very different from the Kantian or the Rawlsian way. One does not start with "the individual and his moral powers," any more than from "the individual and his cognitive powers." Lukács, in *Geschichte und Klassenbewußtsein*,[13] gets it right when he says that the most important thing about Marx is his view that society is a "totality"—that is, it is an entity composed of individuals-in-historically-specific-social-relations, which is oriented toward satisfying historically arising needs and reproducing itself though social action. Lukács adds that one could reject every single claim the historical Marx made, including presumably the labor theory of value, the analysis of primitive accumulation, the laws about the falling rate of profit, the various claims about the role of the proletariat in history, and so forth, and still be an "orthodox" Marxist, provided one thought it was necessary to approach society using the right "method"—and to use the right method was to construe society as a totality (in the above specified sense).

To reject the "abstract" individual starting point is not to deny that there are individuals, to assert that they and their claims are unimportant, or even necessarily to deny that they have the powers the Kantian ascribes to them (at least to some extent and in some contexts). It is to deny that abstract and isolated individuals have a certain foundational status that is sometimes attributed to them. Equally one might well reject the claim that ethics should start from "man is a strawberry-eating animal" and that this provides a fundamental criterion for the evaluation of human institutions and actions. One can reject this view while allowing that it might be a perfectly good starting point for reflections about human society by someone in the soft-fruit business. Rejecting the status of the general claim need not imply denying that strawberries existed, that men, women, and children occasionally ate them, and that for some people this was an important and relevant fact.

Marx, of course, thinks that individuals do have any number of cognitive powers in the following sense: if you take an individual who has grown up in a functioning society, you can theoretically isolate that individual and try to investigate what he or she can or could do. Marx himself puts emphasis on the ability of humans to execute plans which they have elaborated in their imaginations before acting.[14] This does not, of course, mean that the powers thus discovered, and which it is perfectly proper *in one sense* to "locate" in the individual, are not also inherently social in their origin and in their nature. It makes sense if you enter a room to say that she (over there) speaks French, whereas he (over here) speaks Russian, and they (over in the corner) each speak Turkish—it is correct that each has a different power and ability, although what you are doing is merely, as it were, distributing possible social roles to individuals (the role of Russian-speaker, French-speaker, and so on). It is also true that you can get some idea of the grammar, syntax, lexis of Turkish by investigating what this individual Turkish speaker says, what he or she recognizes as comprehensible Turkish. None of this is false, but it does not follow from this that Turkish (or any language) is not also and "inherently" a social phenomenon that can be fully understood only as a way in which different speakers interact with each other.

Language, and hence thought of any degree of sophistication, exists only as a collective social practice activated by individuals. It is true that English would not exist if there had never been individual speakers who made use of it. But it is also true that the language pre-exists any individual speaker; every speaker finds it always already there. It extends beyond the grasp of any individual speaker at any given time—there are English words I do not know and do not use, although I could acquire them—and, in most cases, the language will continue to exist after I cease to speak it; indeed after I cease to exist. There is, however, no royal path either from universal structures of rationality or from my individual consciousness or action to language as a social phenomenon—a point which Herder and Hegel saw clearly, which Kant signally failed to grasp with catastrophic consequences for his philosophical views, and which the late Wittgenstein rediscovered in the 1930s and 1940s. It is for this reason that neither psychology nor the study of the proposition can be philosophically fundamental for Marx.

For Marx, it is a mistake to start with abstract individuals because individuals always grow up as members of a social group and cannot be understood independently of that fact.[15] This does not mean that individuals are "nothing more than" undifferentiated social units or that they can be "reduced" to their social context. To say that society is to be *treated as* a historical totality is not to say that any given theory we may have of it at any particular time is infallible, or actually objectively exhaustive. When Marx speaks of "society as a totality" he is *not* endorsing the existence of what has now come to be called a "view from nowhere."[16] To make this mistake is, in some sense, to drop back to the position of Hegel, who thought that in his philosophy, absolute knowledge was realized: history and system came to coincide, so that his view was at the same time the comprehensible result of human history and a fully self-grasping way in which the absolute realized itself. Individuals as members of human groups have perceptual and ratiocinative powers, but these are not infallible or without historical location, and as a result their views are always perspectival. Marx agrees with Nietzsche that there is no disembodied, absolute knowledge; wherever there is "knowledge" it is a knowledge located in some human individuals or groups (including institutional groups). To say that society "is a totality" is to say that someone (individual or group) must so consider it. Such a person or persons will never be seeing it from "no point of view at all" (or from "god's-eye view" or from the purported standpoint of "pure reason"). I can see my own views as a part of "our" views, and as an expression of a general way of looking at the world characteristic of someone living in southeast Britain at the beginning of the twenty-first century and as integrated into our forms of social reproduction in various ways. Even if I am on some issues individually deviant, I am not deluded enough or self-centered enough to overlook the ways in which I have no more jumped over my own shadow than anyone else has, and my views, attitudes, and desires are (one variant of) those of my time and place, and they will be found to be reflected in what I (and others) take to be "society in itself totality." This reflective knowledge changes the way I think and act in various ways, but need not utterly undermine my use of our available moral language. I may still make judgments; I just fail to make certain claims about these judgments and the status they have, and fail to regiment my moral judgments according to one or another of the philosophical projects that claims on the basis, for instance, of "reason alone," or "reasonableness," or considerations of "reflective equilibrium," to be able to "justify" the priority of one set of them over others. I know that important parts of this language will come to be historically superseded, but do not know which parts, in what way, and what (if anything) will replace them. So their potential historical variability would be an argument against using them only if I assumed that there was some other nonvariable vocabulary and set of concepts and theses to which I might have access and which would be "better" for me to use. We have good reason to think, though, that this assumption is unwarranted. Society, as one might put it, is a totality open-to, open-for, and open-in *praxis*.

Totality

This approach via "totality" means, then, that the human individual, his or her perceptions, values, "intuitions," situation are neither the absolute starting point nor the absolute ending point of thinking about the human good to the extent to which it is attainable through action. In particular I need to call into question my own intuitions, perceptions, and forms of valuation by reflecting on their origin, the context in which they arose historically, the way in which I acquired them, who is benefited and who disadvantaged by looking at the world in this way. The only way to conduct this reflection is through the study of society as a whole and its history, and this is best done as a member of a group; in some sense it can only ever be done as a member of a group, because even an interior monologue is a discussion conducted in a natural language which is an inherently social medium. This is not to deny that sometimes I find myself as an individual in an emergency situation which looks to me like the one the Kantian takes to be paradigmatic—in which I must perhaps act immediately and do not have the luxury of reflecting in common with others and forming my beliefs carefully. Such cases are, however, precisely emergencies.

Post-Christian moral philosophy commonly has three characteristics. First of all, it (at least tacitly) presupposes the priority of the first-person individual perspective and the relation of that individual to a specific action. So it tries paradigmatically to answer the question: "What ought I to do here?" Second, it assumes (with an optimism which originates perhaps in the view that the Christian god is the omnipotent creator of the whole world) that there is a morally acceptable action that can be performed in all circumstances. Third, it assumes that "ethics" is a fully autonomous philosophical discipline with conclusive results that can be expressed in some kind of "doctrine": the injunctions (and/or prohibitions) it provides are certain, fully grounded, and universally valid; they give me a full, definitive warrant for acting. A philosopher, by virtue of his or her special training, can consult the doctrine and on that basis provide guidance for action and orientation in the world.

Kierkegaard brings out the first feature of traditional ethics in the course of arguing against Hegel.[17] One can take Kierkegaard as arguing roughly that Hegel assures me that monogamous marriage is part of the structure of a fully rational society, but this does not answer the real question, which is: "Should I, Sören Kierkegaard, marry Regina Olsen?" In trying to frame the question in this way, is Kierkegaard being profound or narcissistic? Hegel, and following him Marx, would have denied that Kierkegaard's tiny problem had the kind of philosophical priority Kierkegaard wished to attribute to it. This does not mean that Kierkegaard's question and his problem do not exist, that there is nothing anyone could say to him to help him—he may have experienced friends, wise colleagues, a sympathetic pastor (or imam), a concerned uncle, or godfather who could give him what turns out to be excellent advice. It is not even the case that there is nothing helpful that a philosopher—by virtue of having the kind of training philosophers have customarily had in Europe in the past two hundred years—could say to him. Many philosophers were not merely highly intelligent but also strikingly charismatic figures,[18] and perhaps their specific study of philosophy contributed in various ways to making them good at giving advice. However, to say that a philosopher can also sometimes help with practical advice, and that his training has something to do with this, is not to say that the *way* he helps is by consulting his doctrine, nor that the legitimate question of how Mr. SK (or "anyone in SK's situation") should act in this situation is the central one in practical philosophy. Why should not "What shall *we* do?" take priority? And who then exactly is "we"? The people who live, like me, on Tenison Road; my neighbors in the Petersfield ward of Cambridge; other retired university lecturers in the UK; other supporters of the UK's membership in the EU; *alle Betroffenen* (is this a very well-defined category?); all rational agents (why should they be of *special* interest to me and do they include my cat?)?

Even in the philosophical tradition itself there are more than merely traces of approaches that do not give priority to the first-person perspective. If the question is "τίνα τρόπον χρὴ ζῆν" ([In] what way is it necessary to live?),[19] "*Quid agendum?*" or for that matter Lenin's "*Что делать?*" (also usually rendered "What is to be done?"), these are all in an impersonal form (and the first refers to a whole mode of life rather than any specific action). The relation in which any of these questions, or the answer to any of these questions, stands to something that "ought to be done" by *this* specific human agent, is not direct.

To look at the world of human practice systematically from the Christian (and Kantian) point of view, or to start from this question and give it universal priority, is to distort ethical and political thinking significantly, and Marx rejects this distortion. This does not, of course, imply that one "must" or "ought" always to give priority to the collective or a more impersonal perspective, rather than my own individual one. Nor does it imply that there is a universal "view from nowhere" which we can adopt. It is perfectly consistent to deny that the "I"-perspective always has systematic priority without asserting that I "may" never "permissibly" suit myself.

To move, then, to the second of the three characteristics, some of the problems of individuals have no moral solution. If I am a slave in first century BC Rome, should I love or hate my master? It is not clear what it would mean to say that either answer to this question is morally the right one. Of course, this question only arises in a society in which the institution of slavery exists; abolish slavery and the question disappears. This does not mean, either, that we can say that the slave in first-century Rome "ought" to struggle to abolish slavery. This would be a pointless thing to try to do. Marx holds that it is just as useless to tell a slave in a society at a low level of development of the forces of production that he ought to "struggle for the abolition of slavery" as it is to tell him he ought to jump over the moon, because Marx thinks that whether or not slavery can be abolished at any given time and in any place depends on factors massively outside the control of any individual or indeed any organized group. It is perhaps not an accident, but rather something that is grist for Marx's mill, that as far as we can tell *no* slave in the ancient world, not even Spartacus, proposed to abolish slavery. This never occurred to *any* of them as a possibility (as far as we know), and if it had, it would have been an empty thought such as "What would I do if I could [now, that is, ca. 80 BC] fly?" or "How about if my goats could do the cooking around the hut for me?" None of the above means that it might not be good in our society to oppose the continued existence of slavery or its reintroduction, or indeed to impose this (should circumstances permit) on other contemporary societies who do not already accept it.

This does not mean that it is never under any circumstances possible to "abstract" some part of the whole, and study or even teach that by itself—without this possibility human cognition would be impossible. This abstraction is possible and harmless, *provided* you do not falsely think that by undertaking it, you isolate some special property, "the normative," which can be the object of a distinct, self-contained, and fully autonomous discipline, and have thus grounded an ethics that speaks with complete authority to people about how they "must" always act.

To be more exact, if I try to "abstract" the normative in my society,[20] I shall generally end up with a highly complex system of principles, habits, and modes of behavior. Roughly speaking, this system will have two parts (*vide supra*, pp. 94–98): one will contain a set (or various sets) of rules, principles, maxims, and values that will be those that people will publicly profess, with more or less prompting, as describing how their lives "ought" to be organized, or that philosophers can formulate in "rational reconstructions" and get people to affirm. I will call this the "high morality" or the "*Überbau*"-morality of the society. The other part will be the "really existing" morality, which will be what people actually live by. In one characteristic configuration, the "high morality" will be absolutist—"one must absolutely never lie"—but the really existing form will interpret, qualify, and bend these absolutist principles, introduce exceptions, and singularities: "One must never lie, but equally one may not betray a confidence, so when these two principles conflict, it is permissible to be 'economical with the truth'" (or the older: "One must never lie except to protect a lady's honor"). The reason for the discrepancy between the two—"high" and "really existing" morality—that will be given by people in the society is that the "high morality" is literally unlivable: perhaps the occasional saint or hero may make a stab at really living according to its precepts, but no one can expect everyone to be a hero.[21]

So when I, as a theorist, try to abstract in such a way as to formulate the rules of morality in effect in my society, I will in the best of cases end up with an unwieldy and lopsided two-part structure riddled with tensions and contradictions. If I have done my job correctly, most agents in my society will at least recognize my reconstruction for what it is (*modulo* a certain amount of the usual kind of human cantankerousness and countersuggestibility). They might, of course, nevertheless have *different* attitudes toward it. Some might think the "high morality" was based on a set of direct divine commands (or the injunctions of a substitute for god, such as reason); others might have other theories about that. Knowing that my local morality is essentially connected to specific forms of social reproduction will probably change my attitude toward it in various ways, but it does neither constitutes a "refutation of morality" nor does it tell me imperatively how exactly I should act toward this system of rules, virtues, habits, and forms of evaluation. The more enlightened will be likely to think that "the rules of morality" look very much like a set of principles that prescribe what *in general* we need to do for society to maintain itself in existence: a society in which murder, deceit, and envy ("coveting") were really uncontrolled would be unlikely, one might think, to be able to maintain itself in existence for long.

For Marx, the divine command view is palpably false, but when "enlightened" people say "morality is necessary for society to maintain itself," this statement is too ambiguous to be straightforwardly either true or false. By "morality" do they mean "high morality," "really existing morality," or their particular two-part structural amalgam of both? Does "society can maintain itself" mean "*our present society*"? How is this to be individuated exactly? Or does it mean "*any* human society"? Or "any human society above a certain level of complexity"? (What level?) If enlightened people mean by "morality is necessary for society to maintain itself" that our "really existing habits of moral action" are necessary for *the kind of society we now inhabit* to maintain itself, that is perhaps slightly exaggerated, in that it suggests that our actually existing habits are strictly the *only* ones compatible with this form of society, and that is probably not correct. Of course, there is, and always will be, room for small variations and even for reforms. Japanese ethical dispositions and habits in the 1970s were not exactly the same as those in Italy, West Germany (as it then was), or the United States. Nevertheless, these societies were, according to the Marxist analysis, all instances of the "same" socioeconomic formation, which some Marxists at the time called "late capitalism." The exaggeration, however, contained an important grain of insight in that it put the focus on the role that really existing morality played in fostering and facilitating the reproduction of our specific type of society.[22] This, Marx holds, is a society essentially divided into classes, and its really existing morality is a *"Klassenmoral"* much of the actual content of which has the function of maintaining these class divisions and furthering the interests of those who have control over capital. One can assume that Marx would have a certain sympathy with the claim that the reason for the discrepancy between the *"Überbau"*-morality and the really existing morality had something to do with the "unlivability" of the former (under existing economic conditions).[23]

Proponents of the enlightened view, however, tend to confuse the true claim that our actually existing morality contributes to helping *this* kind of society to reproduce itself, with one or the other of two completely different views, both of which Marx thinks are clearly false. The first of these incorrect views claims that our actually existing morality would be needed (or would contribute) to the maintenance of *any* human society (perhaps, any "at a sufficiently high level of organization"). The second mistaken view is that that our *"Überbau"*-morality would be appropriate for *any* society (either "appropriate as a 'high morality'" or even, amazingly, "realizable and appropriate as a 'really existing morality'"). For Marx, however, the "high morality" is essentially a compensatory fantasy generated by, and responsive to, the failings of the social formation in which it arises. As such, it is a deeply distorted expression of human aspirations at a particular time and place; one cannot simply lift it from that context and expect to get anything determinate which could function as a really existing morality in any society. Furthermore, these high moralities derive their binding power precisely from the particular social dissatisfactions or characteristic forms of misery that generate them, and if those dissatisfactions are abolished, the components of the high morality lose their relevance, or change their status and function in unpredictable ways. Perhaps some of the content of the *Überbau* can be reinterpreted, but then the process of reinterpretation will not be any kind of routine transposition, but will actually provide most of the significant concrete content.

To be sure, we can survey human societies and by a process of abstraction and generalization discover and formulate some general rules and principles that (in one form or another) are endorsed by members of most human societies—do not kill without provocation; be kind to children. However, these will be what Marx calls *"Gemeinplätze."*[24] They will be not especially profound and foundational, but particularly shallow and, as it were, "sub-alethic"—too indeterminate actually to have any truth-value on their own, and certainly too unspecific to be a guide to any real human life. What does "without provocation" actually mean? What does "kind" mean?[25]

So there seem to be three results of this discussion. First, in order to understand anything about the morality of any society, we need to be able to give the kind of ideological account I have just given of the role forms of morality play in social reproduction. Second, if we understand that society is a totality and that anything we might say about "morality" will be the result of a complex process of abstraction or of a series of such processes, we will realize that the traditional conception of an "ethical theory" which can be free, self-standing, cognitively autonomous, and yet give determinate, authoritative, fully well-grounded advice on how to live, is fundamentally mistaken. Third, none of the above means that, apart from the usual fallibility of all human judgment, there is any *special* problem with the use of evaluative language. The absence of a separate and completely distinct realm of the "normative" which is an object of study in ethics, in no way means we cannot say it is better to drink this glass of clean water than that glass of effluents from downstream of the huge petrochemical complex, or that we would be better advised to support the development of solar power than to permit fracking, or finally that Mr. Walter Palmer, the Minnesota dentist, ought not to have been permitted to shoot Cecil, the lion, with his bow and arrow, and also that whatever the technicalities of the law, he "ought" not to have shot him. The fact that none of these can be connected to any

set of absolute, invariant, general prohibitions, injunctions, principles, or values is a problem if we think such principles exist, or could
exist, as foundations for "ethics," but not if we do not make that
assumption.

Is There Then *No* Morality?

If one wishes to put it this way, one can say that Marx did have a substantive theory of "morality," although one with a very different
structure from those usually discussed in philosophy seminars.
People are not Cartesian *res cogitantes* or Kantian rational agents, but
rather they live in social groups and have complex desires and needs
and the power (and disposition) to be active in such a way as to satisfy these desires and needs.[26] In this context they develop sets of social rules to govern their interactions with each other: these we call
forms or systems of "morality." The needs humans have include not
only a need to be able to transform the environment in certain ways,
for example, by making water in a river drinkable, by building shelters
for protection from the rain and cold (if appropriate), or by acquiring
and preparing substances that can be used as food, but also and
equally importantly needs for sociability, that is, for having certain
emotionally shaded relations with other members of the group (including relations of intimacy, mutual concern and affirmation,
positive dependency, and a large number of other things). Furthermore, and this is a point Marx emphasizes again and again, the needs
are not static but are *constantly changing* because the process of satisfying our needs (in one way rather than another because they can
usually be satisfied in more than one way) is at the same time the
process of generating *new* needs. People can satisfy their hunger (depending on circumstances) by hunting, fishing, collecting nuts and
berries, herding reindeer, camels, goats, sheep, or cattle, cultivating
rice, manioc, potatoes, wheat, or other foodstuffs. If people cultivate
rice to satisfy their hunger, they eventually acquire/generate a need
for something like chopsticks; if they bake bread, they can use their
hands to eat; if they eat porridge, they may come to need spoons; if
they hunt with a net as individuals, they will probably eventually also
need a knife to clean the game they catch; if they hunt with nets in

a group, they will need enhanced cooperative skills; fishermen may come to need boats. Which particular historical path the development of needs, of ways of satisfying them, and of thereby generating new ones will take is to some extent dependent on the micro-environment in question.

What social rules we develop depend on the needs, desires, and beliefs which we have. The basic mistake of his opponents, Marx often says, and never stops repeating, is to think that current arrangements are not just a passing historical phase, but are "eternal" *(ewig),*[27] and that the concepts suitable for describing current arrangements have eternal application and validity. Perhaps the period during which they were useful and relevant seems "long" by the life span of an individual human—six hundred years or so for feudalism—but still historically it is a transitory moment. Nietzsche says about philosophers that their original sin—he eirenically calls it their "idiosyncrasy"—is their "Egyptianism," their denial of history and refusal to accept that even "categories" or concepts of "reason" are transient.[28] They have a historical origin, develop over time, and eventually lose their identity, become invalid and irrelevant, and pass away. Marx would agree (although he would put more emphasis on the "Egyptianism" of economists).

There is not anything "invariant and universal" about any set of needs or any way of trying to satisfy them. Or rather, one can *say* there is an invariant structure here—"human groups socially transform and control nature to satisfy their interests; their 'morality' is part of this process"—but this is a completely empty statement, useless for traditional ethics because there is no path from it to any kind of universal injunction or decision procedure for any individual. To know that my local morality is part of the process of the self-reproduction of society, or even that it is a strictly necessary part of the process of self-reproduction, does not tell me what to do. Kierkegaard was right about that.

Moral system are an integral part of the social structure, but nothing excludes my judging that, on the whole, any given society does not deserve to survive, that it would, on the whole, not be good for it to reproduce itself.[29] I can make this judgment even about my own society. If I do make it, that shall be on the basis of various other considerations, to be sure, and none of them will be apodictic, categorical, or infallible. Also, even if I judge that it would be a good thing for my society to reproduce itself, it does not follow that I must think I have to give priority to satisfying its needs over following my own desires. Whether or not this is the case depends on the circumstances, and there is no final absolute framework—not even that of "human needs"—to which one can refer which will make it unnecessary to consult the circumstances. After all, it is a *"Gemeinplatz"* that people wish to live, and that to live they must eat, but it does not follow from that that hunger strikes are impossible or "immoral" or *always* a bad idea. As Montaigne,[30] Kierkegaard,[31] and Dostoyevsky[32] all try to argue, it is not even necessary that I be consistent.

"Need" then cannot play anything like the same role in Marx that, for instance, "reason" does in Kant and many other traditional philosophers. For Kant one can discover what one ought to do (or at any rate what one ought not to do) by consulting reason, which is the same essentially for everyone in all societies at all times, and will give everyone in every society and time the same advice. For Marx no one can "consult universal needs," because although in one sense it is possible to affirm some simple, empirical generalization such as that all humans "need" to eat, the purported "universal need to eat" has cognitive content only when its specific historical form is specified, and people can in some circumstances decide to starve themselves to death for perfectly understandable reasons that we have no way of disqualifying a priori as "foolish," "useless," "self-defeating," or "immoral." Despite the absolutely central role of "needs" in human life, you can no more strictly delimit and "close" off a purported "ethical" domain by reference to an absolute conception of "needs" than you can in any other way.

One might wonder whether the above account, whatever its coherency and force against Christian and Kantian style views of *ethics*, was at all relevant to the "normative turn" in political philosophy. If, however, the whole project of isolating and studying "the normative" does not make sense, then it seems odd that political philosophy should be expected to turn to and orient itself on what would then be the "nondiscipline" of normative ethics.

To be sure, to return to my three points about post-Christian ethics above, it does not seem obviously the case that Rawls gives special priority to first-person questions about what individuals should do, although he does give great weight to individuals' moral powers. However, starting from our own "moral intuitions" and imposing the veil of ignorance means that there will be no possibility of serious ideological criticism; it will not be possible to mobilize historical and sociological knowledge to criticize these initial beliefs. The "reflective equilibrium" eventually attained, then, will just be a version of our own original prejudices write large and surrounded by a normative halo. Finally, if one does give up the clear intention of the early work, which was to give a theory with the traditional Kantian kind claiming normative authority based on universal reason, and if one represents Rawls's position, as he comes close to doing himself in the later work, merely as just an expression of the worldview of Rawls's "fellow-citizens" in the United States, the scope of the theory contracts more considerably than I think Rawlsians would be willing to admit. The actual success of the Rawlsian counterrevolution shows, however, that it would be a mistake to underestimate the rhetorical attractiveness of appeals to "moral intuitions" and "fair distribution" (as against, for instance, a theory of human needs and their multiform modes of satisfaction), even for people who seem to have little to gain from it and much to lose.

I said at the beginning of this essay that I would concentrate on what seemed to me to be positive aspects of the legacy of Marx. These included an emphasis on the historical and concrete nature of claims about what was good and what people should or ought or must do, a rejection of moralization, the idea that society was to be seen as a totality (without assuming that this implied the existence of a "view from nowhere"), and the theory about "abstraction," its virtues and limits. In conclusion I would like just to mention one important negative aspect: the emphasis on ever-increasing industrial production. Action to satisfy human needs is tacitly assumed by Marx to *require* ever-expanding production. If we are to survive as a species, however, we will have to break with this obsessive pursuit of cancerous forms of exploitation of nature. Presumably, we might be able to detach human activity directed at satisfying needs as much as possible from the cycle of ever-expanded industrial production, especially since we do not actually need significant further expansion of industrial activity to give a reduced human population a highly attractive life. How such a detachment might be possible, and what exact form it could take, is anyone's guess. Perhaps the way forward is the cultivation of human needs for increased and increasingly sophisticated forms of sociability and of self-expression that do not require increased material production. This clearly will not be possible under capitalist conditions, which is just to say—what is news to no one except the especially benighted—that although our future is unsure if we rid ourselves of capitalism, it is only too sure that without radical change in our present economic arrangements our prospects are bleak indeed.

Wem angesichts der Vergiftung unserer Erde
nichts einfällt als die Frage nach dem Bruttosozialprodukt
Dem habe ich nichts zu sagen[33]

8

Economies: Good, Bad, Indifferent

—◦◦◦—

It is well known that the term *economy* comes from two Greek words meaning "household" (οἶκος) and "regulation, organization, or management" (νέμω=νόμος), so it seems that the repeated appeals by Angela Merkel to the virtues of the proverbial "Swabian house-wife" as a guide to how to run the German economy is not simply a rhetorical flourish which she pulled out of the air or her own fertile Mecklenburgian imagination, but has some historical root.[1] Presum-ably the normal Swabian housewife has some kind of view about what kind of life she and her family *must* live, what they require, or what they "need," as we may say about the "necessities" of life, and she feels it to be her responsibility to try to satisfy these needs with the resources available to her. This way of thinking about her situation—that there are imperative necessities that impose themselves on her "objectively," that is, as if from the outside, and to which she has no alternative but to respond—seems perfectly understandable.[2] Nev-ertheless, the notions of "need," "necessity," or "requirement" are problematic in a number of ways. Roughly speaking, "needs" seem to cover requirements in at least three different dimensions: one can distinguish (at least) natural or biological, moral, and sociocultural needs.[3] So they "must" have food in sufficient quantity and of suf-ficient nutritional value to allow them to survive for the foreseeable future—this is a kind of natural or biological necessity. They must

117

also have sufficient space in their domicile so that members of different gender groups and generations are not promiscuously forced into what are considered to be immoral forms of intimacy—a moral necessity. Finally they must be able to clothe themselves in what they and their neighbors will consider an acceptable way—at some historical periods, such as in the High Victorian era, it was socially impossible for a man or woman to appear in public without headgear of any kind. It is said that at certain periods a man who went out in the streets of London without *some* kind of head covering, a hat or cap of some kind, would have been assaulted.[4]

In addition to these things which she and the other members of her family "must" have (food, clothing, shelter) and that they "must" be able to do (get medical services when ill), there will probably be some things that although not strictly part of what the Swabian housewife, or anyone else, takes to be "necessities" are nevertheless positively desirable or are objects of aspiration. They are not "needs" but things people want or desire or wish to have: the walls of the rooms in the house do not need to be repainted regularly, but a new coat of paint every decade or so is highly desirable, a bottle of Trollinger every day is a very good thing, although no one thinks it an absolute *necessity*, similarly for a dish of meat on Sundays rather than just *Spätzle*, a new hat or new car or new television every five or six years.

Starting then from the way the Swabian housewife sees her world and her tasks, we notice that she makes a conceptual distinction between two broad *categories* or families of things: one the things she *needs*, or requires or must have or thinks are essential, and the other the things she wants—or wishes or desires to have, might like to have, or would prefer to have (rather than not to have). Within these two broad categories, there will be further differences that will be relevant for some of the various decisions she might make. Thus there may be things she actively wants and has pursued for a long time (although she does not, perhaps, think it is essential or necessary to have them); then there may be cases in which she has a momentary whim. In yet other cases she might clearly and always pick A over B if she were forced to choose between the two, but the choice itself is not one she is either forced or keen to make, so the preference for A over B is clear but generally irrelevant or motivationally inert.[5]

Despite any number of differences *within* each of these two categories, it is extremely important to see that there are important structural differences between the members of the first category and those of the second. To ascribe "needs" and to ascribe "wants" are conceptually very different things, and each of these concepts operates according to a completely different logic. A want or desire is primarily some kind of positive subjective impulsion toward an object or an action, that is, it is an incipient movement that comes from "within me." To speak of wanting (in my case) is to speak of what I want, as if I were the initiator trying to do something. The notion of a "need" is, in contrast, construed as in principle "objective" (rather than merely "subjective"). There is some kind of external necessity imposing itself on my *nolens volens* from without. A "need" has the structure of a *conditio sine qua non*. I may want or desire to drink a cup of tea either because I like the taste of tea or because I think it is good for my health, or in order to ingratiate myself with a tea merchant from whom I am about to solicit a favor, or for any number of other reasons either individually or altogether. I may, of course, form the idea of an "unconscious wish," which presumably is a wish that is in some way postulated to account for some of my actions, although I am not aware of having it. Still the ascription is, and must be "subjective" or perhaps "subject centered" in that it must finally be based on and refer to an impulsion or inclination or tendency that *I* experience or that *I* exhibit in a certain direction, even if I am not consciously aware of it.

In contrast, "Jerome needs x," for example, water, means: "water is *necessary* to Jerome [*for* y]," or "if Jerome does not get water, then no y," or "unless Jerome gets water, no y."[6] So the question is what is "y." Sometimes the answer is obvious: "y" is just the continued existence of the entity in question, in this case me. So "Jerome needs water" means "if Jerome does not get water, he shall not survive." This is a preverbal, nonsubjective structure that exists in the world and is rooted in the nature of things, specifically in human biology, whether I or anyone knows about it or is able to formulate it in thought or language. In principle I can be said to "need" some re-cherché protein or vitamin, or to "need" a surgical procedure of some kind, on the basis of some scientific account of human physiology, without that ascription being at all based on any impulse I myself have to seek out that protein or to cajole a surgeon into performing the operation. If I happen to experience a tendency to eat fruits that contain the necessary vitamins, this will be an accident, an idiosyncrasy, or the result of a complicated (and "objective") evolutionary history of the species, but the description of the case as one in which I "need" the vitamin certainly does not depend on the fact that I actually happen to want to eat food containing the vitamin. I may desire to eat oranges without needing to eat them, and my actually eating them, or even seeking them out with great effort and eating them greedily, is not *by itself* evidence that I *need* them.

My desire for something may be more or less strong, but no amount of strength of desire *alone* turns a desire into a need. To say it is a need is not to say that it is of some given strength, but to make a completely different kind of claim about it: that without it I shall seriously malfunction. It *might well be* that if certain kinds of desires establish themselves very firmly and centrally in me, and I structure much of my action around them, it is *more likely* that unless they are satisfied I shall fail to survive, and this will often make it difficult for me to distinguish in my own case what is a desire and what a need, but this epistemic difficulty in no way implies that desire and need are the same thing.

In the above discussion "need" is used in the strictest possible sense of the word, but usually the term is used in a very much looser sense, where the "y" means not "life, sheer continued survival itself" but something more like "flourishing" or "healthy functioning." Still the ascription will have the same objectivizing *conditio sine qua non* structure, that is, "Jerome needs y" will still mean "Jerome cannot fully flourish without y (whether he knows that or not)." Thus, all humans need air to breathe in that they will die within a few minutes if they do not have it, but one can also perfectly reasonably say that humans "need" a certain minimal caloric intake each day. If I fail to get 1,000 calories a day, to be sure, I shall not immediately die, but if the deprivation continues, I shall gradually become more lethargic, more susceptible to diseases, less able to discharge the usual activities of a human being successfully. In what follows it will turn out to be rather important that "need" designates a sine qua non rather than something which I (or anyone else) positively want, desire, or pursue for its own sake.

Ascription of "need" is highly context-dependent for a number of reasons, some of which have already been discussed—is a "need" a sine qua non of mere survival or of flourishing, and then in what sense of "flourishing"? The contextual nature of needs becomes particularly clear in the case of addictions. If Jerome is addicted to morphine, there is a clear sense in which he does not merely want to have it; in fact he may not *want* to have it at all, but be trying to break his habit. He "needs" it because he will exhibit clear pathological symptoms if he does not get it: he will get the shakes, have headaches, vomit, and so on. So relative to his current physiological condition, he clearly has a "need." On the other hand, if he continues in this addicted state, he will suffer serious long-term damage to his health, so he in an obvious sense "needs" to get rid of the addiction. The fact that what he "needs" changes depending on the context chosen does not seem to be an objection, and the fact that one can give this complex account of his needs, *independently* of knowing whether or not he *wants* to continue in or to terminate the addiction, would seem to underline the importance of distinguishing between what he "needs" and whatever he might want, wish, or desire.

If the previous discussion is at all correct, what I, or we, "really" need and what I, or we, *think* we need can be two quite different things. In the case of biological needs this is clear. A woman in one of the few surviving tribal societies in our world may think with perfect sincerity and complete conviction that her infant "needs" to wear an amulet in order not to be struck down by malaria or some other serious disease. Equally a child may actually need something the chief carer does not know it needs, in which case the child will most likely die. There might, of course, be evolutionary reasons why what humans need in order to survive biologically cannot depart *too* greatly from what they think they need, but that is a separate question. To understand the decision situation in which an individual finds him- or herself *as defined in the narrowest way possible*, that is, in the micro-situation, it is probably enough to focus on what that individual believes he or she needs because that is what will have a decisive influence on how the person in question decides to act. "Real" needs will assert themselves to the extent to which those whose real needs are not satisfied will in fact malfunction—whatever, in the given context, "malfunction" exactly is taken to mean. So, if one wishes fully to understand what has happened and will happen in a given society, it is not sufficient either merely to understand what the real needs of the population are or merely to come to know what the members of the society *think* or *believe* they need. It is certainly not enough to understand what they actively want or what they would prefer.

To some extent even "natural" or "biological" needs may differ from one society to another: protection against cold will be more imperative the farther north one goes, whereas protection against certain diseases that are transmitted by insects may become less necessary. Obviously the "moral" and "social" needs will also differ from one society to the other, and the distinctions between these categories cannot be more than rough and ready. If I will be assaulted on the street for not wearing a hat in such a way as to suffer serious physical disability, then having a hat to wear is not, as we might say, a *mere* social necessity. This also points to a number of further ambiguities in the use of the term *social necessity*. On the one hand, it can mean "something that is necessary if *any* human society at all in a form we can recognize is to survive." This would presumably include certain restrictions on violence, sexual and family life, and some minimal forms of reciprocity. This is easily confused with another requirement: "something that is necessary if human society *at some specified level of complexity*, for instance, as an industrial or postindustrial society, is to survive." These requirements might include a variety of provisions such as having a legal system, literacy, some minimal calculating devices such as an abacus or one of the highly complex and expensive electronic toys now produced in the Orient and sold to replace the abacus (MACs, PCs, and so forth), and so on. Finally, there might be a set of specific requirements that need to be fulfilled if *our* society (that is, early twenty-first-century Western European society) is to be maintained. Obviously this is not the end of the story either because one can still disagree on what "our" society means—backwoodsmen in the UK will disapprove of describing it as "European" and insist that it be properly called "British" or "English" (or whatever), and even those who agree it is "West European" may not agree on what this means "must" happen if it is to remain so. Is it a requirement, for instance, that traditional Christianity retain a central position in societies of this kind?

Equally what will count as a "social" and what as a "moral" necessity will clearly differ from one society to another and on one's perspective: Many of the things which we external observers consider to be "merely social" needs—either in the sense that they must be satisfied if the society is to retain its identity or in the sense that they are strictly imposed by direct social forms of action *as if* they were absolutely necessary—will be construed by those who labor under them (or impose them on others) as deeply "moral" requirements, such as many of those imposed on women in some countries. In many such societies women cannot appear in public without conforming to very strict demands that are not rooted in any obvious biological or moral requirements—at least in the view expressed by most Western commentators on such matters, who, of course, might be wrong about what "morality" requires.

Finally, there will a difference in perspective. The "necessity" in claims about "social necessity" will face in two different directions at the same time. On the one hand, it will refer to that which *must* be done if society (as defined in some particular way) is to reproduce itself. On the other hand, it will refer to the "necessity" imposed on the members of society, that is, the way in which members of a given society are *forced* by it to act in such a way as to do what they think "must be" done. There might, then, be things that would have to be done if that society were to survive that no one in the society knows anything about, and there might also be things the members of the society believe (correctly or incorrectly) need to be done for the society to survive, but that they do not—perhaps because they cannot—impose on people. Thus, for instance, a Protestant in the early modern period might have thought that society would survive only if it remained pleasing to god, but that it was pleasing to god *only if* everyone in it *voluntarily* heeded god's word. For such a person it would make no sense to try to *force* people to heed god's word, *although* that was essential for social flourishing, if not survival.[7] So what really is necessary, what they think is (really) necessary, and what they enforce, and thus make "socially necessary" in that sense, can be three different things. Perhaps it really is necessary for society to continue to exist that they punish murderers, and perhaps some kind of primitive lynch justice is the best that can be arranged in a society of a certain kind, but what if they lynch me because I have blasphemed their god on the grounds that he (or she) will avenge himself (or herself) on them for my transgression? When the Roman soldier exposed his bottom in the Jewish Temple and pretended to fart in the direction of the assembled pilgrims, the resulting riot was in any case comprehensible, given the ritual beliefs of the populations in question.[8] It makes little or no difference whether the god exists or not, or, for that matter, whether their society would actually able to maintain its coherence without this particular belief or not. To repeat then one must distinguish:

a) It is *really* a social necessity; without it their society will dissolve (usually this in fact means: "*We*, the observers to whom I am now addressing myself, believe their society would fall apart if it failed to have this feature" or "Idealized social researchers who know as much as it is possible to know about such things would judge that this is necessary for social survival").

b) *They* judge (correctly or incorrectly) that this is a social necessity.

c) They impose this *as* a social necessity on all who come within their power.

The result for me will be that I am subjected to what I will (rightly) perceive as a "necessity" coming from outside me. If the society *imposes* requirement X by law or other effective means (ostracism, lynching), then I who am subject will perceive X as a need even if X is not in fact necessary for social life, and even if I judge that it is not so necessary. Note that this distinction is not the same as that between what I really need and what I merely think I need.

This raises a possibility that seems so deeply rooted in human nature that it is hard to dislodge it. That is the idea that the really important notion in economics and particularly in the political management of economics is not that of preference, want, or desire, but that of "need." What an economy is most centrally about is the provision for human *needs*. This has absolute priority, especially vis-à-vis the satisfaction of mere desires, aspirations, preferences, tastes, or vagrant velleities. If this idea were to be correct, it would expose a fundamental deficiency in all those theories, including most current economic theories, that attempted to describe and explain human behavior as being directed merely to the maximization of preferences. That this idea is deep-seated is no guarantee that it is true, but it is reason to investigate it with some care.

Thus there is a well-known anecdote about a conversation between Jean-Paul Sartre and Fidel Castro in 1960. Sartre had been traveling around Cuba and accompanied Castro on a trip to the northern part of the island. Everywhere they went, it is reported, Castro was immediately surrounded by small groups of people who clustered around him and talked about their situations and their needs. These were formulated as a series of demands: here they had to have new tractors, here the irritation equipment was inadequate and would have to be replaced, here they needed better-quality seeds, here the living quarters were a source of disease. After a while, Sartre noticed that there seemed to be no end to the stream of demands based on what people claimed to "need," and he asked Castro a pointed question: "What if they were to demand the moon?" Castro's answer seems to have made a deep impression on Sartre: "If they did demand the moon, then the reason would be that they needed it; then one would have to give it to them." This, and similar experiences, persuaded Sartre to conclude that human "needs" and the various ways in which they could be satisfied constituted the only possible foundation for a decent form of politics.[9]

This anecdote indicates the ease with which there can be slippage, particularly in political contexts, between speaking of "needs," "wants," and articulating and presenting "demands." The ease of the slippage does not mean that the distinction does not exist and is not important. "Needs," as mentioned above, purport to refer to a nonsubjective structure of necessity to which we must accommodate ourselves, and wants or desires are subjectively motivating states. "Demands," on the other hand, are not in general themselves parts of any nexus of natural necessity and do not present themselves as such even if they formulate what are rightly taken to be rooted in objective facts about the situation or in human needs. Rather "demands" are discursively structured speech-acts in which certain claims are made and presented as to-be-satisfied under all conditions. For needs to become "demands" they must be linguistically formulated by someone in some form and brought forward in some context. This is one of the reasons control over the forms and modes of speech in a society is of great political importance. If a sufficiently developed language is available, we will be able to formulate demands that go beyond what we really "require" in order to survive and satisfy what are our needs (in the strict sense), and in fact every known human language, as far as we can tell, is sufficiently developed for the formulation of such demands to be possible in it. Once language and processes of collective discussion of the kind with which we are familiar in all human societies known to us are in existence, one can come to formulate "demands" that are not based on anything that could *antecedently* have been called a "need." Thus prisoners might demand better food for all those incarcerated while admitting that the food already provided was "adequate" for all human needs. In addition, people might in discussion even go beyond anything the participants in the discussion would antecedently have recognized as one of their own "desires" or "wants." In discussion, that is, people can certainly discover that they have wants they did not know they had, but they can arguably also come to *develop* new wants they did not have at all. A certain strand in recent economic theory has tried to downplay, or even deny, the existence of change in wants, desires, tastes, and preference,[10] preferring instead to speak of changes in people's beliefs about costs, particularly opportunity costs. This, of course, flies in the face of all our experience, but that, in itself, might not be an objection, if one could give some *positive* reason to make this assumption, or if it could be shown to help us understand some phenomenon that would otherwise remain inexplicable. This, however, does not seem to be the case, although this claim clearly depends nontrivially on what one might mean by "understand." If those who propose this view suggest it *merely* as one way in which one *could* look at aspects of our human life that might throw some light on a variety of human phenomena, then that is a claim one might be willing to accept, provided one had some examples of ways in which this mode of analysis had shown itself fruitful and enlightening. That might well be possible. If, in addition to this, the claim is that this is the *only* way in which it makes sense to look at human life, or the only "rational" way, or that this is the way humans, including politicians, "must" or "should" think about life when they are making decisions about how to act, one would need some further argument about what "should" and "must" could mean in this context and why in particular this mode of thinking is thus mandatory.

In the Cuban anecdote both Castro and Sartre seem to move *directly* from the fact that a certain demand is formulated to the existence of an underlying need which it articulates. If this is not a mere mistake, but rather has some systematic basis, then one might wonder what this basis is. The prominence of appeal to "needs" in political argument would seem to have two sources. First of all, in politics often one person or group confronts another with differing interests, desires, tastes, and preferences; it can be a good strategy to distance my demands as much as possible from my own mere preferences, for why should *my* mere preferences take precedence over anyone else's? To speak of "needs" provides at least the verbal cover of purported "objectivity" and this may give me an incentive to present my demands under this guise. Second, since politics is often about getting attention for one's own projects in a competitive arena, it can make sense to exaggerate its merits or the dangers of what will occur if it is not adopted. This is especially easy for most people because my own preferences and desire do often present themselves with an urgency to me that others' desires do not have (for me). Both of these tendencies may contribute to turning "I want" into claims that I need. Exculpatory contexts may generate a similar phenomenon. So it was often noted in the descriptions of the rioting that took place in London and other British cities last summer that the businesses that seemed most often targeted were those selling clothing and electronic equipment such as mobile telephones. Book-shops on city blocks that were completely looted had been left un-touched, indicating the irrelevance of the printed word to the per-ceived need-structure and also the desires of the young people in question. Some of the participants in the rioting who were inter-viewed stated: "We looted these shops because we needed new trainers." It is then tempting to reply to this: "To have new trainers is not a human 'need' in the strict sense, but rather at best a wish or desire that is comprehensible under certain social circumstances, namely, in a highly consumerist society in which these shoes are a symbol of status." The sociological and historical variability of the structure of human needs must be granted, but the question remains whether it is not still necessary to distinguish between the basic or elemental need to have *some* kind of footwear in a cold climate—even though one knows that certain people, such as Russian peasants in the early twentieth century, will have of necessity done without them—the general human need to dress in a way that is (minimally) socially acceptable, and the *mere* aspiration to cut a figure in front of people by sporting particularly fine clothing.

Clearly in some contexts social demands such as that one wear a certain kind of shoe can become internalized to such an extent that the entity *will* malfunction if that demand or wish is not satisfied. Still it would seem extremely rash to take anyone's own word for this, namely, his or her own claim that he or she would seriously malfunction, at face value. Perhaps the difficulty here, then, is not so much with the concept of a need, but with permitting self-assessment of psychological and social needs.[11] To permit self-assessment, or at any rate to allow it to be considered definitive, would in any case be inherently at variance with the whole point of introducing "need" as a category, which is to move discussion away from exclusive dependence on first-person and overtly subjectivist expressions of desire or preference.

The ability to go beyond a given state of needs and need satisfac-tion is one of the most important positive forms of social progress. At a certain point we are no longer satisfied with food consisting of uncooked flesh ripped from animals, and begin to need cooked food;[12] equally we are no longer content simply to allow people who get pneumonia to get better or die, but we "need" antibiotics. Eventually people may begin to believe they "need" mobile telephones and other expensive gadgets to avoid social death, and perhaps a day might eventually come when that became true. Thus, one could easily imagine a society, in fact predict its advent, in which mobile telephones were equipped not just with the usual tracking devices, as at present, but also with identity cards that had to be presented in a wide variety of circumstances; failure to carry these electronic devices would be an offense. Under such circumstances, one really would have a "need" to have one.

Equally it is a form of progress when we come to be able consciously to set ourselves goals that are incompatible with our biological needs (and are known to be incompatible with them). The hunger striker, martyr, self-sacrificing witness are all rightly admired, even by those who may not share their goals. What the martyr does is change the context, or the parameters within which the need-structure stands, and that gives it its meaning. Now "I need" is not relative to physical survival or even a form of "flourishing" that has any particular biological basis. Rather, "what I need" is an ideational construct: Socrates "needed" to continue to philosophize;[13] the Waldenses "needed" not to live, but to live according to a certain religious doctrine. What Socrates did during his life cannot be interestingly described as "changing his wants, desires, and preferences." It is true that one can say that at the end of his life he "preferred" to die than to give up philosophizing, but that is partly a consequence of his changed need-structure. To be sure, in *some* sense it is Socrates himself who has changed the need-structure by construing the active philosophical examination of life as his ultimate sine qua non, but he did not "change his need-structure" *merely* by *saying* something, by merely coming to believe something he had antecedently not believed, or by merely "changing a (or his) preferences" in anything like the sense in which we usually use that term. His adopting of the philosophical life is not at all like my ceasing to like Oolong tea because at one point in my life I drank too much of it, my coming to acquire a taste for the work of a composer whose work I previously rather disliked, or my suddenly deciding I would prefer to spend a holiday in Greece next summer rather than in southern France. To say what "more" must be the case, beyond changes of belief and preference, so that one can say that Socrates now "needs" not what the normal fifth-century Athenian male needs, but something altogether different, is a complicated issue, and there might well be different stories that would have to be told in the case of Socrates, Mani, Saint Polycarp, the Cathars, Jan Hus, and Bobby Sands. From the fact that the story that must be told will be both complex and, perhaps, specific to the individual case one cannot conclude that it is a mistake to recognize "need" as a category distinct from "want/wish/desire."

The issue of Socrates and his "need" to continue to philosophize has often been taken to be connected with issues of identity—Socrates would not be the man he was, if were to stop philosophizing (and he knows it)—and with the notion of a moral or existential form of necessity. If something is really part of my identity or some form of action is existentially necessary, then we can speak of it as part of the need-structure (for that person or persons).[14] If Luther really did say "Hier stehe ich; ich kann nit anders" at the Diet of Worms, the necessity invoked there would ground a need-claim. Again, for obvious reasons we should be highly wary of accepting self-assessment of such "need-claims" at face value, but that is no argument against the existence of a distinct category of "need."

Very strong desires may, as it were, "look like" needs, but needs and desires are still structurally distinct. At this point one might be tempted slightly to change the definition of a "need." Instead of a strictly objectivist view—a "need" is a sine qua non of proper, healthy functioning or of flourishing—we might move to a slightly different view, namely, that a "need" is what I would give up on only if forced, or that I would be willing to risk something serious to attain. Wotan wagers, and loses, one of his eyes in order to marry Fricka.[15] Loss of an eye is certainly something that one would be hard-pressed to deny was detrimental to the functioning of the human organism, although one can physically survive such a loss. Risking one's eye is certainly a token of seriousness of desire, and conceivably getting some sexual partner or another is a deeply rooted desire that moves most humans very strongly, but it still does not seem to be a need for each human individual. Until in vitro technology is developed further then it is today, it is, of course, a need of the human species that enough individuals find partners.

The process of developing needs can take a distinctly perverted form, and so a "false need" can mean not just a misconception of what one truly needs, but a correct perception of a need one thinks the agent in question ought not to have acquired or developed. Instance of this second kind are addictions of all kinds. Here one might distinguish in the way people who stand in a certain Aristotelean tradition do between the responsibility one has for what one does while drunk and responsibility for getting drunk.[16] So similarly one might wish to distinguish between being addicted, say, to heroin, making oneself addicted, and allowing oneself to become addicted. If one is in a serious car crash and is pumped full of morphine for so long that one becomes addicted, then there is nothing "false" about the need thus acquired. So "false need" may refer to a "need" that is not really a need or to a need acquired under conditions that are somehow thought to be deviant.

Despite the vagueness of the concept of a "need" and of the conditions of its application, Sartre was obviously of the opinion that one could not sensibly do politics without it,[17] and this does not seem self-evidently a foolish position to hold. Political demands are sometimes the true expressions of real needs, sometimes they are linguistically distorted expressions of what are real needs, sometimes they express nothing but mere human wishes or desires.

To be sure there is nothing inherently wrong with a human desire or a political demand that expresses a "mere" desire, wish to inclination. In even mildly "democratic" political formations the fact that a significant number of citizens has a sufficiently strong desire for X to bring it forward as a political demand is at least minimally and prima facie legitimate. To say that it is prima facie legitimate, is not, of course, to say that it is a good idea.

To return to Merkel's mythical Swabian housewife, she is assumed to have a limited and *fixed* income, and to be trying to cover necessities, maintain the recognized standard of living, and realize some modest aspirations on that. So she has an incentive to reduce expenditures as much as possible, that is, to be frugal, thrifty, or "economical," that is, not to dispose of more of the fixed and limited income on essential needs than is absolutely necessary. This can then move from avoidance of waste to increase in resources/income. Of course, there will be strict limits within which this will be possible, and that, if she exceeds, will turn her from a housewife into an entrepreneur (if on a modest scale).

Furthermore it is assumed that the *Hausfrau* in question has an income, or access to resources that are what one might call crudely commensurate with what is required to lead the traditional form of life. That is, she has decisions to make because she has almost enough to cover expenses, *if she is careful*. If the woman in question clearly does not have "enough" in any sense, for example, if she is locked up in Guantanamo Bay or Abu Ghraib or wandering with her half-incinerated children through a post-nuclear wasteland waiting for them to die from radiation sickness, there would be no pressure on her to make economic decisions, although, of course, she might well have to make other decisions.

The term *Swabian housewife* then refers not just to a person with certain habits but also tacitly to a whole sociocultural landscape within which such a person with such habits is located. These habits make particular sense if there is a certain substitutability between different possible inputs and outlays. She can buy thread at €1 a spool in a stall in the market or thread at €1.50 at the local shop, and one is, for *some* (although perhaps not for all) relevant purposes "the same" or "just as good" as the other. Or she can buy a thread that is cheaper, poorer quality, but looks just as good, if her purpose is aesthetic, or if it is for an ephemeral purpose. Alternatively her children can eat potatoes which they plant in their own kitchen garden, rather than chips purchased at the chippie's. Substitutability requires that there be a certain flexibility in the way in which needs can be satisfied. Otherwise there would be no *choice* confronting the housewife. We can have *different* sources of calories and protein. The children can eat rice and beans, beef patties, or tofu salad, all of which may contain a sufficient number of calories and some proteins and necessary vitamins. This means that a dish of rice and beans can in some contexts—for some purposes, such as the satisfaction of certain basic biological needs—be "substituted" for a small dish of tofu or meat. It can "count as the same" in *this* context.

Of course, any particular woman in Nürtlingen, Lauffen, or Pforzheim, or, for that matter, in the Chancery in Berlin, may fail to be a good and virtuous "Swabian housewife," that is, she may fail to be frugal, economical, or thrifty, and she may fail for any number of reasons, through ignorance of the true costs of various courses of action, through "moral" failings of one kind or another (alcoholism, sentimentality, and so on), through failure to have the skill to negotiate the best possible deal with the suppliers of goods and services, and so forth. Still, it seems natural to evaluate the actions of the housewife by using the complex vocabulary of human virtues and vices. The "good" housewife is frugal and thrifty as opposed to profligate or extravagant. These virtues, and the corresponding vices, are highly context-dependent,[18] and so saying when a certain person is exhibiting one of these virtues or vices is no easy task.

A certain kind of frugality that made sense in a small household might be self-defeating in the long run if applied to industrial production, education, or experimentation. Perhaps it is necessary to do a 100,000 experiments extended over years, all of which "fail" in order to discover the one particular combination of components that will eventually cure a particular disease (without killing the patient by producing lethal side effects). Similarly, we might need to start training a thousand engineers or historians or philologists at university for six or seven years, so that half a dozen excellent practitioners will emerge at the end. There may be no known way to speed up or rationalize the process because it is virtually impossible to detect the complicated conjunction of abilities and motivations that are a prerequisite for high achievement until the process is virtually over. Once one has invested in the huge apparatus required to train a thousand candidates, it makes little sense to try to fine-tune the process because the possible forms of "quality control" are so crude as to be virtually useless. It makes more sense to find some dignified and moderately useful employment for the nine hundred mediocre engineers at the end of their training. If one tried to make the discrimination too early, most of the five or six genuinely gifted candidates, who would at that point have been invisible to any process of selection adopted, will be likely to be excluded.

To be so obsessed with the avoidance of "wastage" as not to be able to countenance educational and experimental activities seems short-sighted and counterproductive, provided one has the available resources. In addition to the *bonne femme suabienne* there is the pathological Swabian housewife. For instance, thrift in the form of saving money, reducing consumption (not just excess or useless expenditure), becomes not a way of maintaining a traditional form of life or a means to more rational satisfaction of aspirations that require some planning, but an end in itself. The housewife who keeps careful track of her expenses and avoids excessive waste is not the same as one who keeps her family on short rations, and then is found after her death to have a large hidden cache of untouched provisions that during her life she could not bear to open.

Merkel's Swabian housewife is a very different model of economical behavior from the Grantham shopkeeper in the 1920s and 1930s who was Margaret Thatcher's *beau ideal*, or from that of the landowner who employs both German and Polish agricultural laborers, which was analyzed by Max Weber.[19] The housewife will have objects and activities in mind. She will use thread of poorer quality for clothing that does not need to withstand hard treatment, cut the bread thinner so that the loaf lasts longer, and so on. Some of this might be monetarized, but that is a separate issue. Although there are economies in which shops operate by barter, the shopkeeper however will be likely to be dealing with activities and objects that are *already* monetarized. Running a shop is closer to the ideal model of running a "business" than the Swabian housewife will ever get in her domestic economies. A new blouse for her daughter is never *merely* one more tin of peaches bought or sold in the shop, and the loaf of bread is a *direct* object of consumption; for the housewife and her family this will have various consequences. The housewife can be thrifty, generous, or extravagant. Do these terms even apply to the shopkeeper? Can she—qua shopkeeper—be generous, or, for that matter, thrifty, as opposed to rigorous (or lax), careful (or reckless), calculating (or heedless)? Is it *obvious* that when we wish to evaluate an economy, we should ignore these moral judgments?

In one of his early discussions of economic rationality, Weber considers the possibility of increasing agricultural productivity by paying higher wages. The idea is that people will work harder if the wages are higher. This, Weber claims, works for German workers but not for Polish workers. Thus, Weber claims, if landowners increase the wages of German agricultural workers, this gives them an incentive to work more and harder and thus raises the yield from the land. So it is economically rational for the landowners to raise the wages for German workers. The case, he claims, is completely different for Polish agricultural workers. They have a traditional fixed standard of living that they wish to maintain and will work as long and hard as is necessary to do that—eight hours a day five days a week or ten hours a day six days a week. Once they have earned all they need to maintain their traditional way of life, they stop working. Prima facie this seems completely "rational"; why work unnecessarily? To increase their wages is merely to permit them to *reduce* the hours they work, and thus to reduce the amount they produce. So if the aim of the landowner is to increase production, it is economically irrational to raise wages. One would be very tempted to say that in this case it is not that German and Polish workers are, as it were, competing against each other in a common game with agreed-on rules, and then one group is better than the other, but they are playing different games altogether. The main difficulty, then, for the East Elbian Junker is *not* to get the Polish workers to work, because they are perfectly willing and able to do that, but to get them to play the German game of "work." Weber might say "change their work-*ethic*"; not to get them to be "more rational" but to change the "rationale" their work has for them. One might even say that the task is to bring them to change their traditional "identity" and adopt a new one. If so, it would not be utterly surprising that a minor increase in their salary had little effect on them.

It has often been pointed out that many economists think that the Swabian housewife is a tremendously *poor* model for a government trying to run, or at any rate manage, a national economy. If "times are hard," the Swabian housewife might try to reduce her expenses; this might be both a rational and a good thing for her and her family. However, if in times of financial stagnation *all* families reduce their expenditure, then, at least this is the claim made by many economists, the financial situation in general is likely to decline further.

One influential school of economic thought, often called "Keynesian," claims that the same is true of the government. It is rational for it to spend in times of restricted economic activity, and reducing governmental spending in time of economic contraction is suicidal. This partly has to do with the limited scale and the fixity of the situation within which the housewife finds herself compared with the size and openness of a larger economy. Partly it has to do with the possibilities a government has through legislation to force certain outcomes; a government has a different relation to the credit system than an individual has. Finally a government can, within limits, encourage or discourage economic growth.

If, then, there are significant differences between the situation of the housewife, that of the 1920s shopkeeper, that of a national government trying to manage a middle-range economy in 2015, and that of a (hypothetical) agent or institution overseeing the global economy, is it obvious that these can reasonably be ignored? Under what circumstances?

One obvious difference between the situation of the Swabian housewife and the global economy, of course, is that the global economy has no single recognized agent who is "in charge" of it in the way in which the Swabian housewife is considered to be in charge of her household—and to say she is considered to be "in charge" does not, of course, mean she actually does control or even could control what happens there, but merely that she is in some sense held "responsible" for what happens. To define what that "responsibility" is, is no easy task because much of what actually happens will clearly depend on factors utterly beyond her control—how many members of the family get ill, what happens in the wider economy to influence the prices she has to pay for basic commodities, and so on. Furthermore, there is a difference between running a household that is clearly embedded in a wider economic environment that provides the conditions for its continued existence and the situation of a (at the moment hypothetical) manager of the global economy who would encounter natural limits of various kinds—the limited nature of fossil fuels—but who, whatever else might be true, would not be embedded in a wider *economy* in a similar way.

Economy in the sense of thriftiness is understood by almost everyone as at best an instrumental or subordinate virtue (like the virtue of consistency—for everyone except the Kantian). No matter how thrifty, we would not necessarily call a woman who made ends meet by selling narcotics on the side and inflicted gratuitous suffering on her friends, relatives, and associates a *good* person. There are, of course, very different ways of approaching the question of morality. Some think it refers merely or primarily to whether a given individual action is licit or not. Others that it refers primarily or to a great extent to our evaluation of the continuing qualities of character a person exhibits. Still others that the "goodness" of an action is to be judged by whether its consequences are beneficial. Brecht took an extremely non-moralizing view about what one "needs must do."[20] There might be, he thought, nothing wrong with selling narcotics—even highly harmful ones—if that is what one must do to survive. Even those who took this view, though, might distinguish between those who did what they must in order to live and those who *gratuitously* inflicted more suffering than necessary.

We have now moved from an adverbial usage of "economy"—to do something in an economical way—to a substantival one. The Swabian housewife considers her various household activities in a certain light, or under a certain aspect, as potentially instantiating certain properties (such as efficiently, fitness for purpose) or as needing to be organized according to certain principles (for example, of parsimony).

Now, however, we speak of "*the* economy" as if it were a specifiable and distinct sector of society, and as such is something distinct from religion, education, the kinship system, the Foreign Service, and so on. It has, of course, often been noticed that not all societies acknowledge this distinction, and that attempts to enforce it will lead to misunderstanding. Does the fact that this is an abstraction have any consequences for what we can know about this domain? Why construe "the economy" as a separate and distinct entity that could be considered on its own and as subject to its own laws?

If we go along with this reification, it is possible to adopt at least two completely different approaches to the question of evaluating an economy. The first one might call the nature-centered or natural-istic approach,[21] and associate it with the name "Aristotle." This approach starts from the observation that we often use the central evaluative term *good* as an adjective in conjunction with a noun. Thus, a good cat is one that can do well what cats "normally" are expected to do, or even "must" do if they are to survive, that is, it can hunt, eat, and reproduce. Some conception of a "goal" seems presup-posed here. On the other hand, it does not seem to be whimsical to see a cat as an animal oriented toward the goal of surviving and re-producing. "Evolutionary theory" may tell us a lot about the mecha-nisms through which cats over the millennia have become good survivors, but that is a separate issue. A good knife is one that cuts well. One does not understand cats at all if one does not understand that and why they need to be able to run and hunt, and one does not understand them fully unless one has some knowledge of how the different parts of the cat come together to allow it to do what it has to do. The same is true of the knife.

One natural extension of this way of thinking is to appeal to sus-tainability which might be thought to be the economic equivalent of the survival of a biological entity. Thus, Richard Raatzsch argues very powerfully for the claim that "sustainability" is not a merely op-tional feature of an economy, but that a teleological orientation to-ward a certain minimum sustainability must be part of the very fabric of anything we could reasonably call a human economy.[22] This is no doubt true, but it does not definitively settle the issue. After all, sus-tainability is relative to a certain period of time. Does the economy have to survive for a year, a decade, or a century? It is not at all ir-rational, at least not prima facie irrational, to think that our best economy should be one that might last ten millennia at most. How would we decide it was the "same" economy that survived? What would be the point of demanding that it be able to survive for longer than that? Would the demands for being sustainable for ten years necessarily be the same as those for surviving for a century? Fur-thermore, not *all* we want or expect of an economy is that it "sur-vives." We might perfectly legitimately want it to *change* in various ways, not merely to stay as it is; for instance, we might wish it to change in the direction of greater efficiency or of more equal distribution of benefits. Even if we make mere "sustainability" our only criterion, it is perfectly possible that there are a variety of different but equally sustainable forms an economy can take. So (a limited form of) sustainability seems at best to be a necessary condition or a framework for something to be an economy at all, and thus a minimally "good" economy.

There is, however, also another way of thinking about this issue, which is centered not on the nature of things and human economic activity as a response to that, tracking it in a more or less successful way. This other approach, which we can associate with the name "Hume," begins from our own highly variable and subjective forms of desire and valuation. To say that something is good is to say that I (or we, or "one") approve(s) of it, and this notion of "approval" is finally cashed out in terms of some agent's desires, wishes, and preferences. So if I like foie gras, I may also ceteris paribus approve of force-feeding geese in a certain way to produce it. Then a "good" goose is not necessarily one that will live a long life and reproduce itself, but one that will be biddable and produce the requisite pâté when appropriate stuff is thrust down its throat. This second, "subjectivist" approach is ambiguous or indeterminate in that it is unclear whose wants are canonical and definitive: those of observers or those of participants. That is, is the Brazilian economy at some point in time or during some period "good" (or "bad") by reference to the general evaluative preferences of someone like me who is an observer but not a participant in it, or by virtue of satisfying the wants and desires of Brazilians? Whose judgment is to count and how much? The Brazilians' or mine (or those of the directors of those international corporations trying to expand their profits in Brazil)? The wishes of the goose, or of eaters of foie gras?

We seem, then, to have found (at least) three dimensions along which we might evaluate a set of economies or an economy as good, bad, or indifferent: satisfaction of needs, sustainability, satisfaction of wants. For some it might seem natural to think that we could appeal to a fourth dimension: "rationality" here, and this might be useful if we could be sure that we had a clear and agreed-on idea of what exactly "rationality" is. Unfortunately, such an appeal would be an instance of what has been called "obscurum per obscurius." If we do not antecedently agree on which economies are better than which others, we are unlikely to agree on which of the many standards of "rationality" that have been proposed are better than others. Thus the appeal to "rationality" would be a pointless detour.

In this way Max Weber makes an important distinction between what he calls "formal" and what he calls "substantive" rationality.[23] Weber was notoriously highly pluralistic about the kinds of value-judgments he thought people could make, in this respect a bit like Hume. Thus people in a certain society may well value absolute equality very highly or they may have some notion of "merit" or "desert" such as that those born to particular parents thereby "deserve" more—more political power and authority (as in monarchies and aristocracies) or more economic resources and power (as in all known liberal democracies)—than others do, or they may give priority to certain religious values that are nonegalitarian. A certain system is substantively rational if it, by its normal mode of operation, generally realizes some value to a very high degree. There are no "inherent" restrictions on what the substantive value might be. Thus a legal system could in principle be thought to be very value-rational if it produced to a very high degree a redistribution of property from the poor to the rich.

Formal rationality in contrast is not connected with an assessment of the value of outcomes, but of the nature of the procedures by which the outcomes are reached. A formally rational procedure is one where the individual steps are clearly specified, transparently presented, usually in sequence, where reasons are, or at any rate can be, given for the move from one step to the next, and so on. An increase in formal rationality need not mean an increase in substantive rationality. A *qādi* with no formal training, who is perhaps even illiterate and who consults no complicated code, may give perfectly satisfactory legal judgments and in fact a *qādi* with broad human experience and sympathy might do a better job of dispensing justice, that is, satisfying whatever "substantive" conception one wishes to use than trained lawyers who follow the book. The demand for increased formal rationality has grown in the recent past in Western Europe, but it has coexisted with a demand for the realization of various substantive values. In a way, for Weber, our recent history is one of the conflict between different conceptions of "rationality."

This discussion started from a clear distinction between "needs" construed as "objective" requirements, necessities, and so on, and mere "subjective" wants, wishes, desires, preferences. This was a distinction within the way various people, including both participants in a given social formation and theorists studying this formation, saw or interpreted the world and their place in it: something was *construed* as one or the other. Upon closer inspection it then turned out to be more and more difficult in most cases to make the distinction as clear and sharp as it was intended to be: Do the looters really have a need or just a desire for new trainers? Is Wotan's action toward Fricka an indication that he "needs" her or merely wants her? When the Waldenses allow themselves to be burned at the stake rather than renounce their religious views and practices, does it make sense to speak of this situation in terms of their mere preferences *or* did anyone need to refer to a set of objective needs at all?

The distinction between needs and desires is mirrored in the difference between the two philosophical approaches just discussed, that is, between Aristotle and Hume.[24] Either one starts from nature or objective reality and sees humans as essentially responding to this. The real world out there imposes demands on us to which we respond, and it has inherently attractive and repellant features we naturally track, or try to track, as best we can. This tracking mechanism is the essential origin of human valuation. If one takes this view, it will seem plausible to give centrality to some notion of objective human needs and then of desires that correctly respond to the objectively attractive features of our world and situation. The alternative is that humans are free desiring machines that produce lists of preferences. The mechanism by which these lists are produced is unimportant, provided one knows that its operation has been unimpeded by external factors, and the relation of these desires, wishes, and wants to the world reduces itself to a discussion of the extent to which and the circumstances under which they can be realized (individually and collectively). Here "preference" is king, and anything that resembles it sufficiently to seem an alternative, but is not identical to it, is to be "reduced" to it in one way or another.

Philosophical discussion is often structured as if the first of these two approaches, centered around "objective necessity" and need, or the second, centered around (subjective) "preference," must win across the board, but I merely note that that need not be the case. Even if I take the general "objectivist" point that *some* kind of minimal stability or sustainability must be part of any economy, this will not necessarily allow me to discriminate between the specific forms of economic activity between which societies now need to choose. It will mean that I cannot choose *ad libitum* as some modern followers of Hume perhaps envisaged, but it will also mean that there is not only room for choice but a need to choose or determine which form is to be considered "better" from among those that are minimally sustainable.

It is possible to be so impressed by the difficulty of distinguishing between political demands, (mere) human desires or preferences, and needs (of different kinds) that one tries to abandon the whole concept of "need" as a serious component in politics (and economics). I shall follow the usage of Adorno in using the term *positivist* to refer to an approach that asserts that expressed preferences are to be taken at face value, and never to be questioned. Adorno connects positivism with inappropriate priority given to "immediacy." Liberalism, which fits neatly into the schema of positivist economics, calls this "non-paternalism." Actually there are at least two distinct forms of anti-paternalism. First, there is a "cognitivist" version. No one else can know better than I can what I want. This is distinct from more moralized approaches, such as the claim that although I might in some cases know what is good for you better than you do yourself, I may not or generally should not try to change your mind, or bring it about that you change your mind, or force you to do what I know is in your interests (even if you do not know) or force you to do what is best for you *while claiming* that I am not using force. Needless to say, these may all be distinct cases.

One can find a particularly clear instance of the kind of thinking Adorno called "positivist" and that gives a perfectly direct answer to the question of the relation between needs and desires in the views of thinkers who are called representative of neoliberalism. This strand takes up a line of argument I mentioned earlier when discussing the tendency in politics toward inflation of terminology and dramatization. "I need" is taken by the neoliberal *always* to be no more than a dramatization or a mere intensification of "I want," not as a claim with a different kind of structure.

The typical "neoliberal" position has two major components.[25] First, it takes liberal anti-paternalism to its final conclusion, namely, that all desires and preferences are to be taken at face value and as equal. Second, it constructs an idealized model of a "free market" as one wholly without any internal political interference. The state is there only to protect life and property and enforce contracts. This "free market" is then asserted to be an image of the optimal solution to the basic problem of humans who need to live and work together, namely, that of the coordination of action.[26] This ideal "free market" is supposed to be self-regulating and particularly rational in that it is supposed to ensure maximally efficient use of resources and optimal satisfaction of human needs and wants.

The neoliberal position does not lack a certain prima facie plausibility for agents in societies of a certain kind because it does seem to describe some historically transient and relatively superficial aspects of the world that present themselves to individual economic agents in a certain position. However, even the most superficial observer cannot now, that is, after 2008, fail to conclude upon reflection that whatever else is true of the "free market," it is most definitely not self-regulating. Anyone who continues to believe this must have been asleep for the past five or six years while the purportedly "self-regulating" financial markets broke down.

So if rationality includes minimal self-sustainability, neoliberalism is nowhere. In addition, the notion of rationality is particularly relative and context-dependent. There can be situations in which it is perfectly rational to demand something that is impossible. Famously some students in Paris in 1968 did exactly this with their motto: "Soyez réaliste, demandez l'impossible." After all, there is no a priori requirement that one negotiate, much less that one negotiate constructively and in good faith at all. Whether or not that is a good idea depends on the context. If one really thinks that the society is completely corrupt or about to collapse in on itself, perhaps it is in no way unreasonable to put to it demands that cannot be satisfied.

This might be a risky or even a very dangerous strategy; many people, especially those who are relatively satisfied with the status quo might think it a criminal thing to do, but that is different from saying it is inherently irrational.

Many situations can be described in a variety of different ways and that includes being redescribed so as to show an underlying rationality where one initially seemed to be lacking. So Nixon's attempt to convince foreign governments that he was a lunatic—the "Madman Theory"[27]—was, after all, a conscious ploy on his part to increase his power by convincing others that he was not necessarily bluffing when he threatened the use of nuclear weapons. They were supposed to believe that he was deranged enough actually to *use* these weapons, even though it would have meant suicide. A lunatic in control of nuclear weapons might be thought to be politically more powerful in certain negotiating situations than someone who was known to be sane. The more "flexible" the notion of "rationality" becomes, the less useful it is likely to be in giving us guidance about how we should ourselves act.

In the neoliberal universe everything is reduced to a single commensurate dimension. All there is are human desires, of different intensities, and the different intensity can be measured by the single yardstick of how much money people are willing to give for the things in question. Of course, neoliberalism has not actually fully succeeded in transforming any society into a place in which human organs can be sold ad libitum to the highest bidder, all drugs are unregulated, mandatory forms of social insurance are banned but slavery is permitted, and so on. Nevertheless it has played an important role in setting the terms of political discussion.

In some ways Sartre and the neoliberals succumb to parallel but inverse errors: he purported to take any and every political demand that got itself articulated as the expression of a need that ought to be satisfied; they accept any expressed demand, just as they accept any desire or preference, at face value. At the same time, they know that only those that are compatible with making a profit in the free market have any chance of being satisfied. In neither case is a distinction between a need and a (mere) desire recognized. Multilayered accounts that have a place for qualitatively different "needs" and "desires" are more difficult to maintain but they allow at least the possibility of radical forms of criticism.

Neither Aristotle nor Hume is "right" and "wins" the argument. Rather the distinction between "needs" and "desires" is one it is important for us to make, if we are to be able to lead a fully human life, have some distance to our own actions, set ourselves long-term goals, and engage in any form of criticism. We might be tempted to interpret our "needs" as strictly objective, and our desires as strictly subjective, on the models, respectively, of Aristotle and Hume, but that is a mistake (in both cases). Of course, we do fail to continue to live if our body has no water for several days running, but our basic *human* need for something to drink even at this basic level is not simply identical with that biological fact, but is something in every concrete case structured by our desires, wants, beliefs, and their history. Equally one cannot understand our desires as *fully* self-subsistent independent of the world in which we find ourselves and with which we are always engaged.

In the above discussion no mention has been made of what one might think is a further important concept in the political discussion of economies. There are "needs," "wishes/wants," and (political) demands, but also "interests." When in Brussels in early December 2011 David Cameron vetoed the proposed package of reform for European finances, he did so in the name of the British national interest, not of British preferences or British desires. To be sure, "British national interest" in fact was his personal political interest in making a symbolic gesture that would please one wing of the Tory party that had general reservations about him.[28] "Interests," whatever exactly they are supposed to be, are not identical with mere preferences any more than "needs" are. At a minimum they refer to the considered preferences one would have if one had optimal information and reflected carefully.[29] Reference to "interests" is part of the pre-neoliberal vocabulary of traditional politics, and so it is not surprising to find politicians who have no considered opinions or deeply held theoretical beliefs themselves appealing to them in symbolically highly laden situations, even if in other contexts they use the language of neoliberalism.[30]

What is important and can be learned perhaps from Adorno more clearly than from others is not so much the indispensability of the category of "need," but the absolute importance of retaining in place a conceptual scheme that allows one to reject the glorification of "immediacy" in the realm of preferences and desires, and also to reject the liberal taboo on cognitive paternalism. "Need" is important because it is one of a whole battery of terms that gives us a standpoint for criticizing raw desires and preferences.

If economists find this world of vagrant and perhaps impossible wants, contextually specified and historically changing needs, preferences, and interests simply too complicated, then the reply should be that the world is as complicated as it is. If they argue that they "have to" restrict themselves to something clear, shapely, and "operationalizable," because otherwise their subject could not function as the mathematically organized discipline it is, the use of "have to" should tip us off that something is wrong. The tail should not wag the dog. It is a bit like the joke about the man who lost his house key at night at a certain place on a dark country road. He looks for it obsessively under the next lamppost ten meters away because that is the only place where there is any light. If the economics currently practiced cannot give a plausible account of human life, perhaps the conclusion to be drawn is that it is a discipline with inherently limited capacities, a kind of glorified bookkeeping, important enough in its way, but not a model for understanding anything especially interesting about human societies and certainly not a major source of substantive guidance for politics.

This chapter then must end with a practical aporia of a kind that is familiar to modern people in a number of areas of our lives. We can clearly see the utterly destructive consequences of remaining with a "positivistic" account of the realm of human desire. If we stay with this, the world as we know it will pretty clearly suffocate on its own toxic by-products within the foreseeable future (if it does not end in a nuclear conflagration before that time). On the other hand, we have no idea how we could plausibly find a way of getting out of the positivist state because all existing authorities have lost their authority, and we do not see how it would be possible to establish any other that would have any standing.

One might think that this aporia is simply something we have to learn to tolerate, as an ineluctable constituent of the human condition. Or one might think, as Adorno seems to hold, that it is a feature of *our* life in this form of society, and as such something no individual or groups can escape simply by his, her, or their own actions. It was perhaps also a feature of most historical societies, although few people in any of them realized this because the human tendency to self-delusion and wishful thinking, straightforward political and economic oppression, and the social power and intellectual prestige of institutions such as the church made it difficult for them to see this. The question is whether or not it is an invariant feature of all possible human social life, but no one at this moment knows how to answer that question authoritatively.

9

Can the Humanities Survive Neoliberalism?

—⟡⟡⟡—

I WOULD LIKE TO focus here on neoliberalism with special attention to its relation to one group of purported theoretical pursuits that are called in English "the Humanities," and within the Humanities I will be particularly concerned with the subject about which I know most, namely, philosophy.

For the moment I would like to try to begin in a rather "nominalist" way, meaning by that that I shall not try to give anything like an account of the essential properties of certain activities, but simply a list of the subjects we usually call (in English) "the Humanities." These will include centrally the systematic study of language and literature, music and art, philosophy, the historical and comparative study of religion, and most of the more traditional forms of history. It will not usually include physics, zoology, astronomy, or geology; these will usually be classified as belong to the natural sciences.[1] In the modern world at any rate the Humanities constitute a series of academic disciplines that have their central locus in universities. To establish its credentials as a proper subject of university study, a discipline has to contain some kind of theoretical component; practical skill alone, no matter how impressive, will not suffice. In fact, to call "the Humanities" "academic disciplines" is to distinguish them from

148

various forms of disciplined practical activity such as the activity of writing novels, composing music, or conducting forms of religious worship. The relation between theoretical and practical components will differ depending on the specific domain studied. Thus, in the case of something like music, we actually find a tripartite structure: there is musical performance, which is a practical activity taught in conservatories, and "musicology," which is a theoretical study of the principles of music (and perhaps of its history) which is nowadays taught in universities. Both of these are distinct from musical composition. On the other hand, history seems inherently an activity with no "practical" aspect in the relevant sense. And there is great disagreement in the case of philosophy. Many people have held that doing philosophy is completely distinct from studying it, but others have denied this.

I note that this theoretical focus contrasts with the situation of some of the precursors of "the Humanities." One of the most important of these precursors was ancient rhetoric, the cultivation of effective and beautiful speech. Old-style rhetoric, that is, was *practical* and also organized around basically aesthetic principles and notions about what would be politically effective. Philosophers, of course, from the beginning had a slightly different take on speaking and writing. They were keen to wrest control of the study and use of the spoken and written words away from professional speechwriters, and they were particularly eager to moralize the whole enterprise of learning. To learn to speak well was supposed to be *part* of the project of becoming a morally better person. The philosophers' approach was theoretical and moralizing, and devoted to the claim that morality *required* a theoretical framework of some kind. Later the Christian churches in the West took over the structuration of education in the precursors of the disciplines we call "the Humanities," attempting to enforce doctrinal orthodoxy and subject them to a control based on an assessment of their possible effect on religiously conceived form of moral behavior. With secularization the religiously based moral dimension became rather less important, and eventually seemed to fall away almost entirely, but the emphasis on having a framework that was in some sense "theoretical" seems to have remained important. The social position of the practices that constitute the Humanities (and that constituted their predecessors) is also an important factor in understanding their structure.

Hegel noted the difference in the social position of philosophy between the ancient and the "modern" worlds in a famous remark in the introduction to his *Rechtsphilosophie:*[2]

> In our modern world philosophy is not practiced, as it was among the ancient Greeks, as a private art, rather it has an existence which is visible to anyone and impinges on the public *(eine öffentliche das Publikum berührende Existenz)*, either primarily or even exclusively in civil service *(im Staatsdienst)*. Governments have demonstrated their confidence in the scholars who devote themselves to this subject-matter in that they rely on them completely for the development and content of philosophy . . . but often this confidence has been but poorly returned . . . This would not matter, if it were not the case that the [modern] state did not contain within itself a need for deeper culture and insight [among the citizens] and did not demand that science [*Wissenschaft*] satisfy this need.

The first thing to note about this passage is that Hegel operates with a relatively naive and underspecified distinction between "public" and "private." Ancient Greek democracies provided a variety of kinds of public spectacle and of opportunities for education and training, particularly in the form of the development of the military capacities of young citizens. In addition to these, there was a variety of "private" forms of training available. So we are told by Plato that Themistocles had his son trained in particular recherché forms of equitation, so that he learned, for instance, to throw a spear while riding a horse.[3] Presumably Themistocles will have hired a private trainer for this. The ancient world had, it should be noted, a third category. Just as Roman law recognized three categories—public, private, and religious—so in Greece in addition to "public" and "private" forms of instruction, there were "secret" or "esoteric" ones, for instance, those associated with divination, with cult practices, and with the mysteries. The mysteries were full of *arreta*—things that should not be mentioned. Philosophy, Hegel is right, was not part of the public provision of educational opportunities and was also, with the possible exception of the Pythagoreans, who seem to have been something between a philosophical school and a religious sect, not a form of esoteric wisdom. However, at the very beginning of Western philosophy stands a disagreement between Socrates and the sophists about a number of issues, not least of which, however, is the appropriate form for the teaching, learning, and practicing philosophy. For both Socrates and the sophists philosophy was in one sense a "private" art, as Hegel states, but for Plato there was the utterly essential distinction that the sophists charged money for their instruction, whereas Socrates never took a penny and was eager to speak with *anyone* without charge.[4] There are, then, at least two kinds of "private" philosophizing: uncoerced conversations with Socrates that took place outside the nexus of money, and formal paid instruction from a sophist, who was a kind of educational proto-entrepreneur. In the passage by Hegel quoted above, one will also notice that he moves from speaking of philosophy having a public existence to discussion of the needs of the state, and even the government. I merely point out that the identification of "public" with "state" is not really correct. This is especially the case if one is thinking of educational institutions. After all, for a *very* long time the Catholic Church played an extremely important role in education and in the cultivation of the precursor disciplines to the modern "Humanities," and in many countries there still are Catholic universities. The Catholic Church, however, is not a private corporation in anything like the sense in which Siemens or BP is a private corporation; on the other hand, the church is not, in most countries, part of the state apparatus, much less a part of the government.

So to return to the question of the relation of public and private, it seems that one must make at least the following four distinctions:

  1) A distinction in the kind of ownership/management where there are three interesting possibilities:
     a. Owned/managed by the state/city, or some strictly public organization like the police force or army.
     b. Owned/managed by some other public body (such as a "trust," church, and so on).

      c. Owned/managed by a private individual or corporation.
2) Accessibility:
      a. Open to anyone (really anyone).
      b. Open to all those who satisfy some relatively general and universal criteria (for example, examination results, ability to pay fees, and so on). The question then arises whether the "criteria" are intrinsically connected with the goal of the institution (access by some academic criterion) or not (access by ability to pay fees).
      c. Not open to anyone (instruction given by *Hofmeister* or *Hauslehrer*).[5]
3) Fee-paying/non-fee-paying.
4) Profit/not-for-profit.

As I mentioned earlier the Humanities are now to some extent defined by their location in a modern university. There seems to me to be little doubt but that this has had *some* advantages for them, if only because they retain some of what public standing, authority, and prestige they continue to have in modern societies through their indirect association with what are called in Britain STEM subjects (science, technology, engineering, medicine). People are understandably impressed by the development of new techniques for transplanting human organs, quicker means of communication, less labor-intense ways of performing everyday tasks, and a bit of the prestige generated by these technological advances gets transferred from the natural sciences to their sister disciplines in the universities, including the Humanities. The disadvantage, which is the reverse side of this reflected glory, is that the Humanities come under even greater pressure to assimilate themselves, their methods, goals, and standards of evaluation to those in currency in the natural sciences. Above I spoke of the shift from the ancient study of rhetoric as a practical activity structured by aesthetic and political criteria to more modern modes structured around "theory." Now, in addition, the Humanities seems to be expected not just to be "theoretical" but also to adopt the research-centered structure and organization of natural sciences. By "research" I mean a certain ideal type of intellectual activity: it is a temporally extended process that can be analytically subdivided into individual steps, some at least that can be to some extent routinized. At the end of such a process, if it has been successful, stand "results" (what in the UK are now technically called "research outputs"). These "outputs" or "research results" are sets of distinct propositions or formulae that can be detached from the context of investigation and published separately. Although a particular research result can be isolated, it is also the case that the individual research process and its result can be seen smoothly to fit into a larger socially structured context of other research projects and their results; that is, it can be integrated into a larger whole that counts as a "science" and has a minimally cumulative structure.

Of course, it might well be that the ideal-type of "research" that I have described above is not really instantiated in all, or even in any, of the natural sciences. On this point I would like to remain in a state of skeptical suspension of belief, but whether or not this is a correct description of research in natural science, it does seem to me that, whether correct or not, some such conception like this informs public attitudes toward scientific research, and that means also the attitude of the politicians who are responsible for setting educational policy. Perhaps certain low-grade kinds of archival or historical research can be forced into this model, but it seems obviously completely inappropriate as a description of the way the central humanistic disciplines actually operate and also the way in which their practitioners think about what they are doing. Until very recently the Humanities were not about reaching "results" that could be formulated propositionally or mathematically, but rather were about learning to develop increasingly differentiated and sophisticated structures of perception, thinking, and reacting, about asking questions, about constructing and evaluating different points of view, and so on. Through this process people were supposed to acquire an ability to deal with themselves, their past, their world, and others in a free, less rigid, and less constricted, and hence—it was assumed—more satisfactory way. Processes of research that come to a successful conclusion generate new information and new theories that can be applied; the goal of the Humanities, however, is not information, but some kind of transformation of the person. It is true that this goal is perhaps most explicitly formulated in ancient philosophy, where it is clearly connected with acquiring a certain kind of theoretical insight. This insight is supposed to lead to practical wisdom and is connected with gaining the ability to lead the right kind of life. This ancient view, however, had not been completely lost even up to the middle of the twentieth century. The hope that was constitutive of the Humanities was for a life transformation that was not the *exclusive* prerogative of philosophy, but to some extent shared by all the humanistic disciplines. As an essential component in a system of universities, the Humanities were supposed to contribute in some way not to providing jobs for the boys, but to helping maintain a public space of enlightened discussion that was of great cultural and political importance.

This brings me to neoliberalism. One can think of this doctrine as constituted by two theses. First, a rather speculative ethical and political thesis about the nature of the good life for humans, and, second, a set of interconnected claims about a fictional or theoretical entity called the "free market" that was supposed to have certain properties.

The first, philosophical, part of neoliberalism comprises a certain form of individualism. It is the human individual who is the basic object of ethical concern and bearer of whatever values there are. The good life must be the life of the human individual, and its goodness is constituted by a triad of three components: welfare, as measured by the level of access to goods and services, the satisfaction of desires, and freedom. There is not really any significant theory about the relation between these three because most of the supporters of neoliberalism simply assume in a naive way that what people want basically is access to goods and services, and that freedom either simply consists in such unhindered access or can easily be obtained if one has such access. To be slightly more exact, the "freedom" in question is a regime of strictly enforced property rights, plus the right to unfettered economic enterprise and consequent consumer choice.

The second part of neoliberalism is its theory of the "free market." This is an idealized model of transactions between individuals who are imagined as being completely independent of each other, not tied by existing bonds of any kind, and who meet to exchange goods and services motivated solely by "strictly economic" motives, which means by the intention of maximizing the results of the transaction along some abstract dimension, such as "utility" (or slightly, but only slightly, more concretely "money").

Obviously no such market ever existed, the idea of it is a kind of utopian conception, but that is not in itself necessarily an objection, because the question is whether it is a useful conception or not (and, if so, in what sense of "useful"; useful *for* whom? *For* what purpose?). What is odd about the free market is not that it is an idealized and imaginary entity, but rather that it is thought to be "natural," self-regulating, and "maximally rational/efficient." To say that it is "natural" is an important part of the ideology because in fact one of its main goals is to protect the interests of entrepreneurs and corporations against what they perceive as unwarranted depredations by politicians, either in the form of regulation or taxation. The idea seems to be that if it were once admitted that the market is a social construct, rather than some kind of natural phenomenon, this would immediately raise the question whether it could be constructed in *one* way rather than the other. It is this possibility that must be excluded—think of Thatcher's "there is no choice" and "you can't buck the market"—and the appeal to "nature" is what serves that purpose. To be sure, the state, as the sphere of politics, does have a role in neoliberalism, but it is severely limited and essentially negative. It is to prevent violence and fraud, and to enforce contracts; anything else is both morally illegitimate and economically destructive. The associated claim—that the "free market" is "self-regulating"—apparently is a derivative of the so-called law of supply and demand, which suggests that an equilibrium between these two will be reestablished, if it is disturbed by "external" factors. Even if we knew what an "external" factor was exactly and if this "law" turned out in some sense to be true and contentful, it is unclear why it should be thought to be especially important or humanly appealing. After all, it says only that equilibrium will eventually be reestablished, but not either when it will be reached or what the actual content of that equilibrium might be. If there is no demand for my apples, but I continue to show up at the market every day, there is a disequilibrium, which can be remedied if I die of starvation and thus do not show up on the market square. This is no consolation to me. Equally, as Keynes remarked, in the long run we are all dead, so a process in which equilibrium is reestablished after five hundred years might not be of much interest to any of us.

So, even if one accepts the neoliberal framework, but tries to apply it to a span of time that is relevant to human beings, say, forty years, there is no guarantee that anything like "equilibrium" will be attained. Also simple observation should have sufficed to indicate that, whatever the a priori arguments from economics, the present system has not shown itself to be self-regulating in any humanly interesting sense, and there is absolutely no reason to believe that this is because deregulation has not been carried out sufficiently thoroughly. What one might think should have been the final nail in the coffin of neoliberalism was the rush by members of the financial services industry, who for decades had preached that any intervention by the state was harmful, but suddenly changed their tune entirely and called for massive state intervention to save the banks during the recent financial crisis. Which was forthcoming in many cases, and has actually worked in the cases in which it was tried. It is hard to see how the ideology of neoliberalism could conceivably survive after this, but to jump to this conclusion would be to overlook the investment that established and powerful economic actors have in the maintenance of an ideology that gives them a way of presenting the pursuit of their own narrow advantage in a beneficent light.

These, then, are some general reasons for skepticism about the neoliberal project. However, there are also some further deficiencies in the program if one thinks specifically about the Humanities, the funding of universities, and education in general.

Neoliberalism is loud in its praise of the efficiency of the free market and of its role in fostering the maximization of autonomy. However, the theory of the "free market" depends on a number of assumptions that make it an especially inadequate model for educational processes. First it assumes perfect knowledge on the part of the consumer:

a) Consumers know what they want; they are the final court of appeal about their desires, wants, and interests.
b) Consumers know about the goods offered for sale.

The first of these two assumptions is a version of the general liberal thesis that is sometimes called "anti-paternalism," but the second goes beyond anything assumed by older figures in the liberal tradition. In some simple cases, it might not be implausible to think that these two assumptions hold, and in fact the even minimal ideological effectiveness of this assumption depends on this plausibility. I go to the market square, meaning the concrete bit of paved space in the center of the town in which I live, to buy apples. I know I want apples and know that different kinds exist, some of which I like better than others.

In general, however, the idea that I always know better than anyone else what is good for me—or even what I want—is one that seems grossly to contradict everyday experience. In my own case I am only too aware that in the past I have made very significant mistakes in the judgment of my own desires, wishes, and interests. Even if my friends, empathetic but disinterested, observers, professionals, and experts of various kinds who have to deal with me are too polite to say, I now know that in many cases their judgments about me and my behavior would have been right whereas I was wrong.

This principle of anti-paternalism that stands at the core of neo-liberalism is, however, multiply ambiguous. It does not have to be at all the same thing to say that:

1. I am the final judge of what I want

and to say that:

2. I am the final judge of what is good for me, or what is in my interest.

Clearly neither of these is identical with:

3. I am the final judge of what is good (*simpliciter*)
4. I am the final judge of what it would be good for me to do.

If, for the sake of argument, we put aside for the moment the other versions and start from the formulation "I am the final judge of what is in my own interest," this statement is still not completely univocal. There seem to me to be several ways in which it can be taken:

A. "Whatever judgment I happen to make about my own interests is in fact infallible."

So if I happen to think that the glass in front of me, which actually contains sulfuric acid, is full of water, my judgment, when I am thirsty, that it would be in my own interest to drink the contents of the glass is infallible. That seems highly implausible.

A second way to read the thesis is:

> B. "Any judgment an individual makes about his own interest ought always to be treated by others, especially economists and politicians, *as if* it were infallible; that is, it ought to be taken at face value, not to be interpreted away, questioned, ignored in the name of some higher good or greater wisdom, and so on."

However, if my judgments about my own interests *are* not infallible, why should they *always* be treated as if they were?

A third reading of the thesis is:

> C. "Every individual is *in principle* capable of learning what is in his own interest, and whatever he defines as 'in his interest' at the end of a learning process should be accepted."

This formulation would be genuinely informative only if it were to be associated with a clear further specification of what a "learning process" was and how such a process could come to an "end." The minimalist or default position for such a "learning process" would be that it was one in which I endogenously changed my beliefs about what was in my own interest in response to new information, that is, information I had previously not had. So I change my views about whether smoking is in my interest by virtue of acquiring some new information about its effects on my health. The most interesting cases of "learning," however, go beyond the mere assimilation of new and useful factual information. Thus in the nineteenth century there was a whole subgenre in German literature of the so-called *Bildungs-roman* that had as part of its essential content the narration of a process of development in which a young man not only changed his views about his interests in the light of new information but actually came to adopt a new way of living and an associated new set of interests. Often part of the point is that at the *start* of their process of learning, individuals are not in a position to see things correctly and to evaluate the information that may in some sense "in principle" be available to them. The central figure must become other than he is in order to make himself able to learn from what he sees, hears, and experiences. Perhaps the best example here is not Wilhelm Meister or *der grüne Heinrich* but Wagner's Parsifal. At the beginning of the opera Parsifal is really *"der reine Tor"* and what characterizes his immature status is that he is not even able to ask the right questions about the strange ritual-events that are taking place around him. Thus he asks Gurnemanz, *"Wer ist der Gral?"* to which the only answer is that even to ask the question in this form betrays a complete lack of understanding of what is going on (*"Das sagt sich nicht"*), because the Grail is not a *who* but a *what*. At root an innocent sexually immature boy (*"Knabe"*) is not in any position to learn anything about the situation of the knights of the Gral. What changes things for him is Kundry's kiss, but that is not best understood as a form of transmission of information. There are, then, processes of learning that are not mere sequences of assimilation of new information but also changes in one's way of life with attendant changes in one's very modes of perception, in the direction of one's curiosity, in the ways in which one processes information, and in the structure of one's interests themselves.

The early Marx makes the central point here with all requisite clarity:

[Nur unter gewissen Gesellschaftsbedingungen] wird ein musikalisches Ohr, ein Auge für die Schönheit der Form, kurz, werden erst menschlicher Genüsse fähige *Sinne*, Sinne welche als *menschliche* Wesenkräfte sich bestätigen, teils erst ausgebildet, teils erst erzeugt . . . Die *Bildung* der 5 Sinne ist eine Arbeit der ganzen bisherigen Weltgeschichte. Der unter dem rohen praktischen Bedürfnis befangene *Sinn* hat auch nur einen *bornierten* Sinn. Für den ausgehungerten Menschen existiert nicht die menschliche Form der Speise, sondern nur ihr abstraktes Dasein als Speise; ebensogut könnte sie in rohster Form vorliegen, und es ist nicht zu sagen, wodurch sich diese Nahrungstätigkeit von der *tierischen* Nahrungstätigkeit unterscheide. Der sorgenvolle, bedürftige Mensch hat keinen *Sinn* für das schönste Schauspiel;

der Mineralienkrämer sieht nur den merkantilen Wert, aber
nicht die Schönheit und eigentümliche Natur des Minerals;
er hat keinen minerologischen Sinn.
  (Marx, *MEW*, Erg. 1. S 541)

The natural sciences tell us how to represent complex crystalline
structures in a mathematically perspicuous way, what chemical properties different minerals have, and how they can be worked and
used. The Humanities are structured around an attempt to awaken
and cultivate what Marx calls the "mineralogical sense" by initiating
processes of learning in which we transform ourselves into creatures
who have an interest in "the beauty and specific nature" of minerals.
If the anti-paternalist neoliberal states that the final question is "What
does each individual in question value, desire, and believe is in his
interest?," the traditional response of the Humanities would have
been that the questions they raise have a kind of priority, namely, not
what *do* individuals value, but "What *should they* value?," where the
concept of "should" is construed as broadly as possible, and the
specification of the content of *"should"* is *itself* part of what the Humanities investigate. The world of transformation of our habits of
seeing, feeling, and wanting is the world in which the Humanities
are at home. This is a world to which neoliberalism has no access and
about which it has nothing to say. Education is not a commodity or
service like others because it is explicitly directed not at providing
people with something they know they want, but changing the nature and structure of our beliefs, desires, wants, and interests. This
emphasis on the structured change of beliefs, preferences, attitudes,
and interests is what distinguishes the Humanities "in their highest
vocation" (Hegel's *"höchste Berufung"*[6]) from neoliberalism in any
form. One of the most rigorous and influential proponents of neoliberalism, Gary Becker, devotes much time to discussing a basic
assumption he makes, which is that people never change their preferences, they merely respond differently to different perceived
opportunity costs.[7] Students are not like the autonomous consumers
of neoliberal theory because, one is almost tempted to say, "by definition," they are not agents at the end of a *Bildungsprozeß*, but rather
at the beginning.

There are several distinct lines of reasoning that one might mobilize against the central neoliberal conception, that of "freedom."
First, "freedom" is not exhausted by the conjunction of the right to
secure ownership of property, the right to taking certain types of
unregulated economic initiatives, and free consumer choice among
a large universe of alternatives. At the very minimum it must also
comprise some condition to the effect that the individual subject who
is free is both well informed and enlightened about his or her own
desires and interests. Premature exposure to uncontrolled choice
among uncategorized "options" may well in fact have the effect of
confusing subjects and preventing them from coming to develop a
well-grounded sense of what is in their own interests. Especially in
view of the existence of addictive options that offer corporations the
possibility of effectively enslaving individual consumers (cars, drugs,
cigarettes, electronic gadgets). Second, even if one did, for the purposes of this argument, suspend any reservations one might have
about the neoliberal idea of freedom as essentially ownership, entre-
preneurship, and consumer choice, the "free market" does not obviously provide me with unlimited consumer choice. Rather, I am
systematically offered only such options as will be compatible with
the continued existence of a particular market structure. I may have
free choice among dozens of brands of soap or toothpaste, but if my
basic preference structure is one in which what I *really* want is to live
in a society where there is security of employment for everyone, no
advertising on the streets, the expectation of a reasonably comfortable retirement for any except the most feckless (or even *including*
the most feckless), public institutions such as newspapers, radio, and
universities in which informed, open discussion of human life is
possible, these will most definitively *not* be on the list of things a
"free market" will in fact provide. Part of our human freedom is our
ability *collectively* to think about the future and take care for it. Neoliberalism is committed to the view that we ought not to make use
of that ability, but leave the future to *individual* planning and "the
(free) market." It is hard to see this as anything but an attempt at
human self-mutilation.

It is, of course, perfectly possible to argue that the Humanities
could never in any case live up to their ideal vocation. The dream

that there could be a public social space in which we could study and participate in rationally controlled processes of self-transformation in which our desires and interests became more enlightened might just be another lovely illusion. Just as, then, there were precursors of the Humanities, there might also be successors to them, if, for instance, neoliberalism were to be able to refashion the universities completely in their image. The universities would then become factories for the production of a certain kind of luxury good, or salons providing a certain prestigious service, that is, something like a jeweler's workshop or a high-class massage parlor. Neither of these are vantage points from which one will be likely to satisfy the traditional aspiration of the Humanities to contribute to a general improvement of human cultural and moral life.

10

Identification and the Politics of Envy

—◦◦◦—

IN 1844 MARX WAS living in Paris, and for his own edification he wrote a series of texts that in some sense represent his first theoretical breakthrough in coming to a new understanding of the society in which he was living. These texts remained unpublished during his lifetime, but have since come to be known as the "Economic-Philosophical Manuscripts (of 1844)." In an oft-cited passage of one of these texts, he discusses what he calls "crude and thoughtless communism" (*der rohe und gedankenlose Communismus*).[1] This text reads:

> [Der noch ganz rohe und gedankenlose Communismus will] *alles* vernichten . . . was nicht fähig ist, als *Privateigentum* von allen besessen [zu] werden; er will auf *gewaltsame* Weise von Talent etc.abstrahieren. Der physische, unmittelbare *Besitz* gilt ihm als einziger Zweck des Lebens und Daseins; die Bestimmung des *Arbeiters* wird nicht aufgehoben, sondern auf alle Menschen ausgedehnt; das Verhältnis des Privateigentums bleibt das Verhältnis der Gemeinschaft zur Sachenwelt . . . Dieser Communismus—indem er die *Persönlichkeit* des Menschen überall negirt—ist eben nur der konsequente Ausdruck

des Privateigentums, welches diese Negation ist. Der allgemeine und als Macht sich konstituierende *Neid* ist die versteckte Form, in welcher die *Habsucht* sich herstellt und nur auf eine andere *Weise* sich befriedigt. Der Gedanke jedes Privateigentums als eines solchen ist *wenigstens* gegen das *reichere* Privateigentum als Neid und Nivellierungssucht gekehrt, so daß dies sogar das Wesen der Konkurrenz ausmachen. Der rohe Communist ist nur die Vollendung dieses Neides und dieser Nivellierung von dem *vorgestellten* Minimum aus. Er hat ein *bestimmtes begrenztes* Maß. Wie wenig diese Aufhebung des Privateigentums eine wirkliche Aneignung ist, beweist eben die abstrakte Negation der ganzen Welt der Bildung und der Zivilisation, die Rückkehr zur *natürlichen* Einfacheit des *armen*, rohen, und bedürfnislosen Menschen, der nicht über das Privateigentum hinaus, sondern nicht einmal bei demselben angelangt ist.

[The still rather crude and thoughtless communism wishes] to destroy *everything* that is not capable of being possessed as *private property* by all; it wishes to abstract in a *violent* way from talent, etc. Physical, immediate possession is for this type of crude communism the only goal of life and existence; the category *"worker"* is not transformed-and-done-away-with (*aufgehoben*) but extended to apply to everyone; the relation of private property remains the relation of the community to the world of objects . . . This form of communism, by negating the *personality* of the human being everywhere, is precisely nothing but the consistent expression of private property, which is this negation. The envy that forms part of this form of communism, an envy that is universal and has constituted itself as a power, is the hidden form in which greed takes hold and satisfies itself, and it does so merely in a different *way* from the way in which such greed satisfies itself in current forms of society. The thought implicit in any instance of private property as such is envy and the desire to flatten things down, *at least* as turned against any *richer* instance of private property, so that this ever constitutes the essence of competition. The crude communist is only the full-blown form of this envy and of the desire to flatten everything down to some merely *imagined* minimum. He has a *specific limited* measure. This apparent transformation/ abolition of private property is not genuine appropriation of it. How little this is the case is indicated by the fact that this crude communism abstractly negates the whole world of culture *(Bildung)* and civilization, by its return to the *natural* simplicity of the *poor,* crude, human being who has only few needs, a human being who is not beyond private property, but who has not yet even reached that stage.

By "crude communism" Marx seems to mean a modern equivalent of the kind of social and political regime that, following Aristotle's discussion in the *Politics,* was traditionally ascribed to Plato's *Republic*[2] and is usually expressed by the formula: "community of goods, women, and children" (ἐκεῖ [scilicet, in Plato's *Republic*] γὰρ ὁ Σωκράτης φησὶ δεῖν κοινὰ τὰ τέκνα καὶ τὰς γυναῖκας εἶναι καὶ τὰς κτήσεις [as Aristotle puts it in *Politics,* 1261a]). This Aristotelean version of Plato is written from the traditional male perspective, so the tacit assumption is that "communism" means equal use of goods *(by all the men in the community),* equal (sexual) access to women *(for all the men),* and equal disciplinary control of children *(and women by all the men).* Given Plato's views about the equality of men and women, his version of "community" would have a different structure from that described by Aristotle.

The Greeks, of course, had no concept of a "right" and so, a fortiori, nothing like the notion of a modern property right, but if one tries, however, to imagine an analogue to Plato's version of ancient "community" using the modern discourse of property rights, one gets something like: each (adult) member of the society has an equal common *"ownership-right"* to all the goods produced, and parallel equal access, control, and use rights to all other adult members and children. This means, Marx claims, that the society as a whole has a relation to all objects, which is like the relation that in the nineteenth century an individual owner had to objects that were his "private property." Marx's characterization of this as "crude" communism already indicates that he does not see it as an especially attractive way of organizing society. In fact, he says that it, as it were, exhibits some of the moral deformations of our society, associated with the

institution of "private property," in an even more intense and con-
centrated form. It is, as he says, a "universalization" of private property, not an overcoming of it.

A proper, properly humane form of society, Marx claims, would
not simply reproduce the mechanisms of private property while uni-
versalizing and equalizing them. It would not be structured around
the legal fixation of an absolute right to use or abuse, merely redistrib-
uting the participation in the exercise of such rights equally
throughout the populations, but would find some way of allowing
people to have access to and be able to use what they needed without
recourse to such an abstract framework of rights. How exactly a society like that would be organized, if not around property rights to
labor power and its products, is extremely difficult to say, and Marx
gives us practically no help because of his opposition to utopian speculation, but still that seems to be a different question from the one
at issue here.

Marx's own view, of course, is that absolute or abstract egalitarianism is incoherent because people in fact are all different and any
attempt to make them the same along one dimension will simply
increase difference along some other dimension. To think that
there are two opposing views called "egalitarianism" and "anti-
egalitarianism" makes sense only if one misunderstands the nature
of the concepts of "equal" and "unequal."[3] These are not substantive,
categorical concepts like "blue" or "wet" or "sharp," which designate
some feature of the world, but they are what Kant calls "concepts of
reflection," which locate something corelatively *on a particular scale*,
and no scale has any absolute priority. Choice of one scale rather than
another is a pragmatic (or political) decision. Two things are not
just equal in the way they can be blue or sharp, but they must of
necessity be "equal *in some respect*," and whether or not we call them
equal or unequal depends completely on the respect in which we
choose to compare them. With sufficient ingenuity *anything* can be
described as a state of equality or of inequality, depending on the dimension along which comparison is being made. The British NHS
is "equal" because everyone gets free health care, but unequal because those who are more frequently ill get more care than those who
are not. The chaotic, "pay-as-you-go" forms of health care available

in the United States can also be described as equal to the extent to which those who can afford it can get the same level of care, and as unequal because some people who need it get treated and others do not. Describing anything as "equal" or "unequal" per se is cognitively completely empty, but it can also be actively misleading: it has the *appearance* of being substantive. The reason for this is that more often than not some one scale of comparison is singled out, usually tacitly, as the only one relevant, and all other scales are ignored. What this means is that an ideal of "absolute equality" is not merely unreachable but literally incoherent, because there is no naturally or absolutely given standard or respect with reference to which one *must* compare them. Or rather, there is one such standard and that is complete identity, but this is politically completely irrelevant, if not incoherent. Political proponents of absolute equality do not mean that every person should be identical to himself or herself, or that society as a whole should be equal in the sense of being identical to itself, because that is not an ideal to be aspired to, but something that is in any case true of every society no matter what its internal structure. The illusory temptation to absolute egalitarianism is one that arises in a society dominated by private property, because in such a society there *does* seem to be *one* designated yardstick or dimension for comparison that in fact overrides all others and that is the amount of private property one owns, usually measured in monetary terms as the "market value" of one's property. Thus arises the illusion that all one would need to do would be to equalize ownership of private property. Crude communism draws the "egalitarian" conclusion from that illusion, and if one could get rid of "property," one would also pass outside the realm in which egalitarianism would even seem to make any sense. The "crude communist" pursues the false goal of overcoming the deficiencies of a regime of private property by equalizing the distribution of property.

In addition to giving a description of what he takes this "crude communism" to be, Marx also gives a further diagnosis of it relative to a characteristic set of emotions associated with it. The form of reductive egalitarianism the crude communist preaches, and of which, if he is actually honest and authentic, he is an instance, Marx says, is nothing but the full establishment of universal envy as a major social power. Even this envy, Marx holds, has a "capitalist form" because it is pain that results specifically from the observation that another has more property than I do (not from the fact that he or she is handsomer, quicker on his or her feet, or more intelligent than I am). The poor take it very much amiss that the rich possess more than they do, and the imposition of egalitarianism in the form of a restriction of ownership to an equal share in collective property, and the denigration of anything that cannot thus be shared and possessed equally, is thus the revenge of the have-nots against the haves. Two strands come together here. One is a claim about the role of envy and the second the idea that envy "becomes established as a power" in society. I think these are actually intended to be two slightly different things. To "become established as a power" need not be a throwaway remark because much of Marx's early social theory is Hegelian in inspiration and thus it is obsessed with the issue of how human powers (in the widest sense) come to establish themselves as separate social institutions. Thus from a sufficiently global point of view, the police in a certain society are, roughly speaking, nothing more than a structured way in which the forces and powers available in that society are deployed to ensure order of a certain kind. The police, that is, have no access to some supernatural or occult source of extra power; whatever power they have is a power humans in the society grant them. On the other hand, the whole point of having something like a police system is that these powers are lodged in a separate institutional structure in such a way that makes them not immediately under the direct control of those over whom they are exercised. Politics, as we usually understand it, is par excellence the realm of such an institutionalization because it has to do with the attempt to wield, resist, evade, or influence the power of that great separate institution, the state. One of Marx's claims, as we know, was that the state as such an institution would wither away, and he often expresses this by saying that *politics* will cease. This does not mean that there will be no more conflicts of power, merely that they will not take a specifically political form, that is, they will not take the form of a struggle for control of the state apparatus. So the act of taking control of part of the state apparatus, such as the police, is merely a preparatory and transitory part of a revolutionary process. The real revolution, Marx holds, starts afterward when people begin to develop forms of social interaction that replace those associated with that particular institution, which we today call "state," and render any form of state regulation of social and economic life superfluous. It should be obvious, he thinks, that there is no way in which we might say how such rules will look. Totally new conditions will require innovations in our modes of behaving toward one another, and our ways of regulating such modes that cannot be anticipated. Utopian speculation, thus, is pointless. I want to suggest, then, that *"der sich als Macht konstituierende Neid"* does not merely mean that envy will be a powerful motivation for people, but it also means that envy that will be congealed, as Marx thinks many human powers have come to be congealed, into an institutional form and will become part of the political structure of the radically egalitarian state as it exists under crude communism. In such a society, if it could become a stable and relatively enduring one—something one has good reason to think Marx would think highly unlikely— taking a Stradivarius away from a gifted violinist will not be something in need of special explanation.

This line of argument from envy to egalitarianism is, as far as I know, original to Marx. In the ancient world there is a similar line of argument in books 1 and 2 of Plato's *Republic*, but the apparent similarity makes the differences even more striking. Thus Glaukon at the beginning of book 2 of the *Republic* speaks of the canons of "justice" in distribution as arising as a kind of rational compromise. Everyone would really like to take or get assigned as much as possible, but each rationally fears that some stronger person will *also* want to take as much as possible and thus in a free-for-all they will end up with little or nothing. So they agree on equal shares for all. Note that envy plays no role in this construction although fear does. The reflective preference the weak have for having equal shares for all rather than allowing the strong to have more is a perfectly *rational* preference, based on fear of what otherwise would occur. If I know I am weak, of course I prefer for all to have equal shares rather than to be dominated by the strong. Rational fear is, however, one would have thought, a completely different emotion from envy.

The purported connection of envy and egalitarianism is one that was to have a long history after Marx, mostly of course in the form of appropriation by figures on the political right who were keen to reject some *specific* demand for a particular kind of equality for specifiable reasons.[4] Usually this takes the form of claiming that envy was a kind of anthropological invariant, which cannot be abolished, and the necessary persistence of which would make any form of egalitarianism impossible. This, of course, is multiply irrelevant to Marx, who first of all nowhere asserted or implied that envy could be abolished, although he thought the form it took could be transformed. Marx thought that the envy that comes to be universalized in crude communism has its origin in the particular extreme form of envy generated by individual property relations in a capitalist society, but this, too, in no way implies that there could be any form of society in which no envy at all occurred. Marx's basic criticism of capitalism, after all, was that it subordinated diverse individuals in their variable manifold richness under repressive abstract categories, such as money or mere notional units of homogeneously conceived labor-time. So he was against the rigid domination of these categories over human life, not against the fluid play of natural human emotions; he was against envy generated, if one wishes to put it that way, by "artificial" differences in wealth, social status, and political power, not against the envy of one man against another for being quicker and more reliable at doing mental arithmetic, or of one woman for another who can run faster or is more charming, more witty, or intelligent than she is. What is wrong with capitalism, Marx says in the passage from the "Philosophic-Economic Manuscripts" cited at the beginning of this chapter, is that it abstracts from real "talents" and replaces them with abstract symbolic differences calibrated finally in monetary terms. Second, Marx in any case did not take "egalitarianism" as a positive social ideal, because he thought that as such a general ideal it would be incoherent. Marx would be perfectly happy and could perfectly consistently grant the merits of various *specific* equalities, but in each case he would be arguing for a specific equality in a specific dimension of human life for a particular reason. Thus, it makes sense for all the runners in the race to be equal with respect to their starting time because we want to discover which one can run quickest over a given distance, and we can tell that most easily if they all start together. Yet it is easily imaginable that in some situations—say, in a situation in which very young children compete in running against adults—assigning different starting points to different children would count as providing equal chances.

Up to this point I have assumed that the notion of "envy" was clear enough for us to take it for granted, but is it really so clear what we mean by "envy" and how, exactly, it comes into this discussion? Envy seems to be a complex emotion with a rather obscure genesis and a number of historically highly variable forms. Despite this, there would seem to be at least two properties that something would have to exhibit for us to call it "envy." First, envy is a human emotion involving three variables. Paradigmatically, I envy you *because* of some property that I take you to have and that for the purposes of discussion is assumed to be some kind of good, or I envy you *in some respect*: I envy Mary her green thumb, Victoria her fluency in Russian, and Adelaida her way with cats; I envy Teddie his complete inattentiveness to his environment; I envy Michael his library. So there is a subject of envy—in this case me—a person who is the object of envy: Michael; and finally a good that is the cause of envy: Michael's library. This tripartite structure of two persons and some good is part of the basic framework that must be given before one can begin to consider whether one is confronting a case of envy. Second, "envy" must be some kind of painful or negative or distressing emotion. If I am pleased that you have some good, for instance, I shall be said to admire you, or, if you are a close relative with whom I identify in an especially strong positive way and you have achieved something good, the emotion I feel might not be envy, but, for instance, disinterested pleasure or pride.

One traditional analysis that proceeds in this way is that which Aristotle gives in the *Rhetorica*, in which he defines an emotion which he calls "φθόνος" as "being distressed (λύπη) because someone else has good fortune or is well-off (εὐπραγία),"[5] where presumably "being well-off" can encompass either what are sometimes called "goods of fortune," such as possessions, valued objects, or wealth; physical or psychological properties, such as swiftness of foot; a persuasive manner or social relations, such as having many friends, social position, winning contests; or finally positive states of soul, such as courage, satisfaction with one's life, and so on. I will assume all these can be referred to as instances of εὐπραγία.[6]

This seems at least to be moving in the right direction, although there are two queries that immediately arise. First, does one really wish to speak of envy as such a passive state of being affected? Do I really envy you if I am merely distressed by your good fortune? Do we not rather actually use envy in the full-blown sense only when we are not merely distressed, but when this distress moves us to some positive act of hostility? Not that we necessarily act on the hostility, but feeling the distress is not in itself enough. The schema that I envy you if I am pained by your good fortune seems to cover a number of different kinds of case that it is important to distinguish. First there are cases in which you have some good fortune that pains me, so that I wish you did not have that good fortune. You are my enemy, and it pains me to see that you enjoy such ruddy good health; I wish you dead, or gravely and painfully ill, or at any rate not in such a state of enjoying such visible and uninterrupted robustness. Here one might say that in cases like this I might say "I begrudge you your good health" *(mißgönnen)*, but I would not really say "I envy you," unless I was myself in poor health. So, one might claim, there is a comparative element in "envy" that is essential to it. Let us then call the first kind of case "envy (=begrudging)" and the second case, where the comparison between your good fortune and my lack of good fortune is constitutive, "negative envy." However, I also in everyday life repeatedly say that I "envy" people when I by no means wish that they did not have the good fortune I lack. I can say (and have said) "I envy Michael his library," meaning that he has a stock of books that is definitely much larger and in some respects better chosen than mine, including rare works it would be very difficult for me to acquire. This good fortune of his pains me, because I would like to have such a library and do not, but I do not wish that he did *not* have that library. Rather I am *pleased* for him, but I wish I had one like that, too. The comparative element in this is important, as it was in the second case, but this is a kind of positive or constructive envy. In addition, we can nowadays use the term *envy* in a full-blown way but also metaphorically, as a form of mere politeness, as an exaggeration, or as a kind of joke. So I may really and vividly envy a person who has been a long-standing rival and accomplishes something I have tried in vain to achieve, but I may also say (perfectly truthfully) to the taxi driver that I envy him his detailed knowledge of the geography of London. I do not mean by that even that I would myself prefer to know the city better than I do, because I do not finally care *that much* about the geography of London. I am certainly not in any serious sense "pained" by my lack of knowledge or his superior state of knowledge. To say I envy him his knowledge of London is not false—knowing London is something I fully recognize as a good thing; a world in which no one had this knowledge would be lacking something. Nevertheless, I cannot honestly say that I feel deprived or pained by my relative ignorance—although it is a good, it is not *that* important to me. This is at best a mere shadow of real envy. Actually this kind of "envy" looks very much like a case of rather disinterested admiration, which is usually taken to be something like the opposite of envy.

There is a second question about Aristotle's analysis arises with regard to the *reasons* for which one is pained. To say that I am distressed, in the sense either of simply being made sad (the weaker, more passive case) or being made hostile (the more active case), by your good fortune does not seem sufficient as an account of envy, at any rate if one thinks that such an account should allow us to distinguish "envy" from some other phenomena. If I am distressed by your good fortune, but that good fortune consists in occupying the only source of water on the island, then my "distress" is more likely to be a kind of fear than envy. I am distressed because I fear what that good fortune means for me: I am suddenly at your mercy. Aristotle, as usual, is analytically useful here because he does pay attention on the *reasons* for which I feel pained and/or hostile, specifically mentioning that envy is to be distinguished from fear. That is, if I am your neighbor and know that for years you have wanted to build an addition to your house that will have the effect of overshadowing my garden, but that you have not been able to do this because of lack of cash, the news that you have come into an inheritance will not fill me with glee. Still, it would seem odd to say in this situation that I envied you your good fortune. Rather I am disturbed because I *fear* the consequences of that good fortune for me. The reference to the effect on *me* is not essential to this argument. If I have sufficient imagination, I can be pained by the thought that a developer in Italy has had the good fortune to acquire funding and licenses to build on a historically significant or especially beautiful site, even if I will myself never be in a position to visit that site. This, too, is not really envy but fear about bad consequences of what is for someone else a stroke of good fortune.

At this point Aristotle makes a further instructive distinction by referring to a distinction that he posits between three slightly different terms in Greek for forms of pain at another's good fortune.[7] The first is a set of related terms frequently used in a wide variety of contexts in Homer, but that by the fourth century had become slightly archaic: the verb νεμεσᾶν, the verbal noun τὸ νεμεσᾶν, and the noun νέμεσις. This is usually translated "indignation" or "righteous anger." The other is the term that is most usually translated into English as "envy": φθόνος. The third set of terms is associated with "ζῆλος" usually translated something like "emulousness."

The distinction between the first two of these is that τὸ νεμεσᾶν really has to do with quasi-moral disapproval, as Aristotle puts it (*Rhetorica*, 1387a): εἰ γάρ ἐστι τὸ νεμεσᾶν λυπεῖσθαι ἐπὶ τῷ φαινομένῳ ἀναξίως εὐπραγεῖν ["For if we assume that being-indignant is being distressed at a faring-well which seems to be undeserved"]. Νέμεσις seems originally to have been the emotion a person feels toward another when the other shamelessly goes beyond the bounds of what is "appropriate" or decent. The gods feel it when humans get above themselves, and Aristotle claims then that it is the correct name for the emotion I feel toward you, if I have a morally tinged disapproval of the fact that you have enjoyed some undeserved good fortune. This, Aristotle says, distinguishes it clearly from φθόνος (that is, from what we call "envy"), because φθόνος completely lacks the quasi-moral dimension of νέμεσις; in envy, in contrast to νέμεσις, notions of what is warranted, appropriate, deserved, or merited play no role. Aristotle writes (*Rhetorica*, 1387b23): εἴπερ ἐστὶν ὁ φθόνος λύπη τις ἐπὶ εὐπραγίᾳ φαινομένη τῶν εἰρημένων ἀγαθῶν περὶ τοὺς ὁμοίους, μὴ ἵνα τι αὐτῷ, ἀλλὰ δι' ἐκείνους ["envy is a certain distress caused by the fact that some other people like oneself seem to have done well with respect to the aforementioned goods. The subject envies these others not because s/he wants the goods in question for himself/herself, but because *they* have them"].

I "envy" you merely because you possess some good, have some stroke of good fortune, or are signally well-off, regardless of whether that is deserved or not, and even if I do not myself wish to have the particular good or benefit you enjoy. So if you cheat to win the race against me, and I am hostile to you *because* you cheated, that is "righteous indignation" (νέμεσις), but I may envy you your success, even if you did not cheat because (as we would say) I begrudge it to you that *you* win. To be sure, we may surmise, acts of hostility properly thought of as instances of "envy" may for various reasons try to sanitize themselves by presenting themselves as expressions of "indignation," but that does not show that there is no difference between the two. This is all perfectly compatible with Aristotle's theory, provided that one admits that there are some cases of genuine νέμεσις, and that not everything that presents itself as indignation is really envy.

Aristotle, however, also distinguishes envy from "zeal" or "emulation" (ζῆλος) (*Rhetorica*, 1388a32): εἰ γάρ ἐστιν ζῆλος λύπή τις ἐπὶ φαινομένῃ παρουσίᾳ ἀγαθῶν ἐντίμων καὶ ἐνδεχομένων αὐτῷ λαβεῖν περὶ τοὺς ὁμοίους τῇ φύσει, οὐχ ὅτι ἄλλῳ ἀλλ᾿ ὅτι οὐχὶ καὶ αὐτῷ ἔστιν ["for if emulousness is a certain distress caused by the fact that some other people who are by nature like themselves seem to possess certain valued goods, which it is possible for people to acquire. People are emulous not because someone else has these goods, but because *they* do not have them, too"].

This distinction, too, is conceptually clear enough. In emulation I am pained when you get some good because I want that good myself; in envy I might or might not want the good you have myself, but the point is that I do not wish *you* to have it. In envy I am focused on the person or persons whom I envy, not on the good he or she has or they have, which is not, of course, to say that the good involved is completely irrelevant (as it might be in the case of mere irrational, or, as we say, "blind," hatred). I begrudge you your having that good or your doing well, even if I do not myself aspire to having that particular good. This deeply nonconstructive aspect of envy—what I really want is for you *not* to have the good—is one of the reasons this emotion has such a bad press in Aristotle and others. What I really want is not attain or possess the good you have or indeed any discernible objective "good" but that *you* not fare well.

One final aspect of the analysis remains. Aristotle is clear that I envy only those whom I perceive to be "like" me. How much "like" me, and in which respect(s)? This has been a highly controversial claim, but it does not seem to be simply one of those Aristotelean throwaway remarks, a comment to which he has given no thought, because it recurs several times in his writings, and indeed in other ancient works. The idea might seem intuitively to be something like this. The peasant in a society in which social hierarchies are taken seriously may *hate* the aristocrat, and might even zealously wish to emulate the aristocrat, having the goods the aristocrat has, but strictly he does not *envy* the aristocrat. Once social hierarchies break down and once the Christian message of universal moral equality has had time to percolate throughout society, the way is open for *universal* envy, but that is because in such societies *everyone* is construed as "like" or "equal to" all others. Envy makes sense only among equal competitors in the *same* game. So I have to make a twofold imaginative leap. I need to have activated a rather complex kind of identification: this young woman whose speech I can scarce understand or this terminally self-satisfied government minister is really "like me," a human being and co-citizen of the European Union and United Kingdom of Great Britain and Northern Ireland. In addition to this I must imaginatively construe the two of us as engaged in some kind of competitive project in which we are rivals. "Similarity" means some kind of equality, and to be a competitor or rival means for there to be some kind of common framework within which comparative loss and gain or advantage and disadvantage can be calculated. These are also two ways in which envy is different from simple hatred. I can hate almost anyone, and perhaps it is even possible to hate non-human entities, but I envy only those humans who are sufficiently like me to be some kind of rivals or competitors. I hate enemies, but a competitor is not per se my enemy. In fact, there is some evidence that certain Greek thinkers thought envy was particularly closely connected to friendship, that it was a particular perversion of friendship or of a relation much like friendship.[8]

Recall, too, that what really irked his opponents was Julius Caesar's "*clementia.*" One might think that "clemency" just meant kindliness, a relaxed tolerance or forbearance in the face of error or miscreance and hence that it was a human virtue; in the context of the politics of the Roman Republic, however, *clementia* was much more ambiguous than this would suggest. The reason is that it could be thought to be a virtue that was associated with pretentions to kingship. To be clement was to exercise a free choice vis-à-vis someone who was in one's power, and to be fixedly and universally clement could be construed as being or claiming to be above the fray, as a king was constitutionally. An aristocrat in the Roman Republic was supposed to take the others *seriously*, engage and compete with them on terms of rough equality, and *not* to be above the battle with them. Too much clemency expressed the wrong attitude, as if one did not consider an opponent a possible threat or competitor.

At the end of the civil war one of Caesar's great adversaries, the arch-Republican Cato, committed suicide rather than surrender to him. On this occasion Caesar is reported to have said Ὦ Κάτων, φθονῶ σοι τοῦ θανάτου·καὶ γὰρ σύ μοι τῆς σωτηρίας ἐφθόνησας[9] ["Cato, I envy you your death because you envied me my sparing of you"]. Here instead of "envy" we would probably say "begrudge" in the second part of this (although Caesar uses the same word in Greek for both): Caesar envied Cato because Cato has begrudged Caesar the opportunity of showing clemency to Cato. That is, Cato knew that Caesar would *not* kill him but would spare him, and that this would be seen as yet another instance of Caesar's "clemency" and would thus contribute to consolidating Caesar's pretention to be above the fray. Caesar thinks that this pretention is justified because he deserves the status he claims, so for him Cato's refusal even to be put in a position in which it might be thought that he could possibly accept Caesar's clemency is merely an instance of envy on Cato's part: sparing Cato was a good (because an expression of Caesar's superiority) and Cato was distressed at the thought that Caesar might have that good. Cato's own views about this are not recorded, certainly not as pithily as Caesar's, but we can assume that, if they had been recorded, and if he had been speaking Greek rather than Latin,[10] he would have denied the charge of envy and said he felt not φθόνος but νέμεσις, since he thought Caesar's airs of superiority were unmerited—or, at any event, ought not to be in any way recognized or tacitly acknowledged in a republic. Caesar in the first part of his statement admits that he is pained by the fact that Cato possesses a good, namely, the good of refusing to allow himself to be treated as a person toward whom it would be in any way possible to show clemency. So, too, that in modern English we usually say that I "envy" someone some good, if I *lack* that good. Not, of course, that I necessarily want that good myself, but I do not want you to have it. On Aristotle's analysis of the Greek expression there is no such implication. I usually envy you if I am distressed at your good fortune, when I am less fortunate but I can in principle speak of envy if I am pained at your success *even if am equally fortunate myself.* Here, of course, Caesar is in a situation in which either the broader Greek sense or the narrower English sense would apply. Cato *has* the good fortune of a death that demonstrates irrefutably that he was a man of a certain kind; Caesar, even if he at the moment has a firm sense of his own superiority, has not yet had the opportunity to show this by granting clemency and seeing it accepted by Cato. Nor can he even (yet) show his equality to Cato by a similarly appropriate death.

This example shows that in the discussion up to now we have abstracted to some extent from one final important aspect of situations in which we speak of "envy." We have treated the "things" that are the objects of envy—health, intelligence, possessions—as if they were nonpositional goods. My state of health is not directly dependent on your state of health; you could have a large library and that in itself would not prevent me from building up an equally good one. Not all "goods" that are objects of envy have this property. If you are healthy that in no way prevents me from being healthy, but if you are the winner of the race, I, of necessity, am not.[11] Reputation, status, social standing, however, are all positional goods. To have the standing of being "the uniquely best" (at anything or in any respect), for instance, implies that all others are less good. Once the social world is fully monetarized, positionality becomes a basic property of social life and the way is open for a massive expansion of the realm of envy. Beyond a certain point one cannot compete with others about one's respective "health," but there is always more money to be made, and how much you make determines my position.

It is easy to see how envy can disrupt politics and render forms of social cooperation very difficult. If I envy you, that means that I wish you ill, and do not wish you to have some good, even if I do not myself want that good. This, of course, can put a serious spoke in the possibilities of smooth human cooperation and will do so if there are no stronger countervailing motives. One line of thought that has been tempting to many is the idea that if we are cooperating constructively we should in general be willing to change our society in those ways that will increase our welfare. To "increase our welfare" in turn seems plausibly interpreted as meaning to act so that the welfare of the individuals who constitute our group is improved. In particular it seems irrational to refuse to do something that will increase the welfare of any one member of the group, if that can be done in such a way as not to decrease the welfare of any other member. Increasing the welfare of at least one member while not decreasing the welfare of any other is sometimes called moving in the direction of "Pareto optimality" and is described as a minimal condition of economic and thus also of political, rationality.[12]

Suppose, then, that everyone in some state of society—call it state A—earns between €1,000 and €5,000 a month of disposable income with the exception of a tiny fragment of the population who are disabled or have been exceptionally unlucky. In this state some people might envy others or begrudge them their good fortune in various dimensions. I might envy you your fluency in Russian or I might dislike you intensely and begrudge you your health, your musical abilities, or even the fact that you earn the minimal €1,000 a month. Compare state A now with another state, B, in which some handful of people earns €1,000,000 a month, while everyone else still earns €1,000; then state B is, on this view, thought to be more rational. If you are one of the people who will earn €1,000,000 in state B, and I envy you in Aristotle's sense, I am not likely to support a shift from state A to state B, even though in B I am no worse off. I might even be unwilling to move from state A to a possible state C in which I earn €2,000, while you take in €1,000,000. This might, if one looks at it in a sufficiently detached way seem irrational or even perverse. I seem to be cutting off my own nose, refusing an extra €1,000 to spite my face, as they say.[13] Of course, I might be envious or spiteful, but the impression that that is the *only* explanation of my refusal to move is incorrect and results from a characteristic underspecification of the situations in question. Marx would have said, the situations are described "too abstractly." It is, namely, *assumed* that the *only* thing relevant here is the simple quantitative amount of money available to each person in each of the various scenarios. Now what, Marx would ask, does this difference in level of monetary income *mean?* What will be its systematic effect on society? *If,* and this is a *big* "if," it simply means the amount of money available to each person for purposes of personal consumption, that is, if the money is used merely for buying wine, taking a trip, or making merry with one's friends, that is one situation. However, in our society money means *power.* To have €30 more than I do in your pocket means to be able to buy a better bottle of wine than I can, and that you drink a better bottle of wine than I do will have no effects except perhaps on my "feeling" (if I envy you), but to have several thousand times more money than me in a society where money will buy almost anything means something rather different. For instance, it might mean that are able to send your children to a fee-paying school, thereby draining good teachers, who are a scarce resource, from the state sector. Or it might mean that you can have private medical insurance or visit a private hospital, thereby contributing to the establishment of a two-tiered system of health care, with all the negative social consequences that would have. Or you might even be able to make significant contributions to funding particular political campaigns that, if successful, could change the conditions of life, or exercise influence on politicians in some other way. It might mean that you could buy a factory or a quasi-monopoly on some scarce resource or a newspaper or a radio station, like Rupert Murdoch or Silvio Berlusconi. Exercising the power and influence that possession of huge amounts of money in modern societies can buy is an altogether different matter from having a higher level of consumption, and so as long as differences in income are connected in this way with differences in *power,* it is by no means so obvious that I am being envious rather than rationally fearful if, all things considered, I prefer not to give you that differential power over me. In contrast to "proper" envy, I may not be focused on you, the specific person, or have any negative attitude toward your level of consumption per se.

Rather it is reasonable for me to fear *any* person who has an amount of wealth/power that threatens the health of society. Equally it might be right for me to have "righteous indignation" toward those who undeservedly have an especially high level of consumption. Given the unclarity about what—if anything—constitutes "desert" here, there could be constant grounds for disagreement here, unless one empties the concept of "desert" of its meaning and its ability to provide independent justification by simply *identifying* what someone deserves with what he or she end up with in the chaotic lottery that is the economic life of most modern societies. Neither rational fear nor righteous indignation are forms of envy.

Envy is both painful and nonconstructive, and thus it is understandable that it is an object of disapprobation. As a consequence, to attribute some political initiative to envy is usually a canny strategy, if the attribution can be made to stick. The haves will, thus, have a strong motivation to attribute envy to the have-nots. The fact that the haves even bother to formulate this criticism of the have-nots means that the haves realize that they in some sense *need* some kind of cooperation from the have-nots. Even if what is at issue are not differences in relative power, as discussed above, but mere relative levels of consumption, it is not in general clear why the have-nots should not strive to get as much consumption as possible by whatever means they can employ. After all, greed is not in itself a terribly attractive property, either, and yet it is accepted as a necessary and legitimate motor of our economic activity. If the have-nots adopt a principled strategy of obstruction or noncooperation with the haves and this strategy results from envy, what exactly is wrong with that? Is envy so much less attractive than greed? In addition, in many situations systematic intransigence, which could look very much like a form of the politics of envy, might well result in a bargaining advantage for the have-nots. In that case why would such a policy not be perfectly rational?[14]

I merely note that if one takes the ancient distinction between "envy" and "indignation" (φθόνος and νέμεσις) seriously, the have-nots could always in principle claim that they were not motivated by envy, but by indignation, since in fact most of the most extreme forms of economic difference between agents in our society are due to completely accidental factors, such as being born the child of someone who is wealthy, or being accidentally at the right place in the market at the right time, and are not the result of anything that could be counted as "merit" or "desert." This line of argument is not open to Marx, to be sure, because he has an extremely extensive battery of various arguments, which there is no time now to expound, against taking "merit" or "desert" particularly seriously as cognitive substantive categories, rather than as mere ideological constructs. Still, although Marx would not have taken the view that the poor are indignant rather than envious seriously, because this would require one to have a concept of merited and unmerited economic success, and for Marx no such concept is available, we might wish to disagree with him on this. Surely, we might argue, *sometimes* agents with great ruthlessness and a quickness to deploy low animal cunning are very strikingly successful. One might not morally approve of such personal qualities or find them particularly attractive, but that is a different matter. Why do they not constitute a clear concept of economic desert? Such individual cases are, of course, highly publicized by the powers that be in our society because they reinforce the idea that there is some sense in which "merit" (of a kind) is rewarded. However, these cases seem to be individual exceptions, and in fact are often explicitly presented as such exceptions. *Whatever* "merit" might mean, by no stretch of the imagination could the only son of a billionaire be said to have "merited" his inherited wealth, and in fact accidents, including the accidents of birth, are pretty clearly, as Hayek saw, the key to the prosperity or misery of most people.

How, then, can we deal with this emotion in the political realm? There is every reason to believe that the solution envisaged by crude communism will not work, because it is a commitment to the pursuit of a task that is finally incoherent. If one assumes that envy could be abolished if only the mirage of "true" complete egalitarianism was reached, this initiates a diabolical cycle in which envy refocuses itself on increasingly minor advantages, and it is tempting to think that the remedy for every failure is a search for yet further dimensions of human life that have not been "equalized." Envy, however, turns out to be very sensitive to a number of imaginative constructions: I must identify certain people as sufficiently like me to be possible objects of envy, and I must construe them as rivals or competitors, and these boundaries are not at all fixed in reality. Modes of imaginative identification, however, are notoriously difficult to control. So the project of abolishing or even reliably channeling envy into nontoxic directions does not seem very promising. In principle this still leaves intact Marx's early proposal for a depoliticization of envy, but to accept that in its full-blown form requires one to take on board the idea that politics, including, of course, the whole state apparatus, could wither away. Envy (in its various different forms) will surely be with us for the foreseeable future, and although we can hope to try to manage the forms of imaginative identification (both positive identification and negative identification) so as to control the worst excesses of envious action and insulate the political realm against envy as much as possible, there are probably very narrow limits within which this is possible. Realistically we should not expect to be able to create a totally envy-free politics, and forms of political thought that abstract from the phenomenon of envy have lost touch with reality. Nevertheless, not every political project that might in some way look like an expression of "envy," and that powerful economic groups have an interest in presenting as motivated by envy, really is envy rather than rational fear or righteous indignation.

11

Identity, Property, and the Past

———∼∾∽∼———

THE TITLE OF the recent book *Who Owns Antiquity?*, by James Cuno,[1] the former director of the Courtauld Institute and the Harvard Art Museum, and current president and director of the Art Institute of Chicago, seems to announce a general philosophical discussion along the lines of an early Platonic dialogue in which Socrates asks questions like, "Who has been the real benefactor of the people of Athens?" or, "Can virtue be taught?" or, "What is justice?" Or, alternatively, perhaps the reader will expect a dystopian fantasy like Orwell's *1984*, in which a political party physically "holds" all the levers of political power and, by controlling all the archives in the present, also controls possible interpretations of the past. In fact, however, *WO* does not give a mere semantic or philosophical analysis of terms, nor does it see itself as a work of fantasy. Rather Cuno stakes out what is a clear substantial position on a number of issues concerning the ownership of what are now called "cultural properties," while trying to take into account the real politics of our age.

Since ideas about ownership are almost everywhere deeply connected with other moral, legal, political, and religious conceptions, and these change dramatically through time—slavery, once common, is now outlawed—it would make sense to reflect on the *ownership* of antiquities and of cultural objects of all types historically. In her *Art as Plunder*, Margaret Miles discusses late Roman Republican concep-

184

tions about the role of art in society, and particularly of the ways in which works of art could legitimately be appropriated, owned, or transferred from the control of one person or group to that of another.[2] Her particular emphasis is on forcible or nonvoluntary transfers of control or ownership, either seizure of objects as booty in war or the coercive acquisition of them by the use of constituted political power.

A major source of information about Roman Republican beliefs and attitudes is the series of speeches composed by Cicero to prosecute Gaius Verres, the former Roman governor of the province of Sicily, for his savage and oppressive behavior toward the Sicilians and for various kinds of financial malfeasance. Although the formal charge against him was the rather narrow one of "extortion" (*de pecuniis repetundis: In Verrem* 1.10; *AP* 129–133), an ancient prosecutor had the freedom to range widely over the character and actions of the accused, including the freedom to allude to matters not obviously relevant to the case at hand, and any prosecutor would be tempted to blacken the character of the accused in any way he could, including by appeal to widely shared social prejudices. Thus, Cicero describes in lurid and extensive detail the reign of terror which Verres inflicted on the Sicilians under his rule, including, for instance, his crucifixion of an innocent Roman citizen, Publius Gavius, in Syracuse (*In Verrem* 2.5.158–164; *AP* 133), even though this had nothing at all to do with the charge of extortion. More directly relevant to the charge was the fact that Verres seems to have been an art thief on a massive scale, whose house in Rome was stuffed full of statues, paintings, and other objects forcibly taken from the Sicilians.

Cicero's account makes clear that the Romans of the Republican period made a number of important distinctions between kinds of property. Thus, they strictly separated *res sacrae* (for example, cult statues of gods) from *res profani*, and among the latter they distinguished *res publicae* (for example, statues of municipal benefactors erected at common expense in public places) and *res privatae* (for example, utensils belonging to individual people; *AP* 158–61), and this distinction was connected with different views about the way it was appropriate to treat each such object. The distinction between *res profani* and *res sacrae* seems to parallel the two distinct impulses

that give rise to the physical objects which we call "works of art."
On the one hand, people who live above a certain level of subsis-
tence seem to have an irrepressible desire to make the objects they
use more pleasant and appealing to sight and touch than they would
otherwise be, that is, to decorate them. On the other hand, humans
at least occasionally have experiences of the overwhelmingly impressive, the powerful-but-unpredictable, the uncanny (potentially,
at any rate), the terrifying, in short the "numinous," and they often
try to limit and placate this radical Other by representing and
housing it. One might think of this as the theoplastic or theodulic
impulse. If the decorative is reassuring, soothing, and comfortable,
and has an affinity with the domestic and familiar, with the pro-
fane realm of Roman "private law," the theodulic is what gives to
art its edge, its *frisson*, its infinite aspiration to being taken with ultimate seriousness. This is the aspect of art that emphasizes its close
connection with religion and the sacred (*AP* 4).

If, then, Aristius Fuscus "owned" a nice piece of decorative art, a
pleasingly painted pot or cup or vase, he could transfer it to me by
gift or sale, and if I had tried to steal it from him, Roman private law
might have given him some hope of redress, but who exactly, if
anyone, "owns" the cult-statues of gods in Sicilian temples? In one
sense, the citizens might collectively own it, but this might not be the
end of the story. If the temple really is even potentially the dwelling
place of the god, it might be best to keep the place especially clean,
and in general to act with particular circumspection there, not to
touch, or perhaps even approach too close to, the god's image, and
so on, for who knows what could set off divine wrath and what the
consequences of that wrath might be? To the extent to which people
"believed" in the gods and their power—bracketing for the moment
the tremendously complex issue of what "belief" might have meant
in one or another part of the populations of the ancient world at one
or another time—this in itself created a distinctive form of protection for temples, cult-statues, and so on. This notion of a temple as
a distinctive sacred space "cut out" and set apart from daily life, and
hence not subject to the rules of everyday use, trafficking and com-
merce, is etymologically sharp in the Greek τέμενος and the Latin

templum (the first pretty clearly derived from τέμνω, and the second arguably from some similar Indo-European root).

For those who wish to take art with the greatest possible seriousness, its association with religion and the sacred can be or become problematic—for instance, because religious authorities might try to control certain forms of artistic expression—but it can also have some positive consequences, because as long as the sacred exists, it is impossible for the mundane, the political or the economic, or some combination of these, completely to dominate society. However, as religious authorities—at any rate in the West—began to weaken, and eventually a reliable sense of the sacred began to seem under threat during the course of the nineteenth century, attempts were undertaken to fill the vacant space. It is as if we all felt the lack of the protected space that temples and churches literally, and dogmatically founded systems of belief and action metaphorically, had provided, but without the god who was the traditional protector of the temple and guarantor of the code of conduct. That is, keep the space inviolable, but dismiss the "entity" who used to guarantee the special status of the space as merely imaginary. Art itself was one of the first candidates as a substitute for god, with various nineteenth-century thinkers speaking of the "religion of art" replacing more traditional forms of dogmatic belief and practice. Another candidate, which in fact did significantly more damage than the first, was nationalism. Finally, various other thinkers proposed "history" as a final framework for evaluation to replace god, or "authenticity," at any rate, as the highest value in my choice of the kind of life I wished to live. Durkheim went so far as to propose the cult of individualism as a modern replacement for ancient religious systems. And the twentieth and twenty-first centuries have brought us religions of "human rights" and the worship of the "free market." None of these substitutes seems to have worked very well, although, as we will see later, despite the current economic crisis, the last mentioned has retained some appeal, particularly to those to whom it brings financial or other benefits.

Miles in *AP* also discusses a second major distinction that played an important role in Roman Republican conceptions of the way in which art could be appropriated: that between (time of) war and (time of) peace. What is permissible in one situation—for instance, appropriation of the property of the citizens of a city just defeated by the Roman army as "booty"—would not be permissible in time of peace, because the victor was construed as "owning" the property of the defeated as booty by the laws of war, but the right of forcible appropriation lapsed with the end of the war.

One of the origins of museums is in the exposition of war-booty, where presumably the main criterion of exhibition was not the aesthetic value of the individual pieces exhibited, but the indirect exhibition of the power that Rome had defeated (*AP* 33–34). The need to increase one's own prestige and potentially to intimidate opponents remains one of the major motivations for the public display of objects. A second, of course, is the inherent desire to see objects that have aesthetic value (whether of the more decorative or the more numinous kind). To this will eventually be added the third possible motivation of wishing to satisfy human cognitive interests. This can range from simple human curiosity—"See how peculiar are the pots this other tribe makes"—to the highly sophisticated desire to attain a theoretical understanding of some portion of the past or present. Needless to say these three motivations are not mutually exclusive, and desire for enhanced prestige, easy direct access to beauty, and increased knowledge can easily coexist among those who found or manage museums.

There are individual examples of generals in the ancient world who did return the art looted from defeated enemies, two of them being Scipio and Caesar, but these were, as it were, supererogatory acts of generosity and magnanimity (*AP* 96–104) that did nothing to abolish the validity of the law of booty that was generally thought to continue to hold. The first real systematic break with this tradition was Wellington's behavior in Paris after the fall of Napoleon. Wellington both insisted that arts looted by Napoleon be returned to its original owners *and* did not loot French museums for appropriation of art to Britain (*AP* 332–324).

In principle, we live in a world in which war is no longer a universally recognized way of acquiring rights to ownership over works of art and other bits of cultural property—a Hague Convention and a complex network of further international agreements (*AE* 47–60, 160–168) are supposed to regulate that—and the use of direct effectively unlimited political power in time of peace arbitrarily to confiscate statues and other objects in the way Verres did is also not a pressing contemporary problem. Still, although this does give us some information about what we conceive to be the proper rules governing the ownership of cultural objects—not even the victors in a fully legitimate war automatically "own" the cultural artifacts of the defeated—this is not a fully complete response.

James Cuno in *WO* tries to give just such a fuller account of cultural property, which places it in its wider context. Our contemporary world is full of relatively powerful "nation-states" and politically rather weak international organizations (*WO* 26–27, 40–49). The nation-states differ among themselves greatly both in their power (along different dimensions, as economic, military, diplomatic power) and in the way in which their "identity" is formatted, that is, the way in which they see themselves and the sense they have of their own past (and future) and their relation to it. Some forms of national identity may refer to religious or ethnic ties—it may be an important part of being a Serb that "true" Serbs belong to the Orthodox variant of Christianity; some may make special reference to a specific history, such as the Oath that in 1291 founded the Swiss Confederation. To the outsider, the distribution of "us" and "not us" in many of these cases may seem peculiar. So the territory of the contemporary Hellenic Democracy sees itself as continuous with the number of small democracies that operated on part of its present territory in the fifth and fourth centuries BC, but discontinuous with the Ottoman Empire, which included much of the contemporary Hellenic Democracy during the fifteenth to nineteenth centuries, a period significantly longer than the brief flourishing of the ancient "democracies." There are also differences in the extent to which this process of historical identification is thought to be located in or connected to physical artifacts or cultural products. Thus a religious tradition or form of customary life can be relatively disembodied, but the Parthenon and the Theatre of Dionysus are actual physical buildings. Not all forms of national identity need be based on a positive attitude toward history, be it a religious tradition, a set of established folkways, or a collection of outstanding cultural achievements. Thus the old Soviet Union tried, and can be seen now to have failed, to create a stable identity for its citizens based on a wholesale rejection of the past and a shared commitment to the scientific use of reason to structure human life collectively. Similarly, the United States undertook a more successful experiment in creating a national identity based on a rejection of a European past considered inherently decadent and corrupting, a decision to treat history as if it did not matter in the *novus ordo saeclorum*—as if, in Henry Ford's memorable words, it was "bunk"—and an attempt to make the present and the future *tabulae rasae* for the pursuit of individual human happiness. Depending on the specific role history in general, and the cultural history embodied in physical artifacts in particular, plays in the life of the nation-state in question, one can expect different nations, national groupings, and nation-states to pursue very different kinds of cultural politics.

Who owns antiquity? has a negative and a positive part. The negative part presents an attack on nationalism in general and on "nationalist retention policies" regarding historical artifacts in particular, that is, on laws asserting the ownership rights of individual nation-states over objects found on their territory and making it difficult or impossible to export them. The positive part of the argument can be seen as defending two subtheses. First, that there should now be a completely free and unregulated market for the international sale of antiquities, and second that the ideal framework for the exhibition of antiquities is the "encyclopedic" or "universal" museum of the kind archetypically instantiated by the British Museum or the Louvre, that is, the museum that aspires to be as universal in its coverage of human artifacts, freely open to the public, and maximally cosmopolitan in its orientation.

To start with the negative thesis, Cuno gives four specific arguments against nationalism and "retentionist" cultural policies. First, nationalism is evil in itself, dividing a humanity that should be considered as a single integrated whole (*WO* 19). Second, nationalism is based on a mistake, because "nations" are imaginary political constructs, not realities (*WO* 80, 90, 129–130). Third, to construe cultural property along nationalist lines by asserting state ownership of all historical antiquities is to politicize such property, but this whole domain should not be one in which politics plays any role (*WO* 9, 11). Fourth, nationalist retention policies have been ineffective in stopping the looting of archaeological sites (*WO* 5–7).

The first of these three arguments is slightly vitiated by a failure to be very clear about what exactly is being discussed. Thus, Cuno seems to use "state," "nation," "nation-state," and "government" more or less interchangeably, and there is little clarity about what a "nation" is and how it is related to the idea of the nation-state or to "nationalism." Sometimes belonging to a certain nation is supposed to depend on ethnicity and language, but it turns out that the conflict between Shia and Sunni in Iraq is an instance of nationalism, as is the wearing of Islamic costume (*WO* 131–132). Sometimes Cuno seems to find the very existence of "nation-states" threatening, that is, the very existence of political entities committed to the idea that the boundaries of "nation" and "state" should coincide; sometimes the difficulty seems to be not the nation-state itself, but one specific kind of claim which nation-states sometimes make, namely, their claim to "own" the antiquities that are to be found within their borders; sometimes his difficulty seems to be not with the nation-state but with "the state" tout court, and sometimes the problem is diagnosed as one of "politics," which is a domain of human life about which he is deeply suspicious. Sometimes, finally, the culprit in the drama is not the state, the nation, the nation-state, nationalism, or politics, but the government. To be sure, terms like *nation, nation-state,* and *nationalism,* on the one hand, and *state, nation, government,* on the other, are often used rather loosely, but that would not seem to be an excuse for the extreme slippage between these terms that one can find in Cuno's book. Thus we read: "National governments regulate archeologists working within their jurisdiction . . . As these regulations are in the service of the state, they inevitably have a nationalist agenda" (*WO* 53; see also *AE* 14). "Politics is always motivated by a national, if not nationalist agenda" (*WO* 66). "Recent critical studies of archaeological practice have shed new light on the inevitable nationalism of modern states with a rich archaeological heritage within their borders" (*WO* 83).

If nationalism *itself* is supposed to be inherently evil, because it divides a humanity that is or ought to be a single cosmopolitan whole, then is any division of the human species also inherently evil?

So individual families, or local community groups, or clubs, or political parties are also inherently evil?

The second argument against a nationalist cultural politics (*WO*
124) is that one of the characteristic claims of the nationalist is an illusion. The nationalist claims that all works of art and all significant
artifacts produced in the past in what, say, is now called "Italy"—for
instance, in Sicily—are part of the national patrimony of Italy. This,
Cuno argues, is not true because for most of history "Italy" was a
mere geographic expression, and the island of Sicily had generally
not been thought to be part of it. "Italy" in our sense, that is, as a
nation-state, did not exist until Italian unification in the mid-
nineteenth century. No (Greek-speaking) craftsman in the city-state
of Syracuse in the fifth century BC could have imagined their work
as contributing to "Italian national identity"; therefore, it is wrong
or distorting for the works of such craftsmen to be exhibited in museums devoted to the cultivation of Italian identity. Italy, then, should
not be permitted to claim automatic ownership of objects found in
Sicily, and any existing Italian legislation to this effect should be
considered to be null and void (*WO* 31–40), so objects removed in
violation of its national patrimony laws are not really to be considered to have been "'stolen' in the commonly used sense of the word
in the United States" (*WO* 4). From this, Cuno seems to be suggesting, it is plausible to conclude that there should be no restrictions preventing the entry of objects found on the territory of
present-day Italy into the free international market in antiquities.
Some of the components of this line of argument are undeniably true
and important, but some are dubious, and the parts do not fit together in a way that actually supports the purported conclusion.
Thus, it is true that fifth-century Sicilian craftsmen could probably
not have imagined that their work would be construed as a contribution to "Italian identity," and thus we are putting their work in a
context that would have been cognitively inaccessible to them. However, we have equally little reason to think they intended to make
their pots as a contribution to "the world's common artistic and cultural legacy" (*WO* 18), or that they could have imagined that these
pots would end up in the British Museum. As far as we can tell, ancient artisans intended to produce something for contemporary con-

sumption, for local cults, or as signs of familial or civic pride, not for exhibition in an abstract environment like that provided by universal museums such as the Louvre or British Museum. *Both* "Italian national identity" *and* the "world artistic heritage" are imaginative constructs that would have been outside the ken of the original artisans—"myths," if one likes that way of speaking—and in that respect the two constructs are on a par. If "nationalism" was an invention of the nineteenth century, "cosmopolitanism" was equally an invention of the philosopher Diogenes the Cynic, who coined it as a way of trying to deflect criticism of a way of life that was considered by most of his contemporaries to be politically feckless and morally defective. Finally, the very idea of an "encyclopedic" museum seems to have been an invention of the Enlightenment, and the "free market" is at best an imaginative idealization of certain features that would obtain if the existing exchange of goods in the world was perfectly regulated by a legal and social framework of a certain kind. So that "national identity" is an imaginative construct does not seem a very powerful objection to it.

Sometimes Cuno tries to claim that modern cosmopolitanism is more than just one ideal construction among others, by arguing that it has a real basis in the facts of artistic production. Thus, Cuno argues (*WO* 126; see also xxxv–xxxvi):

(a) No important past culture, including the ancient Hellenic cultures, was completely self-contained in its artistic production, but all *were actually* cosmopolitan from the beginning (because they were open to influences, new techniques, expectations of potential buyers of their artifacts).

(b) Therefore there is something *less* distorting about placing these objects in a modern cosmopolitan museum than keeping them in (merely—or explicitly?—) national galleries.

Although (a) is true, the inference to (b) does not follow, and what is more, it is incompatible with the position Cuno expresses at other points in the book. Thus, at *WO* 124 he had argued *against* nationalism by appeal to the artisan's own *conception* of what he, or she, was doing, and construing that as what was most important, if not

definitive. If those ancient Sicilians had no conception of themselves as proto-modern-Italians, then it is wrong to treat their artifacts in that way. Now there is a shift: it is not the self-conception of
the artisans that is definitive, but what was *actually the case* (regardless of what they thought). So the fact that the ancient Greeks distinguished strongly between themselves and Barbarians, and would
not have been best pleased to be called "cosmopolitans," suddenly
becomes irrelevant. It is unclear how one can have it both ways.

So, pointing out the "imaginary" nature of "national identity" will
not by itself get one very far in the direction Cuno wishes to go. Still,
he might reasonably wish to distinguish between "imaginary" constructs and "illusions." An "illusion," he might claim, is a factual
belief that is (perhaps, "is clearly") false, such as the belief that
Gustave Flaubert invented the jet-propulsion engine in 1870. Many
of the beliefs that are at issue in this discussion, however, do not have
that kind of clear-cut epistemological structure or standing; they are
not claims about "facts" in this sense. Thus, if a twenty-year-old man
born of Greek-speaking Orthodox parents in Athens in 1990 says,
"We invented democracy," this assertion requires of us a very considerable imaginative leap via an understanding of his identification
with the actions of certain agents in the ancient world, but then the
use of "we" generally invites us to take a leap of some kind. However this belief is not in itself straightforwardly false in the sense in
which the belief about jet-propulsion is false. To focus exclusively on
the "truth" or "falsity" of statements like "We invented democracy"
is to miss an important point about them. When politicians during
the French Revolution identified with Roman Republicans, this was
not primarily a way of making a claim about the nature of reality—
"Robespierre *is* Cato, as Cicero *was* Tully"—but of trying to mold
their world, a way of trying to cause their co-citizens to emulate the
(purported) virtues of a certain past way of life.

If there is nothing strictly and factually false and nothing inherently reprehensible about it, why should not the modern inhabitants
of the Hellenic Democracy be permitted to identify with the ancient
Athenians? Why should not we respect this identification? If it is just
a form of self-congratulation, what is wrong with allowing that? In
fact, if this identification tended to give Greeks the force to resist

the fascism to which their country succumbed in the 1960s under
the so-called Colonels, I might well applaud it. If, on the other hand,
it was used to exclude women from political office (by appeals to the
fact that Keisthenes would not have permitted this), I would have a
different and negative attitude toward it. Naturally from the fact that
I find the Greek myth of their identity with certain ancient tribes
harmless in the present political context, it does not follow that I need
approve of all similar myths. In particular I need not approve of
myths that are used for more reprehensible purposes such as providing a legitimation of the forcible ejection of an existing population from a desired territory.

Cuno's third criticism of nationalism, that it politicizes cultural
property (*WO* 11), would be more convincing if one could imagine
that in a world without nationalism cultural property would necessarily *not* be an object of political concern. Cuno's confused failure
to distinguish clearly between the sphere of the state, politics, and
the ideology of nationalism seems to make it difficult for him to take
this point. If declaring all antiquities property of the Italian Republic
is to politicize them, is putting them up for sale on the open market
not to politicize them? Is there *no* political aspect to the massive shift
of artifacts from financially relatively poor, but archeologically rich
countries like Greece, Iraq, and Egypt to wealthy individuals and to
wealthier and more powerful, but antiquities-poorer countries? It is
true that "cultural property is a political construct" (*WO* 9), but the
same is true of "real" property. After all, *all* relations of ownership
and also "property" are equally political constructs. Cuno assumes
that there is something inherently more dubious about nation-states
asserting ownership of antiquities than about a purchaser asserting
ownership. What grounds would one have for that particular assumption? For that matter, why assume that the person who finds
an antiquity has an automatic and impeccable claim or title to it? If
I drop my wallet and you pick it up, is it obvious that you automatically own it? It is not that there is no reason at all to think it is usually best to allow finders to be keepers, but this is not an a priori truth
about nature, or part of the fundamental structure of rationality; it
is, like *all* the above ascriptions of ownership, finally a political decision. Cuno recognizes in principle (*WO* 15) that "possession is power,

and notions of property include notions of control," but does not draw any of the obvious consequences. Even if the power given by money is not "political," is it inherently less reprehensible than that given by political authority, even legitimate political authority? Is "*non olet*" really the final word here, and should it perhaps be inscribed on the new wings of universal museums under the names of their private benefactors and donors?

This leads to the fourth of Cuno's criticisms of nationalism. The looting of sites of archeological interest is a serious problem, and as long as there is a "free" international market in art objects, the poor in countries with rich archaeological heritages have a very strong incentive to engage in uncontrolled excavation in the hopes of finding something worth selling. Such uncontrolled excavation, however, has devastating effects on the archaeological record itself, destroying the "context" that gives found artifacts their cognitive significance (*AE* 33–7, 81–91; *LL* 15–51; *MC* 69–72, 77–78, 222–229). One does not know what the presence of an object in a certain place "means" archeologically unless one knows in exactly what place in relation to exactly what other objects it was discovered. Even the meanest and most apparently trivial object, for example, an ugly, badly thrown pot, can be informative if it is found together with other objects, giving us knowledge about trade patterns, movements of people, social structure. *What* it might tell us will depend on the details of the find, and that is precisely what an uncontrolled excavation would be very likely to destroy.

There is, of course, a perfectly legitimate formalist theory of art that emphasizes the strictly aesthetic value that can be found even in objects that have been extracted from their original context of production and use (see *WO* 9), and arguably it is the undeniable aesthetic appeal of such detached objects that causes people to be willing to pay enormous prices for them, and thus fuels the destruction of the archaeological record. However, regardless of this, a supporter of the cause of "universal, encyclopedic" museums cannot really subscribe to the purely formalist view with too much fervor because part of the point of such museums is not merely to give visitors aesthetic pleasure, but also to give them knowledge. The promise of the universal museum, as Cuno puts it (*WO* xxxi), is that of "the museum as a repository of things and knowledge, dedicated to the dissemination of learning and to the museum's role as a force for understanding, tolerance, and the dissipation of ignorance and superstition, where the artifacts of one time and one culture can be seen next to those of other times and other cultures without prejudice." Thus, such museums include not merely the aesthetically attractive and exceptional, but should also encompass those banal objects that will be smashed by the tomb robbers in their eagerness to get to the potentially sellable artifacts; and it should give an account of the "contexts" that give the exhibited objects their archaeological meaning.

Simply putting all archaeological finds under the protection of a nation-state, however, Cuno argues, has not worked: nationalist legislation cannot be effectively enforced, and tomb robbing and the destruction of ancient sites continue unabated (*AE* 16–17; *WO* 33–37, 40–41, 92–105). The very measures that were intended to preserve the historical record can have the perverse effect of giving people a motive to destroy it, because if *all* export is illegal, tomb robbers have a special positive motivation to mystify and deceive potential buyers about the provenance of a piece.

Cuno has put his finger on an important unsolved problem, but it is possible to wonder whether he has not overstated the lack of effect of nationalist regulatory measures (*AE* 29–30, 119–131). That the present regime for preventing illegal excavation and export in many countries is not very effective does not show that it could not be made more effective. Finally, if looting is the problem, and nationalist measures, or nationalist measures alone, are not the solution, it still does not seem plausible that Cuno's alternative, lifting regulation and allowing a free market in antiquities, will be any more effective in solving the problem.

None of Cuno's four arguments against cultural nationalism, then, in the specific form he presents any of them, seems to have much to recommend it. What, then, about the two contemporary institutions Cuno argues for, the encyclopedic universal museum and the free market in art?

The idea of an encyclopedic museum is not simply that of a place where objects are collected, but rather it is that of a place that instantiates a systematic ordering of all knowledge, and exhibits representative or typical specimens of all (important) existing types of object. Thus, it is not just that the museum collects in principle anything and that it is not partial or prejudiced in any way, but more importantly it embodies and presents a *privileged* point of view. It gives you *knowledge* of things by locating them in their correct systematic context, the context that tells you what they *really* are. This otherwise unremarkable piece of stone is "actually" a prehistoric flint scraper; that object is a Chinese pot from a particular period in a particular style; this is a grave stele from fourth-century Greece. In each case the museum (ideally) lets you understand (better) what the object really is by explaining it, locating it for you in the developing sequence of human artifacts, informing you where it was produced, where used, and where found, what other artifacts it was usually associated with, and what it allows us to infer about the life of the people who produced or used it, making it easy to compare the artifact in question with others. No prejudice is shown in favor of artifacts found in one particular part of the world or at one particular time: flints from southern France lie in the same kind of vitrine as bronzes from Benin, or objects found in Bohemia, Mexico, or China.

There is little doubt but that the universal museum is a wonderful human invention and represents great human cognitive and moral progress, but two questions remain. First, is there really a single, privileged view from nowhere? Could there be competing "universal" views, like the all-encompassing views of European (and world) history one used to be able to find (in the 1950s–1980s) in the museums of the NATO states, on the one hand, and in the member states of the Warsaw Pact, on the other? If there are differences, will they always be politically neutral or anodyne? Was the old Museum of the History of Religion and Atheism that used to exist in the Cathedral of the Madonna of Kazan in Leningrad (as the city was then known) necessarily more universal than a contemporary museum devoted to religious artifacts? If not, is not any universal museum less neutral than it presents itself to be? Second, Cuno claims that "encyclopedic museums are counter-arguments to prevailing tendency to divide the world up" (*WO* 123), yet the view from nowhere, even if it existed, must, paradoxically enough, be concretely located somewhere: the museum must stand in Petersburg, Paris, Mexico

City, Beijing, or Isfahan. Cuno recognizes this in principle: "Museums are there for the public, and that public is always local" (*WO* 13), but fails to recognize that this in itself divides the world into center and periphery. People who now have the good fortune to live in Paris, Petersburg, London, New York, or Berlin, or one of the other cities in which there are encyclopedic museums, will take the Métro, the Tube, or the S-Bahn for an hour or so and have direct access to the universal perspective from which all things make sense, but those who live elsewhere will not perhaps have a similar institutional center within thousands of miles of them. The real effect of this will be to endorse a claim like the following: "We here in the Louvre (or the Hermitage) have the true universal encyclopedic view; you (in Greece, Iraq, China) have only in each case your limited national view; therefore, if you really want to know who you are, what you have done, and thus what you could or should aspire to, come to us; we will tell you through our exhibits." It is not, I submit, hard to comprehend why some Greeks, Iraqis, and Chinese might find this less than fully satisfactory.

To say that one can overcome the difficulty of spatial localization through electronic media or the Internet is not an option for Cuno, because to do that would require him to give up one of the main assumptions of his argument, which is that the cultural benefits of the museum depend on allowing people to have a direct encounter with the real objects themselves. Malraux's *"Musée sans murs"* and Benjamin's *"Das Kunstwerk im Zeitalter seiner technischen Reproduzierbarkeit"* may have correctly drawn attention to various ways in which our experience of art is of necessity different from that of previous ages because of the omnipresence of mechanically reproduced images, but for the modern director the task of a museum is not merely to give a picture or an image, but to allow *autopsia* of the *thing itself* (*WO* 128).

The Greeks do not want even a perfect replica of the Elgin Marbles that is visually indistinguishable from them—they want the very stones themselves, and one can understand why. In a way it is exactly the tension between the highly abstract, theoretical, and all-encompassing perspective that is expressed in the architecture, the mode of presentation, and the labeling of the exhibits in the encyclopedic museum, on the one hand, and the direct encounter with real objects themselves, on the other, that constituted one of the main attractions of the traditional universal museum.

As far as the free market is concerned, there is no reason to believe it will in itself stop looting, or that under such a system individual wealthy buyers will have a strong motivation to give their precious acquired objects to universal museums rather than keeping them for their own enjoyment.

Despite Cuno's self-ascribed "internationalism" (*AE* 18) and his very vocal support for the impartial universal museum as an institution, certain parts of his book breathe a rather different spirit, which is perhaps closer to certain versions of the nationalist view than he realizes. Thus in a chapter entitled "The Crux of the Matter" (*WO* 1–20), we find a series of remarks lamenting the way in which various existing international laws, regulations, and practices purportedly disadvantage *American* museums vis-à-vis foreign institutions, and in a footnote (*WO* 176n27) we read that the strict enforcement of laws devoted to "the international protection of archaeological sites" must be balanced against "the right of U.S. citizens to participate in a legitimate trade in antiquities." At a deeper level, even Cuno's "universalism" has a distinctly American inflection. Its central features are extreme individualism, a general unwillingness to acknowledge the importance of existing historical connections, deep and inherent distrust of the state, and a passionate devotion to the free market. Thus we are told (*WO* 11) that "culture is personal, not national." This statement is a half-truth of the kind that often plays a pivotal role in ideological discourse. I take it that the statement is part of Cuno's general attempt to downplay the role of social groups and collectivities, and to install individualism at the heart of the museum's self-understanding. "Personal" and "national," however, represent a false dichotomy. The Parthenon was not a "national" work of art in the sense that it was produced by a nation-state in order to glorify that nation-state, but it does not follow from that in any interesting sense that it is "personal." "Personal" to or for whom? To/for Pericles? Ictinus? Phidias? Or, to take another example, opera as an institution would not exist without individuals, persons who played the prescribed roles on stage and persons who were sufficiently keen on the institution to form an audience, and each one will have some kind of "personal" attitude toward the practice, but it does not follow from that that one can understand what we call "opera" without reference to various collective, impersonal, and traditional aspects of the genre, the conventions and rules that govern it, and the tacit social context within which it exists. I may "personally" like to whistle along with the orchestra, but the custom is that I do not do that during a performance, so the fact that I do not whistle, although I would rather like to, requires some explanation with reference to traditions, collective expectations, and so on. Similarly, ancient potters did not in general simply produce "pots" in general or merely express a "personal" vision, but rather they created instances of one or another of a highly complex set of *kinds* or *types* of pot—an *olpe*, a *kalyx*, a *psykther*—and one cannot understand what they were trying to do without understanding this nonpersonal aspect of their activity.

Just as in the New World traditional social ties and allegiances and established hierarchies of status were to play no role, and only differences in wealth would effectively count, so for people who hold the ideological position I am ascribing to Cuno, the real historical aspect of cultural artifacts is not relevant; they are detached objects of aesthetic contemplation or academic study, and because they have no organic connection with any place or any population, they become universally and promiscuously available for appropriation or "acquisition" by anyone, which in the contemporary world means "available to purchase by the highest bidder." I have already had occasion to mention Cuno's skepticism about any form of political, state, or government regulation of "the cultural heritage." "States," we are told, "make self-interested decisions" (*WO* 34). (But financiers, art dealers, and, I dare say, museum directors do not?) Furthermore, because national regulations governing archaeological sites "are in the service of the state, they inevitably have a nationalist agenda" (*WO* 53; also *AE* 14). I note again the tacit identification of "the state" and "the *nation*-state," and the elision of both with "nationalism." When the Turkish archeologist Mehmet Özdoğan defends Turkey's policy of state ownership of all artifacts found within the territory of the republic on the grounds that the past "belongs to all of us" (*WO* 85), Cuno's comment is, "How can it belong to all of us if it belongs to the state?" The answer to this would seem obvious if one notes the ambiguity in three different senses of "ownership" or "belonging." Something can "belong" to the Turkish state in the sense that the state affirms ownership of the object, and yet it can also "belong" to all of us because the Turkish Republic exhibits it in a museum open to all, and because it is an object that pertains or is relevant to all of us. Anyone who has trouble understanding how a vase can "belong" to the Turkish state (that is, be owned by) and also "belong to" us (that is, be relevant to us and exhibited so that we all can inspect it) should have equal trouble understanding how if our common cultural heritage ought to "belong to all of us," some of it could be permitted to "belong to," that is, be owned by, private owners or for that matter by the *French* state, which after all owns the Louvre. Should, then, the buying and selling of cultural artifacts in any form, then, be prohibited on the grounds that they should "belong to all of us"? How can the past "belong" to us, if it belongs to—that is, is stored and exhibited in—a universal museum located so far away from me that I will never have any real access to it?

In contrast to his suspicion of governments and states, Cuno is relaxed about the role of private financiers in the control of cultural property. Thus his book contains glowing praise of the "philanthropists and collectors of antiquities" Shelby White and Leon Levy (*WO* 200–201) and less fulsome, but still positive, remarks about the activities of George Ortiz (*WO* 23). Some of the other works under discussion give a very different view of White, Levy, and Ortiz and their traffic in unprovenanced antiquities (for White and Levy, see *LL* 28–35, 44, 71, and *MC* 126–128; for Ortiz, *LL* 30–32, 44, and *MC* 133–134).

To put it in the crudest possible way, the argument of this book can be summed up in one question: "We, directors of the major U.S. museums, at the moment have more money and resources than anyone else; who are *you* to tell us there is something we cannot buy?" To this the obvious reply is: "We are the internationally recognized legitimate government of the Republic of Turkey (or the People's Republic of China, and so on) and we wish to retain these objects in the interests of our respective populations." Although this reply does not *by itself* settle the matter, I submit that there is more to this response than Cuno gives it credit for. The distinguished archaeologist Malcolm Bell III puts the point in a slightly more irenic way (*AE* 37): "We may want to ask whether the claims of foreign museums and collectors are stronger than those of the local community."

At the beginning, I said that *WO* was not a dystopian fantasy, and throughout the book Cuno (*AE* 15) calls on archaeologists to recognize the *reality* of the conditions in which they work, at the mercy of governments who often pursue a nationalist agenda, but the *reality* of his (and our) situation is that he wishes to live in a world in which those with largest checkbooks still can appropriate the world's cultural heritage *ad libitum*, even if much of the historical record is thereby rendered definitively unreadable. It is true this is not a dystopian fantasy, but it is an inappropriately sanitizing and glamorizing account of what is in fact our rather sordid reality. Watson and Todeschini describe in depressing detail the virtually industrial scale conveyer-belt leading from organized tomb robbers *(tombaroli)* in Italy to the Getty Museum in Los Angeles, which in the 1980s and 1990s provided that museum with a continuous stream of antiquities that were looted from illegal excavations or straightforwardly stolen from other collections. While this gained the museum the nickname "Museum of the Tombaroli" (*MC* 87–99), a number of other reputable museums seem to have been only marginally less culpable. This is the reality we must face. It is hard to avoid the conclusion that the only way to deal with this problem is through even tighter legal regulation at the national and international levels combined with the political will to enforce such regulation effectively. This is compatible with a great increase in initiatives for voluntary— or even obligatory—exchange between museums (*AE* 38–41, 116– 117, 155–159), but not with the continued existence of a virtually unregulated international market in antiquities.

12

The Future of Evil

———*ຄາຄາ*———

THERE ARE fashions as much in vices as in virtues, and these are neither completely dependent on, nor completely independent of, changes in social institutions and transformations of the available moral vocabulary. It is often very difficult to distinguish changes in customs or habits, changes in modes of evaluation, and changes in vocabulary. Do vices become extinct, and if so, how does this occur? In his *Summa theologiae* Thomas Aquinas discusses the "vice of *simony*"—the desire or attempt to purchase or sell spiritual powers, then by extension the buying and selling of ecclesiastical office— which he classes among the "vices contrary to religion" *("vitia opposita religioni")*.[1] Simony still merited a separate topological location among the most serious vices in Dante's *Inferno*, but one would be hard put to find a discussion of it in any contemporary work of virtue ethics. It has probably succumbed to a combination of social and economic changes and widespread skepticism about the very existence of spiritual powers. We are disinclined to believe that spiritual powers, even if they did exist, could be acquired by purchase. The result of this is that attempts to purchase nonnatural powers seem pathetically stupid rather than vicious. In addition, changes in the internal regulatory structure and the relative economic position of the church have caused the market for the sale of spiritual powers to dry up to such an extent that it is difficult or impossible for individuals to develop a fixed disposition to try to buy or sell the power of the Holy Spirit or to purchase or offer for purchase bishoprics, monastic offices, or a place in the College of Cardinals. Simony is not the only vice to suffer. The good old Christian vice of gluttony *(gula)* seems to have disappeared, being reinterpreted as a medical condition or a morally neutral, although perhaps aesthetically repellent, lifestyle choice. In the Middle Ages, too, "curiosity," was often considered a vice; it is now no longer considered at all objectionable, but rather is something that, on the whole, we are inclined to admire.[2] If vices, therefore, can apparently disappear, can new ones also come into existence? Was there always as much "pedophilia" and child abuse as there now seems to be? Have the dissolution of social taboos and the omnipresence of news reporting caused something that always existed suddenly come to people's attention in a way it did not previously, so that people are forced to make up their minds about its exact evaluation in a way they could have avoided in earlier periods? Was it always there, but accepted or at any rate tacitly tolerated, but is now very explicitly and vividly repudiated? Or was it previously "hiding" under some other more general term?

One of the ways in which Nietzsche presents his project in *The Genealogy of Morality* is as a historical account of the development of contemporary morality, including the development of our virtues and vices and our conceptions of virtue and vice.[3] His account arises, he claims, out of two philological observations about the history of the word "good," or rather about the meaning and history of some earlier terms (καλός, ἀγαθός, *bonus*) that are usually construed as "meaning the same thing" as our word *good*.[4] The first observation is that "good" (and its historically existing semantic "equivalents") has had and continues to have two distinct opposites: that which is "bad" is definitely not good, and that which is "evil" is also definitely not good, and yet "bad" and "evil" do not mean the same thing. Furthermore, Nietzsche claims, "bad" and "evil" are not merely semantically distinct because, for instance, "evil" is a subspecies of "bad," so that "evil" means "intensely bad" or "intentionally very bad." If that were the case, "bad" and "evil" would not mean the same thing because everything that was evil would also be bad, but not everything that was bad (for instance, that which was merely mildly or moderately or unintentionally bad) would also count as "evil." This simple kind of difference in meaning is not what Nietzsche intends. Rather, Nietzsche holds that originally "bad" and "evil" were used characteristically by the members of two different groups of people, and that they were used in such a way that their extensions did not overlap. This is a very strong assertion indeed. Nietzsche's second historical observation is that the pair "good–bad" is older than the pair "good–evil," and this stimulates him to the hypothesis, to the development of which the first essay of the *Genealogy* is devoted, namely, that "good–evil" should in some sense be seen as arising out of "good–bad" through a revolutionary change in the system of valuation, a "reversal of all values" (*"Umwertung aller Werte"*).

"Evil," of course, is not itself a vice in the normal sense of the term. That is, it is not on the same level of abstraction as proper vices like indolence, cruelty, simony, duplicitousness, envy, or impatience. They seem in the first instance to refer to complexes or patterns of behavior which, to be sure, count as vices only because they form stable constellations that are taken to be the result of persisting psychological states. "Evil," on the other hand, seems not to refer primarily to any externally discernible kind of action, but rather to be a second-order interpretative term, which shows how these individual vices are to be understood by reference to some underlying structure feature that they all have. A very strong philosophical traditional view would have it that although specific vices might fall into desuetude or die out, "evil" is a structural feature of all vices, and so as long as *any* vice at all remains in existence, "evil" will still exist. Christians, of course, have traditionally held that the possibility of doing evil was an inherent part of human free will, so that even a society that, *per impossibile*, was utopianly good would have a use for the concept of "evil." Since for the Christian "free will" had to stand in the center of any ethical reflection, then as long as humanity continues to exist, the concept of "evil" would retain its relevance and its importance: if Christians and post-Christians are right, its future is assured.

Nietzsche's views on this topic were deeply influenced by his study of the Greek poet Theognis, whom he cites in the *Genealogy* as the "mouthpiece of the Greek nobility"[5] and describes in his unpublished notes as "a poet as philosopher."[6] Theognis was a sixth-century

aristocrat from Megara who wrote elegiac distichs of a vaguely ethical character. Many of the verses are addressed to his young boy-
friend, Kyknos, and contain, as is common in works in this tradition
of pederastic pedagogy, advice to him about how to live a proper
upper-class life.[7] It is perfectly true that Theognis was, as Nietzsche
states, a man who formulates in an especially explicit way a certain
self-conception of the Greek aristocracy, but what is almost more
striking about his work is the way in which it reflects and expresses
Theognis's own sense that the world of traditional certainties in
which he had been brought up and had lived was being completely
transformed in radical ways over which he had no control and of
which he deeply disapproved. Nietzsche was obsessed with what he
calls the "slave revolt" of morality, by which he meant the process in
which old aristocratic values of prowess in war, glory, successful self-
assertion, and associated traits were systematically devalued and replaced with virtues of nonaggression, cooperation, benevolence, and
so on. Theognis's own preoccupation is not exactly the same as
Nietzsche's. He is rather sensitive to the destructive effect of new
wealth on traditional social hierarchies, but his particular fear is not
the devaluation of aggression. He is, however, living through a process of "*Umwertung aller Werte*," which has some significant similari-
ties to what Nietzsche calls the "slave revolt," and he observes the
effect of this transformation of society and its values on language itself; the very meanings of words seem to change.[8]

Thus Theognis writes:

> Kyknos, this city is still a city, but the people are
>   different.
> Those who used to have no knowledge either of laws or
>   judgments,
> wore clapped out goatskins wrapped around their
>   middles,
> and wandered about aimlessly grazing outside the city
>   like deer,
> *they* are now good [ἀγαθοί], and those who used to be
>   noble [ἐσθλοί]
> are now worthless [δειλοί , "cowards']][9]

And, in what seems to be a separate passage:

> Kyknos, those who used to be good [ἀγαθοί] are now bad
> [κακοί]
> and those who used to be bad [κακοί] are now good
> [ἀγαθοί].
> Who could stand to see the good [τοὺς ἀγαθούς] having
> less honor
> [ἀτιμοτέρους] and the bad [κακίους] getting honor? A
> noble man [ἐσθλὸς ἀνὴρ] even goes courting [the
> daughter of] a bad man [κακοῦ].[10]

I have translated this in a particularly bald way to bring out the apparent confusion of linguistic usage and the crude juxtapositions of opposites that would be lost in a more idiomatic version. This is a time and a world in which meanings are shifting so radically that it is unclear at first glance what exactly is being said, and contradictory statements seem possible. When Theognis writes that the good are now bad, does he mean that those who were bad (in an agreed-on sense) have now changed their nature and behavior and actually *are* good (in the agreed-on sense), or that those who were (and still are) bad are now *(called)* "good"? Called by whom? Written Greek of the sixth and fifth centuries BC had practically no punctuation and in particular did not have quotation marks, so one could not distinguish in a text between "they are good" and "they are 'good.'" It is difficult to see how one could try to read passages like these without asking what is meant by "good." Are people good by virtue of having some psychological or behavioral properties, by virtue of coming from a respected stable family, by virtue of their wealth, the honors they receive, their position in society? Does "the bad are now good" mean: "men of good families are now no longer given the positions of honor to which they are entitled," or "men who really have merit are not given appropriate honors," or "good families are no longer producing men of genuine merit" (perhaps because they are ignoring Theognis's own eugenic advice),[11] or something else (or all of the above)?

This passage does not support Nietzsche's specific claims about "evil," but it does indicate a complete dissociation of linguistic usage,

with the very same lexical items used to designate that that are completely different, and incompatible. On one usage that was current
in Theognis's society, the former wearers of goatskins are "good" (for
example, they are honored in society and get to marry women from
the best families); on another they are definitely "not-good" (they are
still former wearers of greasy goatskins, and presumably still smell
of cheese and garlic and have unattractive personal habits).[12] Nietzsche's first claim is that just as Theognis noticed contradictory uses
of "good" (and "bad") in his period, so historically there has been
another and philosophically more significant kind of contradictory
use of the term "good" in Western moral theory.

   In *Genealogy of Morality* Nietzsche argues that virtually all forms
of the moral life in the post-Platonic and post-Christian period in
the West, and particularly in the "modern" period, have been inherently both self-deceived and duplicitous in that they *present* themselves as inherently unitary, coherent, and all-encompassing, but are
actually a jerry-rigged congeries of potentially incompatible elements. Whatever modern morality is, it is not a form of *Sittlichkeit*,
that is, a coherent form of moral beliefs and habits of individual and
social action, much as its representatives might protest to the contrary. The *apparent* unity of "good" as a central concept in morality
actually masks the fact that the "good" in question means two very
different things: "good" *as the opposite of* "bad" and "good" *as the opposite of* "evil."

   The body of the *Genealogy of Morality* gives the well-known development of Nietzsche's historical hypothesis. In the first of three
successive treatises, he describes the origins of the evaluative pair of
concepts "good–evil" out of a process of revaluation of the previously
dominant pair "good–bad"; a second treatise treats the way in which
humans learned to deal with their aggression by turning it against
themselves. The third treatise discusses the role the ascetic ideal
plays in the history of morality in Europe. However, although it is clear
that *Genealogy* is supposed to be an essay in "real" history, of the
"gray," dry-as-dust kind, not just a kind of conceptual analysis,[13] it is
not so clear what the point of this historical account is supposed to be.

   Why is Nietzsche telling us this story? What, if anything, are
we supposed to learn from this historical account practically? Is it

supposed to change us and the way we live, and, if so, how? In the preface to the *Genealogy of Morality*, Nietzsche states that his ultimate aim in undertaking the historical analysis he gives in the body of work was to ask the question of the "value of morality." Western philosophers have for the most part simply *assumed* that morality (in their preferred form) had great or inherent or even absolute value, rather than considering in a spirit of genuine inquiry what kind of value what kind of moral conceptions could be expected to have. One way, then, of seeing Nietzsche's overarching project is as trying to ask two coordinated questions, where previous philosophers have asked only one. They asked only, "What is the good?" or "What is the final end of human life?" or "What ought I to do?" But really they should have been asking questions of this form *and also* "What value does the good have?" or "What value does doing what I 'ought' to do have?"

To claim, as Nietzsche does, that "modern" morality is not a seamless whole, coherently derivable from a single concept or a single form of valuation, but is a disjointed compromise conjunction of various different and potentially incompatible parts might suggest that modern morality is completely chaotic, exhibiting no order or structure at all. The structure it has is not an internal logical order, but a rough-and-ready one imposed on it by one specific element that is dominant and that coerces the disparate parts into some kind of co-existence. This dominant element has been Christianity. Nietzsche thinks that Christian and post-Christian forms of valuation have had the upper hand historically in the West for a sufficiently long time now for *their* specific form of valuation, which is based on the dichotomy of "good" and "evil," to have a special standing, not just because this is the way in which Western morality has understood itself, but also because moral views based on this dichotomy have had a real effect in making modern Western populations what they are.

Nietzsche does not think that "evil" and the associated conceptions of sin, guilt, and so on, are *mere misunderstandings* in the sense in which, say, the belief that I have £1,000,000 in the bank is a simple false belief, of which I can in principle disabuse myself by unprejudiced inspection of my bank statement. Sin and guilt are realities, states of real psychic discomfort rooted in my own somatic constitution. It is merely that these states are not, as Christianity would have it, a universal, necessary part of the human psychic apparatus. Rather they are specific psychic *and somatic* realities that have been produced historically, and have been reinforced, if not generated, by the operation of Christian social institutions that have successfully inculcated them in me. It is extremely important to realize that Nietzsche thinks there is no contradiction between saying that sin has a *somatic* component—it is a state of *physical* discomfort—and also saying that I was caused to acquire this physiological state by the operation of specific historical institutions which were ultimately acting under the guidance of Christian beliefs of various kinds. Hegemonic Christianity, through its institutions, *creates* a kind of person. This means, among other things, that replacing Christian (and post-Christian) moral conceptions will not be as easy as replacing my erroneous beliefs about my financial state with correct ones. Simple observation, the use of empirical methods, and even Socratic dialogue with our own contemporaries—or rather Socratic dialogue between Nietzsche and his contemporaries—will not necessarily do the trick because, by hypothesis, those contemporaries are the fruit of two thousand years of the operation of Christian institutions and have a particular somatic constitution, particular acquired needs, particular forms of feeling, and a particular attachment to certain forms of thinking one cannot simply suspend or think out of existence. For this reason, Nietzsche thinks, if one wishes to ask his ultimate question about the value of our morality, it is imperative to try to find a standpoint outside our current ordinary language and the usual empirical generalizations we will be inclined to make if we observe our neighbors. He tries to find this in part by studying the "natural history" of moralities, that is, in a kind of ethnological or anthropological study of other cultures, and also in history. Given his own epistemic situation in the 1870s and 1880s and also his training, the historical approach looms especially large.

Using one of the spatial metaphors Nietzsche often favors, one might say that to see ourselves and our morality in such a way as to allow us to ask the question about the value of morality, rather than simply reproducing slightly sanitized versions of our own prejudices, requires us to find a position "beyond" that morality, and since good and evil basically structure this morality, a position beyond good and evil. It is, of course, one of Nietzsche's most fundamental tenets that placing oneself beyond "good and evil" does not necessarily mean putting oneself altogether outside the realm of morality—of any conceivable morality. Since "evil," for him, is connected with a highly specific form of negation, being "beyond good and evil" does not necessarily mean being "beyond good and *bad*." In addition, the phrase "put yourself beyond good and evil" is not, for Nietzsche, a universal injunction to all humans telling them how they "ought" to live. First of all, Nietzsche does not believe in a single universal moral code for all humans, second, he does not believe in a moral "ought," and, third, he thinks preaching is usually pointless because the very basic level people do not have much choice in being the sort of person they are. Rather, the injunction (*"Forderung"*)[14] is to *philosophers* to free themselves of the "illusions" of traditional morality. The relation of this philosophical investigation to human practice would need to be further explored, and would replay further discussion.

What about "evil," then? Nietzsche thinks that *evil* is a term that has a complex use:[15]

a) To designate a certain type of characteristic action that is the natural expression of a certain human type, that is, of human impulses that are associated with the special unreflective vitality of a dominant social group (especially those that inflict harm on a subordinate group).

b) To interpret actions of the type so designated by relating them to a complex psycho-metaphysics of the soul, freedom, intention, responsibility, and guilt.

c) To express a contra-attitude (of an appropriate kind) toward actions of that type.

He also thinks that traditional forms of Christianity-derived moral thinking have made some kind of tacit assumption to the effect that

d) "Good–evil" is not merely *one* evaluative pair, but that it is fundamental, basic, primordial, or definitive.

To put this in terms closer to those developed by some later philosophers, "evil" has an extension or reference, and a meaning, and using the concept expresses an attitude. The extension of the term is archetypically to the actions of a dominant person acting on exuberant human impulses in such a way as to inflict pain, damage, or harm on a weaker subordinate person. The "meaning" is the whole tacit metaphysical theory of human agency that Nietzsche thinks underpins attribution of "evil" to agents. To say that agent X has done something that is "evil" is tacitly to assume that X has an immortal soul that possesses the metaphysical property of freedom of the will, and that X employs this freedom to decide to inflict harm intentionally. It is further tacitly presupposed that X can and should be held responsible for freely acting as he has done, and should feel guilt. In using the term *evil* to designate such an action (or the impulse to perform such an action, or a person who feels such an impulse), I express my own contra-attitude toward it. This "contra-attitude," Nietzsche claims, arises out of my resentment that X is able to act powerfully in ways in which I would like to act myself, but that I feel myself too weak to do successfully and with impunity.

One part of Nietzsche's own detailed account of "evil' is directed at showing that (b) above is a set of untenable beliefs. He takes extremely seriously the fact that, on his view, (b) requires commitment to a full-blown metaphysics of the human subject as fundamentally an immortal soul having a nonempirical property of free will, and he thinks he has shown that no obvious version of that psycho-metaphysics could actually be true. Another part of his discussion purports to show what strong motives people, especially weak members of dominated groups, might have for believing that "evil" is a well-defined and indispensable concept: it allows them to take revenge in thought on those who are stronger than they are, and they in some sense "need" the imaginary sense of power that this conceptual "revenge" gives them. One might think of this account of the motivation for calling some act or some person "evil" as a further part of item (c) above: the "contra-attitude" was one inherently motivated by a certain kind of vengefulness that arises from a deep-seated need to overcome, even if only in the imagination, one's own sense of comparative weakness.

Let us suppose now for the sake of argument that Nietzsche has demonstrated to our satisfaction that we can no longer hold (b) to be true. One possibility is that "evil" will simply stop being used. After all, the theory on which the application of the concept rests (a metaphysics of human freedom) has been shown to be "refuted." This might conceivably happen, but if Nietzsche's general account is correct, it is highly unlikely, given that "evil" refers in a relatively clear way to a recognized set of properties and that its availability and use satisfies a well-entrenched need for a simple way to express our vindictiveness. It is too useful simply to give up. If we did give it up, our underlying need would probably just lead us to create some other lexical items that essentially served the same purpose.

Nietzsche clearly himself thinks that for most people the project of getting rid of ressentiment is hopeless, because ressentiment arises naturally from weakness and basically one is simply as weak (or as strong) as one is, and there is nothing more to say. "Evil," then, will always have a future, at least with the majority of the members of our society. In fact it seems likely that he expects discourse about "evil" to flourish because with the increasing psychological sophistication and devotion to truthfulness Christianity itself propagates, we will gradually come in some sense to see, or to half see the untenability of the metaphysics on which "evil" is based, but will not, because of our need to express our ressentiment, be able to give it up. A situation in which we almost-see the internal incoherence of a concept that for deep-seated reasons we simply cannot give up is highly pathogenic. The use of the term *evil* will be likely to become more obfuscated, hysterical, and toxic, as indeed it has.

On the other hand, if we *could* in fact get rid of our underlying need to react to our own powerlessness by venting our aggression on more powerful or uninhibited others through labeling them in this way, we might no longer "need" the term *evil* in the same way. Nevertheless, we might think that historically this term has in fact been used to refer to a large number of things that are genuinely especially bad or harmful, although of course they are bad for different reasons from those which would have been cited when Christians characterized them as "evil." The path might be clear for a revaluation of "evil," which might, for all anyone knows, retain the word while reinterpreting its meaning and shifting its extension. Thus we might reserve "evil" for especially serious forms of the bad, or for the intentional infliction of great harm. Or we might have recourse again to Thomas Aquinas and his theory of "capital vices."[16] Thomas held that just as there were (as it were) simple virtues, but also "cardinal virtues," so also there were simple vices and "capital vices."[17] Cardinal virtues were thought to be the "hinges" (*cardo*) on which a good human life turns. That is, they were qualities that were structurally central to the good life, qualities that were not only good in themselves, but that formed the basis of, and brought along in their wake, other good qualities. So, similarly, we might reserve the term *evil* for defects that were not just undesirable in themselves, but also had the property that they tended to bring in their wake many *other* bad things: "vices from which other vices arise" (*vizia ex quibus alia oriuntur*).[18] Thus, one might think that such things as "censoriousness" or "personal vanity" or "officiousness" were bad human traits, for whatever reason, but also that they did not in themselves generate any further harm; they were simple vices. On the other hand, one might think that "avarice" or "duplicitousness" were both bad in themselves, and also caused those who were afflicted with them to develop other undesirable traits. These were "capital vices." One does not have to find these specific examples convincing to take the underlying general point about certain traits playing a more basic structural role in human life than others. Presenting this theory in a convincing form would, of course, require us to have a view about the good life and its constituents, but Nietzsche would have no objection to that, and we would very likely not call the same things "evil" that our predecessors did. What we would call "evil" under this new scheme would depend on the positive view of the good life which we had formed. Provided that the use of this new term was not connected with imaginary vengefulness, it would effectively be a revalued (*"umgewertet"*) concept, that is, a concept based on a form of valuation completely different from that in Christianity. Whether one *calls* this "evil," taking over for convenience the old name, or invents a new name for it is, for Nietzsche, irrelevant.

So we might carve a niche for a post-Nietzschean concept of "evil" if we meant by that concept simply the idea of intentional action directed at producing something we thought was especially bad, particularly if we also thought that the agent should have known and prevented the damage or harm in question. We might be extremely open in giving a further specification of what the signal badness in question meant, and also rather open-minded about what "should have known" means. Nevertheless, it would not be a foregone conclusion that being "evil" (in the transvalued sense) was—hierarchically as it were—the very worst thing there is. Small structural defects in a person's character might not be thought automatically to be worse than anything else one could imagine. An evil but impotent person, that is, someone with a psychological disposition to do that which was bad intentionally, but with no particular power to exercise these dispositions, might be thought less of a menace than someone who pursued what he or she genuinely thought was an acceptable political course, but which was in fact very destructive. In that sense "evil" might well have a modest future.

At this point one might be tempted to object that this whole discussion has focused on the *concept* of evil, or even the term or word *evil*, not on the reality. It is one thing to ask whether we will still use the term *polar bear* in thirty years, another to ask whether any polar bears will really have survived the complete melting of the summer ice at the North Pole that we now expect in the near future. This objection misses the point. Evil is not a thing, a substance, or an objective feature of our world; it is nothing like a polar bear, or a chemical element, or a topographical feature of our Earth (such as an isthmus or a promontory). If Nietzsche is right, not only is evil not a thing; it is not originally even an imaginary term that anyone uses to characterize his or her *own* action. The dominant, aggressive masters in Nietzsche's story do not set out to "do evil," and they would originally never have applied the concept at all. "Evil" is an imaginary characterization used by the weak originally to describe the actions of *others* (who are oppressing them) and applied in a spirit of revenge. With the demise of the spirit of vengeance, the monochrome reduction of the world into "good" (light) and "evil" (dark) that it imposed would come to an end, and a world of complex coloration would appear. We would have moved out of the world of bleached-white classical statuary into a world of highly colored moving images like those in the films of Pasolini or Antonioni. The reflection that many of the "classical" statues were themselves originally clothed in rich fabric and vividly painted might, as Nietzsche hoped it would, help us with the transition. The real question about the future of evil, then, is the question of whether we are able to control or get rid of our need for vengeance.

13

Satire, Who Whom?

—◦◦◦—

SOMETIMES THE EVENTS themselves force us to take a position on the thorniest questions without permitting us the luxury of being able to structure the discussion as we would wish. The lines are already drawn, and there remains at best the possibility that they are not yet set in stone. Such was the situation after the attack on the office of the satirical magazine *Charlie Hebdo* on January 7, 2015. Do you support the freedom to engage in satire and thus—it is assumed even when not explicitly said—freedom of thought and speech, or do you side with the terrorists? This question is a purely "rhetorical" one. That is, it is not really a question at all, but rather a particularly forceful *statement* that conceals itself behind an interrogative form and arranges the space of discussion in such a way that no other answer than the desired one is possible—for who would want to confess to terrorist sympathies? The apparent obviousness of the expected answer is an artifact of the way in which the question is posed. Sometimes certain questions cannot be answered because they do not make sense; they can only be replaced by better but completely different questions.

We know very well the heroic stories of certain great satirists: the Roman poet Naevius, for example, who in the third century BC attacked the powerful Metelli family (although admittedly, his "satire" did not, by modern standards have very sharp teeth). His verses contained, so far as we can judge, no general or fundamental social criticism, but only personal insults (which, moreover, were not even especially witty). For example, his line *"fato Metelli Romae fiunt consules"* ("only by accident did the Metellis become consuls in Rome") is not exactly brilliant—who today would be much ruffled by such a declaration? True, one consul belonging to the Metelli family, Caecilius Metellus, was clearly concerned enough to respond to the poet with a verse of his own, *"dabunt malum Metelli Naevio poetae"* ("the Metelli will give Naevius a nasty surprise"). Needless to say, the level of sensitivity to satire is a historically variable matter through and through. All the same, one might be surprised by the touchiness apparent here, for the Romans—a people of brutal warriors, simple-minded farmers, grasping traders, and decadent aristocrats—hardly distinguish themselves as having a particularly high degree of human or artistic sensibility. They had little reason to be proud of their cultural achievements, which barely went beyond bloody gladiatorial games, and they themselves knew this as well as we do:

> excudent alii spirantia mollius aera
> (credo equidem), vivos ducent de marmore vultus,
> orabunt causas melius, caelique meatus
> describent radio et surgentia sidera dicent:
> tu regere imperio populos, Romane, memento
> (hae tibi erunt artes), pacisque imponere morem,
> parcere subiectis et debellare superbos (*aeneidos* VI,
>   846–853)

["Leave it to others to sculpt bronze more subtly and bring out living faces from marble—I grant they can do that—and they will also be better at pleading cases at law, and will mark out with their stick the motions of the heavens and be able to predict the rising of the stars: You, Roman, remember to rule peoples with your command—these are your arts—and to impose on them the habit of peace, to spare those subjugated, but war down the haughty."]

Many of the ingredients of a glorification of Roman imperialism are packed into these lines: the exercise of power is not simply a way of

affirming one's own position over another, or of enriching oneself,
but an "art" *(artes erunt)* like sculpture or astronomy. It is no pleasure
for the Roman to govern, but a destiny of burdensome responsibility
that is imposed on him: he is relaxed and peaceable by nature, and
so has always to remind himself of this thankless task *(memento . . .
regere imperio)*. It would be an offense against the divine order for
him to let himself go and give in to irenic disposition and thus to
forget to extend the imperial power to ever more distant peoples;
indeed, the latter *need* to be conquered by the toga-wearing masters
of the world. In fact, the Romans must teach the conquered to live
"in peace" *(pacis imponere morem)*. We know, to be sure, that this "pax
romana" did not appeal to all non-Roman peoples, and even the
Romans (or at least some of them) knew it too. In his text *Agricola*,
Tacitus has a British general say about the Roman policy of "pacifica-
tion": *"ubi solitudinem faciunt, pacem appellant"* ("they make a wasteland and call it 'peace'"). And those who are not prepared to be let
themselves be subjugated *(subiectis)* are "uppity" *(superbos)*, against
whom it is legitimate to wage war to the death—that is, until they
too are "vanquished" *(debellare)*.

Intriguingly, the only literary genre that is (according to Roman
estimation) an original product of the Roman spirit is satire: *"satira
tota nostra est"* ("satire is wholly our own") (Quintilian X.1.93). This
assertion depends, however, on a rather formalistic definition of satire:
a Roman satire is a ragtag collection whose contents are a mix of hu-
morous barbs, containing poetic flytes in various meters, biting im-
provised couplets, insulting songs, and perhaps also prose elements.
But at the origin of the poetry of invective that has been handed down
to us we find not a Roman, but the iambic poet Archilochus, who
wrote (in Greek) in the seventh century. Tradition has it that Archilochus wanted to marry Neoboule, the daughter of a certain Lykambes,
but that Lykambes refused to grant the pair his consent to the marriage. This prompted Archilochus to write the following verse:

πάτερ Λυκάμβα, ποῖον ἐφράσω τόδε;
τίς σὰς παρήειρε φρένας,
ἧς τὸ πρὶν ἠρήρεισθα; νῦν δὲ δὴ πολὺς
ἀστοῖσι φαίνεαι γέλως.

["Father Lykambes, what has got into you? Who scrambled the wits you used to have? Now you are a huge laughingstock to your fellow townsmen."]

Lykambes, according to ancient commentaries on the text, hanged himself after hearing these lines—a reaction that, to us in the twenty-first century, would seem exaggerated. But even if this particular report is false, the fact that the anecdote was told repeatedly in antiquity indicates that people at that time saw this as a plausible or entirely appropriate way to respond. According to the Roman definition, these lines of Archilochus's are not satire, since they are not part of a literary work that mixes verse and prose, but on a less formalistic definition, their "satirical" character cannot be denied.

To come back to the conflict between the poet Naevius and the Metelli family, the fact that the consul Caecilius Metellus was able to meet Naevius with the retort cited earlier (*dabunt malum Metelli Naevio poetae*) suggests that Caecilius Metellus, too, was no slouch at repartee, and this could lead us to suspect that what we are dealing with here is no more than a literary game between the two. We also know, however, that Caecilius Metellus had the poet arrested. If this was a game, then, it was not one without real danger to the poet. Augustine tells us (*de civitate dei* 2.9) that in the time of the Republic the publication of libel was subject to the death penalty. It is clear that the Roman consul's quick-witted comeback is only the beginning of a story that is continued with the incarceration of the poet.

In more modern times Voltaire's pleasantry at the expense of the so-called Chevalier of Rohan was a case where the personal insult was part of a general defense of bourgeois meritocracy against the pretensions of the hereditary aristocracy. The point of conflict between bourgeois citizens and the nobility was the question of the "title": who "deserved" which name and which title? Only the bearer of a noble title could get away with having a bourgeois author like Voltaire beaten on the public street without having to fear the consequences. When Voltaire goes on the offensive with "Écrasez l'infâme," he certainly has more in mind than simply crafting personal insults. His ideological victory is rightly counted as one of the most important steps on the way to the liberation of the European spirit.

There is one element that is present to some extent in all so-called cultural works, but that stands out with special clarity in the case of satire: its contextuality. Satire is not in every case subversive, progressive, or praiseworthy. Think, in the ancient context, of Aristophanes, Horace, Juvenal, or Martial: these are traditional (Aristophanes) or conformist (Horace) souls. Think of Jonathan Swift, a stolid Tory, who preaches a politics of religious intolerance; think of the satirical tirades in the works of the deeply anti-Semitic supporter of the Vichy regime during the Second World War, Louis-Ferdinand Céline. Besides, if it is true that bitter satire can inflict deep wounds, it is equally true that "soft" satire may "humanize" its object, as, for example, with the gentle mockery of the British royal family that is sometimes found in England. We are also familiar with festivals such as the "saturnalia" or the "carnival," which have the function of reinforcing social hierarchies precisely by playfully inverting these hierarchies for a limited period of time.

It seems to me of particular importance in the case of satire to distinguish between its possible objects and to take into account, when judging it, the historical context and the specific circumstances that obtain: *Who is making fun of whom? For what reason? And under what conditions?* On the one hand, there is the biting satirical critique of the great and the powerful, which attacks the king of England, for example, or the Metelli family, or an influential institution like the Catholic Church in the time of Voltaire. Along the same lines, we might think of a satire of some typical representative the currently influential ideology of neoliberalism. This kind of satire may perhaps constitute a stimulus to laudable political actions (although one should not suffer any illusions as to their efficacy). On the other hand, there is also a second form of satire, which takes aim at the poor and the abused, the "little people" and the victims of power, and showers them with additional abuse, taunts, and insults—as the German saying has it, "Wer den Schaden hat, braucht für den Spott nicht zu sorgen" ("the joke is always on the loser"). It is a form of blaming the victim. It was the Inquisitors in Spain who forced their victims to wear a dunce's cap at the stake—the burning of the body while still alive was apparently not enough of a punishment.

Do we poke fun at the Inquisitors, or at the victims of the Inquisition? Friedrich Nietzsche justified his distaste for Cervantes's great novel *Don Quixote* by pointing out that Cervantes always takes the side of the Inquisitors and taunts the victims. Thus he writes: "Cervantes could have fought against the Inquisition, but he preferred to ridicule its victims, i.e., the heretics and idealists of all kinds . . . or what else is he doing but mocking when he tells how the sick man is made the butt of jokes at the Court of the Duke? And do you really think Cervantes would not have laughed even at the heretic at the stake?"[1] We would do well to keep in mind this Nietzschean distinction, between derision of the perpetrators and derision of victims, when it comes to the evaluation of satire. Even the most cutting satire is doubtless a poor weapon against the Inquisitors, but someone who "satirically" mocks the *victim* is no plucky champion of freedom. He should be ashamed of himself—as should anyone who helps to distribute this kind of "satire."

Who may make fun of whom? This is an eminently political matter. One cannot escape responsibility for one's own reactions by excusing laughter as a purely "natural function," for while laughter may have physiological roots, it is in the last analysis a human phenomenon, and as such is part of the never-ending *"éducation sentimentale"* of humankind and of each individual.

The images from Abu Ghraib show naked prisoners, forced to form human pyramids or to go around like dogs on leashes. Funny, no? No. And anyone who laughed at this would be doing something morally and politically offensive. The fact that what we are dealing with here are *images*—that is to say, artificial and arguably even artistic products—is in this case not even a mitigating circumstance but an additional outrage. In Abu Ghraib, there is reason to assume, these pictures were not taken only "after the fact," merely in order to document what had happened. The intention from the beginning was to ridicule and humiliate the prisoners, and photographing them in the process was a conscious and deliberate intensification of this humiliation. The pyramids were formed *so that they could be photographed, and in order to degrade the prisoners still further.*

Newspaper cartoons of the prophet of Islam and the images from Abu Ghraib cannot simply be thrown into the same basket. But is the attempt to think about both together so completely absurd? How valuable is the freedom of speech that eggs a lynch mob on? Even the dire and pedestrian J. S. Mill saw that the answer to this was not a foregone conclusion, but it was a question worth asking. How about the freedom to produce images that incite military planners to use cluster munitions, phosphorus shells, and Hellfire rockets on civilians? Aside from those simply and directly killed and maimed by war in Iraq, Afghanistan, Pakistan, and Yemen, how many more innocent Muslims will pass through the gates of Guantánamo? How many people have disappeared into dark corners like the secret CIA prisons in Poland, Romania, Diego Garcia, and other places about which we know nothing, not even a name? According to statistical inquiries, *half* of all mosques in the UK have been hit by an anti-Islamic attack—*half*.

To insult the king of England in 1750, the bishops of the Catholic Church in the sixteenth century, the president of the World Bank in 1990, or the research director of Microsoft today is *in no way* the same as to attack the beliefs—even the ill-founded beliefs—of poor Muslims against whom war has been being waged for countless years. Is the belief that the life of the prophet is an exemplary life really less "rational" or less well grounded than the opinion that the rich in our societies have "earned" their privileges? Or than the doctrine that there is no alternative to our society's policy of wasting resources on a massive scale? Or the thesis that the extreme concentration of economic power in the hands of a few hundred of the superrich will profit the rest of the world as well?

Philosophers are especially adept at identifying and classifying forms of fallacious argument and inference, and doing so has a tradition stretching back at least to Aristotle's treatise on "sophistical refutations." Within the traditional classification of sophism, there is the *"post hoc ergo propter hoc* fallacy (z comes after y in time, *therefore y* is the cause of z). There is also "affirming the consequent": if my cat Tabitha has already eaten, then her bowl is empty; her bowl is empty; *therefore*, she has already eaten (but what if I have forgotten to give her breakfast?).

I would like therefore to introduce a new category of sophistical argument, the "Tony Blair," which hinges on the construction and insinuation of a false dichotomy: "If you are against the invasion of Iraq, you must fully and unequivocally support Saddam Hussein and accept his crimes." Behind such false dichotomies lies deep fear, and

the invocation of this fear has unfortunately all too often shown itself to be an effective political means to circumvent rationality, prevent understanding, and dampen empathy. One might also call this
the *argumentum hystericum:* "Saddam Hussein Can Hit Us in Forty-
Five Minutes," ran the headline in one of the tabloids, and we know
from documents now in the public domain that Tony Blair and his
spin doctor Alastair Campbell worked energetically and strategically
to produce *exactly* this headline. I implore you, dear reader, not to
commit the following Tony Blair: "If you think that it is a shameful
act to insult Muslims with the publication of artlessly obscene images
of their prophet, you are justifying the murder of journalists." No.

To march together, arm in arm in Paris, with Netanyahu, Cameron, various African dictators, and Arab rulers, even if it is under
the banner of "freedom of speech," and even in the absence of a
Rumsfeld, a Cheney, or a Blair: no, thank you.

14

The Radioactive Wolf, Pieing, and the Goddess Fashion

———⟨∿∿∿⟩———

ESCHATOLOGY IS originally the Christian doctrine of the "last things" (τὰ ἔσχατα), and it took two forms: Theories about "the end of days," that is, the way in which the world as a whole, at any rate as we know it, terminates, and views about the end of *my* days, that is, my death. On the traditional view there are four "last" things: death, judgment, heaven, hell. At my death, according to the orthodox view, I undergo a "particular" judgment at the hands (or perhaps eyes) of god, the final *Judex Fortis et Justus*, who issues a definitive ruling about me and my life, assigning me to unending bliss or eternal torment. Similarly, at some point in time our world as a whole will end with an apocalyptic day of reckoning—a day of General Judgment— after which there will be no more Earth; it will itself "die" and there will exist only heaven and hell. Utopian projects are anticipations of heaven, dystopian of hell. In Christianity death is not the end, but merely the beginning of the end. In 2009 Adrian Ghenie exhibited a painting entitled *Dada Is Dead*. Who exactly—or what—is dead in this painting?

There was disagreement about the meaning of "dada" from the very beginning. One of the people who claimed to have invented the word was Hugo Ball, who opened the Cabaret Voltaire in Zürich in

Adrian Ghenie, *Dada Is Dead*, 2009. Copyright © Adrian Ghenie.

1916. He stated: "In Rumanian Dada means Yes Yes; in French it means hobby-horse; for Germans it is a sign of naive silliness and philoprogenitive connection with the perambulator."[1] It is an "international word"[2] representing the vernacular languages of the original members of the Dadaist group who performed in Cabaret Voltaire: Germans (Hugo Ball, Emmi Ball-Hennings, Richard Huelsenbeck, Walter Serner), a bilingual Alsatian (Hans/Jean Arp), and two multilingual Rumanians (Marcel Janco and Sami Rosenstock/ Tristan Tzara). Sometimes, to be sure the benignly philoprogenitive father with his pram loses interest altogether (Ball *also* says that Dada means: "Ciao, please get off my back; see you some other time!"[3]) or even turns into an (anti)philosopher,[4] driven by "demonic skepticism" *("dämonische Skepsis").*[5] Tristan Tzara, perhaps the most energetic and uncompromising member of the original group,

pronounced some of his early Dadaist manifestos in the persona of
the "anti-philosopher" Monsieur Pyrine. Pyrine *en bon dadaiste* was
tolerant of contradiction and immersed in the ephemera of real
history—hence the prominence of newspapers, dated announce-
ments, and so on, in Dadaist collages—rather than being devoted to
a speculative contemplation of the unchanging;[6] he was a lover of
processes rather than "finished products" and of puppets and masks
rather than a Stoic sage with an unwavering character and moral disposition, and an aspiration to assimilate as much as possible to
god's-eye view of the world and its inhabitants.

An artistic movement that began in neutral Switzerland during the
First World War would be unlikely to be completely without any relation to politics. Once again Hugo Ball provides the most telling
comment: "While we were involved in the cabaret at Spiegelgasse 1
in Zürich, M. Ulyanov-Lenin lived just across the street in Spiegelgasse 6, if I'm not wrong [Ball is wrong; it was Spiegelgasse 14] . . . Is
Dadaism as sign and gesture the opposite [*Gegenspiel*] to Bolshevism? Does Dadaism put forward the utterly quixotic, non-functional
[*zweckwidrig*] and ungraspable side of the world in opposition to destruction and complete calculation?"[7] To say that a certain movement
is a "*Gegenspiel*" to Bolshevism strongly suggests at least that one is
playing the same game, just on the other side.

At the end of the war the center of Dadaism moved from Zurich
to Berlin, where in 1920 the first Dada International Fair was held
in the Gallerie Burchard on Lützow-Platz. Ghenie's painting is a reworking in 2009 of a photo that was taken by the photographer
Hannah Höch of that event. The original photo shows walls covered
with politically charged paintings by Otto Dix and Grosz—most of
which were later destroyed by the Nazis—and with the slogans the
Dadaist liked to employ: "*Dada ist die willentliche Zersetzung der
bürgerlichen Begriffswelt. Dada steht auf der Seite des revolutionären Pro-
letariats*" ("Dada is the willful dissolution of the bourgeois world of
concepts. Dada stands on the side of the revolutionary proletariat");
"*Dilettanten erhebt euch gegen die Kunst*" ("dilettanti, rise up against
art"); and "*Dada ist politisch.*" From other photos of the same event
we know that a further slogan was "*die Kunst ist tot; es lebe die Maschinenkunst Tatlins*" ("Art is dead. Long live the machine-art of

Hannah Höch, First International Dada Fair, Berlin, 1920. Photographer
Unknown. Höch seen in profile, sitting on left.

Tatlin"). Vladimir Tatlin was a Russian avant-garde artist who in the
1920s planned a complexly rotating "tower" that was to be a techno-
logically sophisticated steel monument to the Third Internationale
larger than the Eiffel Tower. So at this point Dada had moved away
from the position apparently assigned to it by Hugo Ball and was
hardly still a form of "opposition" *("Gegenspiel")* to Bolshevism, although one could argue that putting up a sign in a gallery reading
"Dada is political," whatever one might think of it as an artistic gesture, was not much of a political act. Still, it is difficult to see how
admiration for *"Maschinenkunst"* is compatible with devotion to
"nonfunctionality" *("Zweckwidrigkeit").*

   In reworking the photo Ghenie changed the brightly lit and perfectly salubrious-looking room in the Gallerie Burchard into something dark, derelict, and slightly sinister-looking. The chairs and
upholstered benches are gone. The walls are soiled and covered
with empty picture frames and with the mere traces of the pictures
and slogans that used to adorn it and seem to have been removed, or

to have fallen away by themselves in the passage of time. The long horizontal picture frame on the left-center of Ghenie's painting surrounded (in 1920) Otto Dix's painting *45% erwerbsfähig*, which is a satirical image of four men who were grotesquely mutilated in World War I. The second man from the right has no legs and is being pushed in a rudimentary wheelchair; the third man from the right is represented with three overlapping heads, which is presumably a way of trying to depict the tremor or nervous twitching of the head he has acquired as a result of wartime injuries. The point, transmitted by the title of the painting, is that, despite their horrific injuries, they have failed to receive a state pension for disability because they were considered still to be "45 percent able to earn a living." This painting was confiscated by the Nazis, exhibited as an instance of "decadent art" at their great exhibition in Munich in 1937, and then destroyed, so Ghenie in 2009 is in fact painting from a photograph of an earlier painting by Dix that has now disappeared, and trying to represent what that earlier painting would have looked like if . . . If what? If it had not been destroyed in the 1940s? What would have had to have happened to it since then for it to look as it does in Ghenie's painting? *When* exactly is the scene depicted supposed to have taken place? Is it a painting of what Gallerie Burchard *would have looked like* in 1945, had it survived to see the Red Army entering Berlin? Or what it would have looked like in 2009?

If one looks carefully at Ghenie's picture, it looks as if part of the paint in Dix's original had run *(zerfließen)*, dripping out of the frame and down onto the wall below it, forming a stain. This stain seems to form the image of a phantom leg on the wall, that is, *outside* Dix's original frame, as if to replace the limb, which the crippled man in the original painting lost in the war. In fact it looks as if the stain forms the image of a military-style boot. The booted foot does not seamlessly connect with the hip of the crippled soldier, but perhaps that is intended. If one thinks of the two major stands in the philosophy of art as emphasizing, respectively, the production of the beautiful/harmonious/well ordered/symmetrical, and the production of the meaningful/significant/worthwhile, then Dada rejected both of these strands. They were, however, obsessively concerned with the limits of meaning: to say that something "has meaning/

significance," however, is usually to connect it with an assumed framework of reference: "that gesture (for example, 'squaring the figs') has no meaning (here in Britain, although it did have a meaning in medieval Italy)"; "to say 'Equal goes it loose' makes no sense (*in English*, although *"Gleich geht es los"* is a perfectly good sentence in German)"; "to rotate your pawn on a given square (rather than moving it to another square) has no significance *(as a move in chess)*." What, then, is *inside* and what is *outside* any given framework is always of importance. Can things slip, drip, or "run" out of one frame into another (from Dix's painting to Ghenie's)? The wooden frame of Dix's original painting does not now define the visual sense of what is inside it. Rather Ghenie represents Dix's frame as "cutting off" the soldier's leg; actually the soldier "has" a leg in the form of the stain on the gray wall that in Ghenie's painting is as "real" as the rest of his body. Has Ghenie "replaced" the soldier's leg? Completed or finished Dix's painting? It would be an odd form of "completion" that turned a picture of a cripple into a picture of someone with a healthy leg. Is this an imaginary or a real replacement limb? What would affirming either of these alternatives amount to? Or are we to imagine that the very passage of time, the "time" between 1920 and 2009, has by itself caused the paint to run? Natural processes, without any human intervention, seem, then, to have created this image of a boot in the stain. To be more exact, natural processes of dissolution (moisture seeping down the wall of an abandoned room) seem to have produced a stain which we with no special prompting "naturally" see as containing the image of a boot. In that case Ghenie is not responsible for changing Dix's image; he has simply painted what the contingencies of the passage of time have actually done. What actually destroyed Dix's original painting, though, was not "natural processes" or "the passage of time," but the historical event of National Socialism.

In Ghenie's painting the carefree and sociable Dadaists of the original photo are now gone, replaced only by the single wolf who now occupies the center of the painting. Although in reality wolves are relatively gregarious animals who live in well-ordered social groups, in the Western imagination the wolf generally figures as a solitary and savage figure. *Homo homini lupus* does not mean that humans naturally form highly cooperative packs.[8] Rather that beneath the thin veneer of civilization and sociability humans really are still "wolfish" to each other.[9] This wolf looks slightly like one of Man Ray's "solarizations" or a "ray-o-gram." A sliver of intense light from the right illuminates his hind quarters. In contrast to the crippled soldier who is "only" an image, the wolf is "real": he casts a distinct shadow in the painting. There is also an odd white light on his ears and eyes. Conceivably that might be the result of another shaft of light or some play of reflection, but it seems to *emanate* from his ears and eyes; is the wolf perhaps ever so slightly phosphorescent or radioactive? The wolf seems to be in a rather self-satisfied state with a slight grin on its face. Perhaps he is pleased to have done something very naughty and got away with it, or he has been sent to stand in the corner or even told to leave because of the way he has behaved, but thinks it was worth it. How naughty would one have to be to be ejected from a Dada event? Or has he just had a good meal (on the corpses of dead Dadaists) and is smiling with repletion? Or perhaps the wolf is simply the last Dadaist, reduced to his true human nature, radioactive but still standing in the now abandoned gallery, and the picture captures his final moment of reflection and perhaps nostalgia before exiting through the door?

In the mid-1930s Walter Benjamin wrote about the need to see art as teleological:[10] technically specific forms of art often seemed to be trying to achieve with great difficulty through "traditional" means effects that would "come naturally" when later techniques were developed. Thus much of late eighteenth-century painting seems to be trying to attain effects that would later come "of themselves" with photography. Dadaism, he claimed, was in one of its aspects the attempt to anticipate film. So the tremor of Dix's war-cripple would be easy to capture with a cine-camera. When Benjamin wrote "every epoch dreams the following epoch,"[11] he did not specify whether the ensuing reality would be a utopia or dystopia, heaven or hell. Part of the mechanism that holds history, especially the history of art, together is the series of pretensions—references to, anticipations of, expectations about the future—and retentions—memories and associations form the past. Man Ray's solarizations and ray-o-grams cannot now, in retrospect, fail to make us think of Hiroshima or Chernobyl, although we know that radiation does not actually make

(Left) Publicity postcard of Hugo Ball in Cubistic Costume to promote the programme of the Cabaret Voltaire in Zürich, 1916. Photographer unknown. Image reproduction courtesy of Wikimedia Commons. (Right) Prisoner being tortured with electrical shocking devices at Abu Ghraib Prison, 2003. Photo by The United States Armed Forces.

humans visibly glow. Equally Hugo Ball's Dada-costume of 1916 must now be seen as a proleptic reference to that great monument of U.S. foreign policy in the early twenty-first century: Abu Ghraib.[12]

The most energetic and uncompromising early Dadaist, Tristan Tzara, stated very baldly *"Dada ne signifie rien."* It is not, however, that easy to imagine anything that fails to signify *at all?* "Meaning" for conscious creatures like us, is almost inescapable; we are virtually condemned to make things make one kind of sense or another. The real question is not whether or not we can find or invent some categories and a framework of reference into which we can fit any given phenomenon we encounter, but whether there is one final set of categories or framework within which we can locate everything, and particularly whether there is one antecedently given set of such categories.

Imagine that I sit down to play chess and instead of making a recognized move, I extend my index finger and rotate it gently in the air in a circular pattern. My opponent might well say, "That gesture has no meaning" and, of course, he or she would be perfectly correct, if it was completely clear that the universe of significance was restricted to "possible chess moves." If, however, the room was very warm and my opponent was seated next to a powerful fan, he or she might take me up on my attempt to change the context and see that my gesture was not intended as a part of the game, but as encouragement to turn the fan on so as to cool the room. So it did signify something, just not anything recognizable as a move in chess. The rules of chess, after all, do not exhaust the realm of that which has meaning. By changing the context we can also see how what means nothing in chess can still have significance—if one wishes to put it this way—"in another realm." Sometimes rule-governed domains are embedded in yet larger rule-governed domains: the individual game of chess may be part of a tournament in which there are strict regulations about how games are played. The tournament itself may be governed by rules set down by a chess federation, which, in turn, may be a corporation subject to legal regulation—different regulations in different jurisdictions—and so forth. The legal system itself may operate in a wider domain of institutionalized and nonformalized everyday gestures, of which my rotation of the index finger might or might not be part. How would we know that such a gesture was or was not part of a given "domain" or that it is right even to speak of a "system" here? The gesture of rotating my finger is not, arguably, part of any existing system of meaning that I activate; it is something I more or less make up, assuming you too will be able to rise to the occasion and "see" the point of what I have done. How I do this, and how you do whatever it is that you do in this situation, is exceedingly obscure, but that is a separate issue.

Must we simply accept that there are different systems of significance—the "universe" of chess, the British legal system, the DIN-system for referring to standard sizes of paper, the Mesopotamian division of the year into a series of twelve months, the set of hand gestures people use to point to things in the environment or to encourage others to perform certain actions (for example, the "stop" gesture or "come on: continue" gesture used by traffic controllers). Some of these may be formal and more or less closed systems, but many of them are open and constantly evolving (hand gestures). In any case, they stand in at best contingent relations with each other, and may not even overlap, for example, the rules of chess and the rules for determining paper size so that one can almost always change the notion of "significance" by shifting the context, or must one assume, as many philosophers, and virtually all Christian theologians, do that this process of changing the context cannot continue *ad libitum:* there is and *must be,* a final framework that is, as it were, the Game of Games, the "absolute" Game we are and *must be* playing, a Game about which the Christian theologian will be happy to give you much more information of a highly detailed kind.

To put this another way, Platonists, Christians, Kantians, and other believers in the Great Game hold that that "nothing can signify nothing at all (because we can always invent a way of accommodating anything as meaningful)" implies "there is one final framework of meaning (which accommodates everything)." This is, however, a bit like saying "no man lacks a (legal) father (because we can always assign him one)" implies "there is one father of all men."

If, then, there is no absolutely final framework of meaning—no god, no fixed and definite structure of "consciousness," no "logic of language"—then "the realm of" meaning/significance, *and our ability to violate* any given structure of meaning/significance may both have radically indeterminate boundaries. What we "can" or "could not" mean will become a matter of having a more or a less fertile imagination, or of our inventiveness, not of "logic." Failing to obey given rules, breaking the code, can be a way of bringing to our attention something, for instance, that our forms of "intelligibility" are more arbitrary than we usually take them to be or even that they are severely limited and deficient. Tzara's *"Dada ne signifie rien,"* then, need not refer to a mere absence—it is not a *nihil privativum*—but it might approach Huelsenbeck's view, which would have it that Dada is "the signifying nothing in which Nothing means something" *("das bedeutende Nichts an dem Nichts etwas bedeutet").*[13] Dada's "nothing" is a *nihil significativum,* as when the accused in a court case fails to enter a plea. That is, the fact that something, say, an event, a gesture, or a "work of art" does *not* signify in some particular way can itself be significant. Thus, if my answer to your question fails to make grammatical (or some other kind of) sense that fact can be significant: I might be confused, a foreign speaker of your language, or trying to make fun of you. If one presupposes a fixed context within which "signify" is taken in an antecedently narrowly specified sense, then it is easy to imagine all kinds of things that "do not signify anything" in that context and in *that* sense. The way we live will determine our sense of what is "intelligible" and if our way of life is sufficiently rigid, unreflective, and conformist, it will be all the more difficult to find any deviancy even intelligible. That Dada means nothing to any of us might reflect badly not on *it*, but rather on *our life* and our conception of significance. So Tzara's *"Dada ne signifie rien"* can be seen to be complementary to the 1920s slogans *"Dada ist die willentliche Zersetzung der bürgerlichen Begriffswelt"* and *"Dada ist politisch."* Dada does not mean anything because it has no place in that bourgeois world and fits into none of its categories; it becomes political to the extent to which it becomes a project of deliberate dissolution. This also makes clear to what extent there is the possibility for collaboration between Dadaism and Marx-inspired political movements, but also the limits of such collaboration. Both Dada and Marxism are committed to the dissolution of the world of bourgeois concepts, but all good Marxists are also committed to "dialectical thinking" and dialecticians, whatever else one might think of them, are rationalists of a kind; one might even say "hyper-rationalists" in that they can find a kind of "logic" (eventually) even in that which seems random, chaotic, inexplicably painful. "Rationalism" in any of its forms is not one of Dada's characteristic stances.

What would it then mean that Dada was dead? Its project of "deliberate dissolution" could be thought to have become historically irrelevant. In Berlin in 1920 the lay-figure hanging facedown from the ceiling has on the uniform of a Prussian military officer but the head of a pig. This work was entitled *Prussian Archangel (Preussischer Erzengel)*, and he held in his hand a paper on which was written, *"Vom Himmel hoch da komm' ich her."* In the original 1920s installation he was represented as being a specter *from the recent past*, but no longer really able to intimidate the members of the public; a figure, at best, of ridicule. He is certainly dead, but part of the point of representing him in 1920 by such a lay-figure was that in one sense he was never really alive. The Prussian officer only ever had such power and authority as he was endowed with by the human collective imagination. Heine once said about Kant that he tried to put a Prussian gendarme inside the breast of each individual human, and so one could also imagine this painting being entitled *Kant Is Dead:* the empirical self with all its inclinations *(Neigungen)* is still there in the form of the wolf, but he is toxic, irradiated, and thus moribund. If the Kantian raised his eyes to try to behold the starry heavens above, he would behold the pigheaded Prussian Archangel, the closest earthly approximation to the ideally Rational Will. By 2009 the public has disappeared, the works of art on the wall, too, are gone or have run and smeared—although the process of smearing has created a new image in the form of the phantom leg—and if *per impossibile* the officer, who is after all only a stuffed doll, ever tried to exercise his imaginary jurisdiction on the radioactive wolf, he would get nowhere.

In another of Ghenie's paintings from about the same time (2008), *Nickelodeon,* we seem to be in roughly the same kind of visual world as *Dada Is Dead.* In both cases we see the claustrophobically enclosed interior of a shabby and ruinous room painted in somber tones of dark brown and gray with a strong sense of three-dimensionality. If anything, in *Nickelodeon* there is an even greater sense of enclosure within a room of phosphorescently rotting wood. The painting is a juxtaposition of two canvasses of 210-cm-by-120-cm positioned side by side, but it is not a traditional diptych because the image spreads continuously over both canvasses and does so in such a way that the vertical juncture between the two panels is still visible. The perspective reinforced by the strong converging lines of the floorboards (and, on the left side, what seems to be a pile of long sections of iron [?] railway tracks) draws both halves of the painting together and also pulls the viewer's eye very powerfully *into* the frame.

Nickelodeon is associated with a series of works Ghenie did on pie fights, especially cinematic-style pie fights of the kind in which Laurel and Hardy specialized. The Nickelodeon was a very early form of cinema, a *Theatrum Mundi* on the cheap for the very early twentieth century. The painting shows a group of men who have just visited a Nickelodeon. The men are dressed in overcoats of a style more characteristic of the middle than of the very beginning of the twentieth century; some of them, a small group on the right, are simply standing together, perhaps talking; others, the figures in the

Adrian Ghenie, *Nickelodeon*, 2008, Copyright © Adrian Ghenie.

center and on the left are beginning to walk forward and slightly to
the left, following the lines made by the cracks between the floorboards. None of the faces of the men are clearly visible; some still
have pie on their faces. Remnants of pie surround the heads of the
two figures on the extreme left, giving almost the impression of a
halo. The face of the figure in the exact center of the painting—the
visible joint between the two panels runs right through his shoulder—
is a white blank. Presumably his face covered with pie, and both of
his hands are raised to the area of his mouth and chin as if the pie were
a mask he was desperately trying to pull off. A pie you have thrown
that covers my face *is* a kind of mask, albeit one you impose on me,
not one I have chosen to put on.

   The Dadaists were in any case very keen on puppets, dummies,
lay-figures, and masks.[14] These pie-masked faces, then, belong with
the *Prussian Archangel* exhibited in Gallerie Burchard in 1920. Puppets and dummies are imaginary others, allowing for a play along
the boundary of the living and that which is not (really) living, just
as a mask can be an imaginary self. The poet Aeschylus is "not there"
anymore, when he puts on the mask, and steps onto the stage. In his
place stands Clytemnestra, who, however, is in another sense not "really" alive. The possibility of this play along the border between

living and not-living, present and not-present, real and not-fully-real traditionally made philosophers deeply suspicious, and the possibility of deception—of hiding one's "real" self from others—that the mask presented was construed as a deep moral danger. The active fascination with and positive valuation of the straddling of these boundaries was one way in which the Dadaist is an "anti-philosopher." Even worse than the possibility that a mask may hide from others my true self is the thought that I might in some way come to fail to have a "real self." Nietzsche's conception of the radically antitraditional philosopher as a person who loved to change masks continuously is the precursor in this of Dada's M. Pyrine, the anti-philosopher. Perhaps Nietzsche suggests the "real" philosopher does not have any final beliefs of his own at all, just as mask adopted for some occasion and *beneath* the mask there was no "real" face, rather only a further mask. And beneath that mask yet another, all the way as far as one might wish to go. Even to speak of a "mask," then, was in one sense a mistake because the term made sense only if "mask" could be contrasted with "real face beneath the mask."

One can trace a similar suspicion of traditional philosophical views about masks and faces back to another figure who lived in the Zurich in the 1830s. Georg Büchner was on the run from the police (for having founded a revolutionary group in Hessen) and also lived for a short time in the same street that in 1916 hosted Lenin and the Cabaret Voltaire. Büchner was the author of *Dantons Tod*, and it was while living in the Spiegelgasse that he worked on the unfinished *Wozzek*. In a scene from *Dantons Tod*, Danton's supporter Lacroix reports on a meeting of the convention he has just attended.

LACROIX: "Und Collot schrie wie besessen, man müsse die Masken abreißen."

This is the traditional view that people can keep certain thoughts, intentions, and feelings locked into their hearts. God, the divine judge, might see this, their "real face," even though they put on a mask when dealing with others. The task of the convention is to tear off these masks and reveal the reality beneath it. Danton's comment.

DANTON: "Da werden die Gesichter mitgehen"

has the implication that the very idea of a sharp distinction between mask and face is inappropriate. If one wears the mask for long enough it becomes reality, and finally what human reality could there be but one shaped by the historical succession of forces of various kinds imposing different "masks," including "masks" endowed with moderate amounts of self-regulation and transformation?

The central figure in Ghenie's *Nickelodeon* is perhaps not so much trying to wipe the pie off as frantically trying to palpitate his face to see if it still exists, and, if so, what its nature is. He is "spectral" because although the upper part of his body is fully realized, the bottom part of his body seems to peter out. The other figures seem firmly planted on the floor, but his legs and feet are transparent—like the "phantom limb" of the cripple in *Dada Is Dead*. In addition, his upper torso seems to be *behind* the two figures on either side of him, and yet his phantom feet are just barely visible, visible enough, though, for us to see that they are in *front* of the plane on which the two figures on either side of him stand. That suggests that he both is *and is not* part of the world of this antechamber. There is something about all the other men, and about the grouping, that immediately makes one think that they are Party members (of what Party one does not know), members of a delegation, plainclothes policemen, or security agents. The Nickelodeon itself, that is, the room in which the audience sits for the performance, is not visible, but in the back depths of the painting in the upper-right-hand side of the right panel, there is something that seems to be a door at the end of a corridor, and that is presumably the entrance to the auditorium itself. The men have just emerged after a performance from this room into a kind of foyer or antechamber. Why would *these* men have pie on their faces?

One possibility is that they have just come from a meeting in the Nickelodeon that has degenerated into a pie-throwing contest. Or are they members of the *Securitate* who have come to close or censor a performance and have been attacked by the members of the audience? This would explain why the men in this group do not, apart from the spectral central figure, seem terribly upset or disaccommodated by what has just happened. This, after all, may be part of their métier, and they also may know that they can return the next day or the day after that, and then the joke will very definitely not be on them but on those who threw the pies at them. Where, though, if this is the scenario, would the audience have acquired the pies in the first place? Is it customary to go to a performance with a proleptic pie in case one feels the need of it? Did they know they might be raided by the *Securitate?* A second possibility is that there was a live theatrical performance going on in the Nickelodeon, but that this performance has taken a Dadaist turn. The Dadaists, after all, were some of the first to reject the idea of a closed and finished "work of art" and of a sharp distinction between performers and audience, just as they wished to destroy the distinctions between art and politics, everyday life and art, poetry and painting, sense and nonsense. All of these ideas were part of the "bürgerliche Begriffswelt" Dada was out to destroy. Dada "performances" were events that did not usually have and follow detailed scripts but evolved unpredictably as they were taking place.[15] These performances could be seen as unique organic processes and any images formed were formed in the way in which the phantom leg in Ghenie's version of *45% erwerbsfähig* seems to have been formed, by the unintended action of natural processes. Usually, too, the audience took an active part in making the performance the work of art it was. The "public" shown in Höch's 1920 photo are not anonymous members of a "general public" but individual recognizable Dadaists: the audience *was* the artists. At one of the very first Dada-events in Zurich in 1916, Richard Huelsenbeck read a manifesto that contained the words: "I hope you shall not suffer any bodily harm, but what I have to say to you will hit you like a bullet" (*"Ich hoffe, daß Ihnen kein körperliches Unheil widerfahren wird, aber was wir Ihnen jetzt zu sagen haben, wird Sie wie eine Kugel treffen"*).[16] So perhaps what has happened here is that the "actors" in the performance have at one point replaced a statement that will hit the audience like a bullet with pies, and have thrown them at the members of the audience, who are the people we see exiting in Ghenie's painting.

A "nickelodeon," however, was not simply a theater, but a *cinema* showing short *films.* So a further possibility is that Laurel and Hardy have thrown pies at the audience, who are seen emerging from the Nickelodeon. Something, that is, has happened to the boundary between the imaginary—what is represented in the film on the screen (Laurel and Hardy throwing pies at each other)—and the "real" men depicted in Ghenie's painting, who presumably constituted the audience. Some of the pies thrown by the actors on screen in a cinema have flown out of the film into the audience and hit some of the people watching in the face. To be sure, to speak of the "real" audience or the "real" men in the painting might seem to be highly peculiar, because, although they are "real," as it were, relative to figures on the cinema screen, they are also figures in a painting (by Ghenie), and so we might think of them as "imaginary" relative to the people around me in the gallery in which I view Ghenie's painting—each of whom presumably has a National Insurance Numbers, valid credit cards, and a unique spatiotemporal physical location.

The *Theatrum mundi* was supposed to give us distance from the events of the human world and allow people to see it as a whole and thereby form an overall judgment about it. Benjamin thought that the aestheticization of politics was a characteristic feature of fascism—presumably be was thinking of phenomena like the Nuremberg Rallies—and that the appropriate response to this was the politicization of art. Whatever exactly he meant by this, he presumably thought it compatible with the application of *some* aesthetic categories to politics and history, as Marx does when he remarks at the beginning of *The 18th Brumaire* that events in history generally happen twice, the first time as tragedy, the second as farce. Here the judgment seems to be that history is a comedy of a sort; not in the sense in which Dante's poem is a "comedy"—ending in a vision of saved human souls in paradise—but a distinctly brutal and absurdist farce in which most of the participants end up with pie on their faces. If Ball was right that the two main alternatives presented by the dissolution of the old bourgeois world in World War I were Bolshevism and Dada, then this painting would suggest that Dada is perhaps not dead, but rather that it should be seen to have emerged victorious over its only serious rival.

One might consider "pieing" (as it is now apparently called) a quintessentially neo-Dadaist gesture because it hovers uncertainly between the real and the merely symbolic—no organic damage or bodily harm is done to those who are pied, but, presumably, it is uncomfortable and embarrassing—and between the ludic and the serious—what might be a joke for those watching could easily be serious for those "pied." People who have been pied, and are widely perceived to "deserve" it—who finally makes this judgment?—like Bill Gates (1998) or Rupert Murdoch (2011), suffer a moment of indignity, but their power to continue to do evil is not seriously reduced, and many of the most active agents of evil, high-ranking agents of security forces, are so well protected as rarely to be possible targets for this kind of action. Finally, pieing will work only on individuals, so corporations, banks, law firms, and investment companies are immune, except through actions directed at representative persons, but pieing the chairman of the board may also backfire in that it can contribute to fostering the illusion that individuals are really responsible for what corporations do. Gates and Murdoch would perhaps like us to believe that they are the very embodiments of their respective corporations and indispensable to the success of the nefarious project of getting monopolistic control of all information and human opinion, but Microsoft and Fox News could easily continue to be forces of darkness without these individuals. Corporations, after all, are really very much like individual persons or even groups of persons are rather than structures of a very different kind,[17] and judgments about their systemic effects do not reduce to evaluations of any of the individuals of which they are composed.

Although the painting is not a diptych, for the reasons mentioned above, the visible crease down the center does raise the possibility that it was supposed to be imagined to swivel on this axis and fold over in the middle. The question would then be which way it was intended to be folded? Since this central juncture runs directly through the spectral figure in the center, if the painting is to be folded, it will pivot on him, but which way? Should the two sides pivot backward, so that the painted surface was on the outside? Then one would have a continuous wraparound scene, perhaps indicative of a panoramic view of the scene or even of recent history. There would, of course, be a vertical strip down the center. This strip would be twice as wide as the depth of the framework on which the canvas is stretched; it would run directly through the left shoulder of the spectral figure in the center, and, for all we know, it might be unpainted. He might then be thought to be a man torn apart by history. If the painting is folded in this way, one might be tempted to open it in the way one opens a book, but would then find that the inside was blank (because one would see the unpainted side of the canvas), like a prayer book with a highly ornamented cover but no text. Or perhaps the painting was supposed to be bent in the opposite way, with the painted side on the inside as if it were precious content protected by a simple canvas cover (the "back" of the painting we see). Here the suggestion would rather be that the painting was a depiction of esoteric knowledge or of a nightmare in the soul of the spectral figure. Perhaps one is supposed to think of the painting as double-jointed: to be opened or closed in either/both direction(s).

Dada Is Dead was a painting based on a historically extant photograph of a (destroyed) painting (which itself represented an imaginary street scene). *Nickelodeon* represents a parallel nested set of different frameworks of reference in which the distinction between image/appearance and reality shifts, and eventually becomes problematic in a number of ways: Ghenie's painted image invites us to imagine a group of men from the 1950s who are exiting a turn-of-the-twentieth-century Nickelodeon or to imagine a (real) group of people who have real pie on their faces that was thrown at them by the imaginary figures on a motion picture screen and a spectral figure without real feet and who exists on a different spatial plane apparently standing among them. What would have been serious and unpleasant in reality (pie in the face) becomes comedy by being presented on film, but then reverts to something serious if the event depicted in Ghenie's painting had actually happened. But it is imaginary.

Much of the interpretation of these two paintings by Ghenie has depended on taking the title of each painting particularly seriously. Using titles in this way, one might think, is problematic. Titles have two distinct origins, and there are two different traditions for thinking about them. In one such tradition titles are construed as completely extrinsic to the work itself. Thus, in the ancient world most works had no titles; they did not need them. For an Athenian the image in the Parthenon did not need a small attached plaque reading *Athena*. The title becomes necessary when the original context is lost—when it is possible to ask about the statue of the young woman with helmet, owl, and shield: "Who is this?" Or if one is running a library or a museum and must have a catalogue. The title, then, is merely a handle, and often a handle assigned after the fact by someone who had no connection with the original process by which the work was produced; it was thus irrelevant to a proper appreciation of the work. This strand gets further support from the view that the "proper" aesthetic reaction must be one to "the work itself" that does not appeal to "extrinsic" or "collateral" information. If the work must stand on its own, by itself without external support, one would be foolish to use a title to interpret the work. The second tradition comes from forms of human self-aggrandizement, especially perhaps on funereal monuments. If I want to be remembered, I may have an elaborate tomb made to draw attention to myself, but the effect will be lost if I do not have my name inscribed on the tomb. Here the "title"—for example, "I am a bronze maiden and have been placed on the tomb of Midas" or simply "CAIUS FUI"—is an essential part of the intention. Or a craftsman may sign a work *"Antiochus fecit"* (for instance, on a pot). Or a political figure may claim credit for something *"M. Agrippa fecit"* (on the Pantheon). None of these is a "title" in the modern sense, but the Latin word from which "title" is derived *(titulus)* means any kind of notice or board, bits of paper, or inscription conveying information.[18] Eventually, the term comes to be used for "information" about the work in what comes to be taken to be the preeminent sense, namely, what its name is. That is, once the viewer begins to need further information about the work, because the context of interpretation is for whatever reason no longer clear, works of art come to seem to need "interpretations." This is likely to be increasingly the case, the more art becomes "autonomous," that is, once the painter is not painting the altarpiece in the Church of the Virgin (where a painting of a young woman in blue with a halo and child underneath a white-bearded old man and a dove does not require the provision of any extra information in the form of a *titulus*). Once paintings become things to exhibit in galleries and the range of techniques, subjects, genres, associations, and so on, becomes unsurveyably large, the question of how the work is to be read becomes an important one. Assigning a "title," then, seems an easy way to convey the necessary information, and determine the direction in which the search for meaning proceeds. Who, however, gets to assign the title? Why will the first painting I considered in this chapter continue to be called *Dada Is Dead* rather than (my suggestion) *Kant Is Dead?* When the National Socialists confiscated Dix's painting, they assigned it additional *tituli* ("degenerate art," "insult to the German military"), attempting thus to control the direction of interpretation. The fact that they failed to succeed in their project, because, apparently, too many of the visitors to the exhibit emerged *liking*, rather than abominating, the works of art exhibited, is not directly relevant to the question of the status of titles. When artists gain a sufficient status and autonomy to do so, they can begin to assert themselves by signing their name to their product and then also eventually they can try to channel the interpretations that will be given their work by assigning titles themselves. Once the institution of the "title" exists and an artist can choose one title rather than another, it becomes possible *not* to assign a title—and this may be significant—or one can decide to assign a misleading, whimsical, or contingent, or even random title. This world of almost infinitely malleable meanings is the one we live in, and we need all the help in interpreting it we can get.

Is the title of Chantal Joffe's 2004 painting *Black Camisole* as significant as *Dada Is Dead* or *Nickelodeon?* Why name an image after an item of clothing? This would, of course, make perfect sense in a catalogue or fashion magazine where types of objects for potential purchase are displayed and it becomes important to be able to refer discriminatingly to one specific type among a large stock rather than another. This might be considered a kind of self-assertion on the part of the commodity in question. The size alone (300-cm-by-120 cm) suggests self-inflation. The fact that the painting is done on board rather than on canvas, the positioning of the sitter, and the relative lack of fine-grained texturing contribute to making it resemble a huge playing card, or an entry in a glossy catalogue that has been blown up into a poster for use on hoardings. We know nothing about the sitter's history, and the painting gives few clues as to the immediate context; it does not seem to be considered relevant. Unless her name is "Black Camisole," for us she has no name. Perhaps she is a fashion or advertising model with the *nom de guerre* "(Miss) Black Camisole."

Chantal Joffe, *Black Camisole*, 2004. Courtesy of
the Artist and Victoria Miro, London. Copyright
© Chantal Joffe.

Since the sixteenth century one of the familiar genres of painting was the depiction of a reclining or semi-reclining (female) nude, the subject originally identified as "goddesses," then (eventually) as courtesans. The women are depicted stretched out on greenery or luxurious-looking beds or couches.[19] The middle of the nineteenth century had its nude images of *grandes horizontales,* of which "Olympia" was perhaps the most noticeable instance.[20] In the twentieth century nudes flowed down staircases (Duchamp) or resolved themselves into multiple angular planes (Picasso). This painting belongs to a historical period (2003) in which the human figure has in general reintegrated itself. The female figure in this painting is not fully nude; she is distinctly upright with neither "nature" nor a couch in sight. In fact the painting seems to go out of its way to emphasize the vertical. It is itself 300 centimeters high and only 120 centimeters wide, and even the background of the painting is a series of striking vertical lines on a simple relatively neutral bluish-gray surface, presumably either the joins between panels or planks, or conceivably a wallpaper of visibly marked by a series of parallels.

The body of the young woman in the painting is disposed so that it seems to fill the space entirely with the top of her head just grazing the frame. She is wearing stylish shoes with very high heels; the frame cuts off the very tip of the right shoe. Even without the shoes, if she were to stand up, her head would protrude out of the top of the painting; the frame can just about contain her. There is a latent energy here, and the formatting is such as would befit a figure of some authority. Altogether we seem closer to the world of Velazquez's painting of the Pope than Titian's Venus, and the young woman in this painting does not need the props of the Pope—jeweled rings, velvet cap, elaborate, thronelike chair—to support that authority. Unless, of course, the authority is given or enhanced by the black camisole she wears. The black camisole suits this blonde sitter, but it is also perhaps the analogue of the flat black cap that judges used to need to put on before pronouncing capital sentences.

The sitter is not depicted as absorbed in any physical activity that holds her attention, such as pouring out tea, writing a letter, or even talking with a companion—she sits up straight with her legs confidently crossed; the insouciance of the crossed legs indicating that she is at her ease and that immediate action is not envisaged, but she is also not absorbed in a reverie or a moment of introspection. She does not have the vacant look of the barmaid at the Folies Bergères in the famous painting by Manet where part of the point would seem to be the extreme contrast between the publicity of the situation, a public bar, and the privacy of the activity. Nor is she depicted with a lot of empty space around her, as if to emphasize isolation. This sitter is half turned away from the viewer with her head tilted back and her nose in the air so that one sees only one eye under the thick black line of an arched eyebrow—the original meaning of "supercilious." Her mouth has no traces of a smile or even a relaxed neutral expression but is distinctly turned down at both ends, and the throat seems tense. Her demeanor is one of slightly aloof and perhaps slightly disapproving detachment from the situation: she is viewing and judging something or someone, not being observed and evaluated.

The garment the young woman is wearing, a camisole, is a halfway house: not properly an outer garment, but also not really a *dessous*. It is in this respect like the "boudoir" in a traditionally furnished set of rooms, which has been described as a space *"situé entre le salon, ou règne la conversation, et la chambre où règne l'amour, le boudoir symbolise le lieu d'union de la philosophie et l'érotique."*[21] The woman would then be, as it were, dressed for philosophical reflection and judgment, and although no one else is visible, she also does not seem to be alone. The special piquancy of the transitional "boudoir" derived from its ambiguous status, straddling the sharp division often made in bourgeois societies between public and private. In our Western societies this luminal position has lost much of its ability to energize and focus attention. The deep décolletage half revealing one breast has in itself so special significance in our post-prurient world and the fact that the position of the sitter reveals much of the bottom half of her very prominent thigh also seems just one more natural fact of no particular consequence. Or is it significant that the left thigh of the sitter is so prominent and fleshy, and is that of particular importance in view of the generally judgmental attitude of the sitter? What, or whom, in any case is she judging so condescendingly? Given her expression and general posture, the judgment does not seem likely to fall out in his (or her or their) favor. Or is the presumed irrelevancy of her seminudity itself a mere appearance; is she perhaps not so much condescending as wary or even apprehensive?

Modern fashion might seem to be a realization of the Dadaist appeal for a breaking down of the "bourgeois" distinction between art and everyday life. After all, the carefully designed and aesthetically vetted items of clothing are intended not to stand in museums as objects of disinterested contemplation, but to be worn by people going about their everyday business. It is perhaps also significant that the camisole as depicted does not conform to the usual structure of such garments. The upper portion of a camisole is more usually in the form of the upper half of the letter *h*, sometimes, to be sure, of a slightly distended *H*, that is, the top is horizontal (or slightly rounded) with two vertical straps over the shoulders. Here the straps are very thick and the top of the camisole is in the shape of a very deep U or V, extending almost down to the navel. The fabric also seems to be oddly bunched near the bottom, rather than hanging crisply or falling naturally. Has the sitter put the garment on negligently? Is she on break between camera shoots? Has she been interrupted while doing something else that has disarranged her camisole? What was that she was doing? Is, perhaps, this camisole supposed to lie like that?

The woman in the black camisole seems to be a denizen of the "flat world" envisaged by Thomas Friedman,[22] without three-dimensionality, nooks and crannies, *chiaroscuro*, the visible signs (or the results) of the passage of time, or, ideally, human inertia, cultural difference, or idiosyncrasy. The same fashion items are actually mass-produced literally anywhere—China, Malaysia, Latin America, Morocco—and given a pseudo-artisanal character by the addition of a designer label. In this world history and ideology are said to be at an end;[23] "one-dimensional man" has become the self-evident only reality;[24] there is a uniform final framework of signification that is to replace history, philosophy, and politics: the consumerist society of late liberal capitalism and its aesthetic subdivision—fashion.

A painting *about* fashion (in whatever sense a painting can be about fashion) is not necessarily in itself an instance of fashion, any more than a painting about an anatomy lesson is an instance of medical instruction or a painting of a fortress is a fortress. On the other hand, in a genuinely flat world, the distinction between painting and fashion can become etiolated. For those at home in the flat world, this is no objection.

Is the woman in the black camisole a competitor in a game, and subject to the rules and forms of judgment associated with the game? What game is that? Glamour, beauty, marketability? If she is a model, are we supposed to be evaluating her? ("She is good at that; she is glamorous; she shows that outfit to its best advantage; that outfit shows her to her best advantage.") Or are we supposed to be evaluating ourselves, taking her as the standard ("Am I as thin/elegant/self-possessed/blonde as she is?") Or is she herself a judge, finding our dress sense wanting? Or a second-order commentator on the game and its rules? Or all three at once? Is she merely subject to rules others impose in the way in which those pied must, at least for a moment, carry around the mask and identity imposed on them by those who throw the pies? Or does she enforce pregiven rules herself? If so, "pregiven" by whom or by what, by what person of what set of systemic imperatives? Does she make (some of) the rules up herself, or does she act *ad libitum* with no reference to rules, engaging in a free and spontaneous act of evaluation? If she does all of these things at once, is it still in any *interesting* sense a "game," and not, for instance, "human life"? Does it matter whether—whatever she is *actually* doing—she *thinks* she is enforcing pregiven rules or making them up (or acting ad hoc)? If it does matter, for *what* does it matter? If she thinks she is enforcing her *own* rules, but is mistaken about that, does that matter?

"X (say, Romanticism, the Temperance Movement, the Third Way, Bi-metallism) is dead" can mean at least two distinct things. It can mean that X was tried out in a serious way and definitely failed or that X has become irrelevant. Both can arguably be asserted of the original Dadaist movement. The "bourgeois conceptual world," with its strict dichotomies, hierarchies, and distinctions it wished to dissipate, has disappeared to be replaced by an altogether "flatter" world in which certain economic imperatives have significantly wider and more uniform sway. From the perspective of theorists like Adorno, the "flat world" would seem to be nothing new, but merely a fuller and more consistent realization of tendencies that made the old world of the bourgeoisie reprehensible. The dissolution of that bourgeois world was clearly *not* the result of Dada's intervention, but of wider social, economic, military, and political forces. So to the extent to which Dada was committed to being the major *means* for that transformation, it failed, and it is hard for us to imagine circumstances under which it *could have* succeeded. Even a Dada-revised and Dada-expanded "art" could not have *that* power. So when Huelsenbeck announced in his 1916 manifesto, "We wish to change the world with Nothing . . . We wish to bring the war to an end with Nothing" (*"Wir wollen die Welt mit Nichts verändern . . . wir wollen den Krieg mit Nichts zu Ende bringen"*)[25] this is a sensible project only if the *"Nichts"* involved means something significantly more than collages, sound-poems, and Dadaist "events." Even throwing pies is no effective alternative to or form of resistance against the armaments of World War I and the unspeakable horrors of the Internet. On the other hand, is concern for that which is *not* part of the flat present really so obviously irrelevant or so obviously doomed to complete impotence?

15

What Time Is It?

—✿—

POEM

WHEN I DECIDED to write something on Bernard Williams and Pindar, focusing on Pindar's *Fourth Pythian*, I discovered that although I still had a battered old copy of the Snell edition (printed in 1964 in the then DDR and acquired in Freiburg in 1967), I did not have any commentaries. Fortunately, I recalled that the Cambridge University Press had just initiated a series of reprints of out-of-copyright works, mostly from the nineteenth century, reproduced from clean copies in the University Library, so I went to the University Press Bookshop and bought a copy of Basil Gildersleeve's edition (text and commentary) of the Olympians and Pythians (originally published in 1885). I had vaguely known of Gildersleeve as an important nineteenth-century classicist, but associated him with a Latin school grammar that was still occasionally referred to in the 1960s. Reading Gildersleeve's Introductory Essay on Pindar, however, I was slightly surprised to find his discussion taking as its point of departure Pindar's relation to the Hellenic "national cause" and his "patriotism." Pindar was a Theban aristocrat and during his lifetime

253

the city of Thebes "medized"; that is, they took the Persian side in
the struggle between the Persian Empire and the coalition of city-
states led by Athens and Sparta that eventually defeated the Persians
at Marathon, Salamis and Plataia. Nationalism was a late nineteenth-
century obsession, but Gildersleeve's concern with it in this context
still seemed misplaced and excessive. One part of his discussion struck
me particularly. "It was no treason," Gildersleeve wrote, "to medize
before there was a Greece, and the Greece that came out of the Persian war was a very different thing from the cantons that ranged
themselves on this side and the other of a quarrel which, we may be
sure, bore another aspect to those who stood aloof from it than it
wears in the eyes of moderns, who have all learned to be Hellenic
patriots. A little experience of a losing side might aid historical vision." The first of these sentences seemed overcharged with content
expressed in dangling subordinate clauses and its clumsily convo-
luted structure strongly suggested to me that the writer had something very pressing on his mind that he was not able or willing to
express in a simple and direct way. Gildersleeve, I then learned,
had been born in Charleston, South Carolina, in 1831, taken a PhD
in Göttingen in 1853, and was the first properly trained North American classicist. He also fought with the Confederate forces in the U.S.
Civil War and was seriously wounded; toward the end of his life he
became a highly articulate defender of the "lost cause" of the American South. He thus lived through a period in which a political
struggle about "states' rights," an issue on which the Southern position seemed constitutionally impeccable, was retrospectively transformed into a national moral crusade against slavery. Pindar's *Fourth
Pythian* is addressed to Arkesilaos, King of the city of Cyrene in
North Africa, for a victory in the chariot race in 462. Arkesilaos's
rule was itself a bit of an anachronism. His was a traditional kingship "by divine right" in a world in which that particular political
form was increasingly unusual, giving way to one or another of the
manifold oligarchic, democratic, or tyrannical arrangements that
came to be characteristic of the second half of the fifth century. In
fact Arkesilaos's father seems only to have been able to maintain himself and his family in power by becoming a "friend" of the Great King
of Persia. In the *Fourth Pythian* Pindar gives a lavish genealogical

account of Arkesilaos's family (back over seventeen generations) and of the divine warrant they have to colonize Africa and rule Cyrene, centered around a clutch of divinely inspired prophecies and oracles, the gift of a magic clod of African earth to one of the ancestors, and numerous mythic precedents. Their divine credentials are renewed again and again in succeeding generations. As Pindar will have it, the various prophecies and oracles refer backward and forward to each other and to what has happened and what will happen. Backward to mythic precedents, prefigurations, and other previous prophecies and divine commands; forward to later repetitions of the divine message, to possible courses of history that *would* have actualized—had various people acted differently—but that now will remain unrealized, and to the eventual fates of various members of the family, some of whom at the time the prophecy is issued are not even as yet born. The result is a dense, multilayered structure of crisscrossing actual and merely possible timelines and nested cross references. Even by Pindar's own standards the poem is complex and it comes very close to giving the impression of ideological overkill. If the dynasty is really that firmly established and its power so clearly divinely mandated, if the gods really did give them with that magic clod the very earth of Africa itself to be their own and rule over, does quite so much fuss need to be made about it? Brecht at one point remarks that we would quickly get suspicious of a person who kept repeating that his shoes did *not* pinch. In fact not long after the poem was written, Arkesilaos was toppled and killed, and the monarchy was replaced by a democracy. Gildersleeve clearly found in Pindar what he took to be a kindred spirit. This attitude "victrix causa diis placuit sed victa Catoni"[1] does probably sharpen one's "historical vision" for the hypocrisies of the victors, and is not lacking in a kind of moral grandeur, but in itself it will not ensure a particularly high level of self-reflection and self-distance. I have not read Gildersleeve's later writings on the American South, so I do not know to what extent he was able to turn his acute, historically informed eye dispassionately, and potentially critically, on his own preferred ideological formation. Inability to learn from failure, setback, defeat, or from being "on the losing side," however, is a serious cultural deficiency. Gildersleeve in one sense had it easy in that he was not even tempted to deny outright that his cause had lost or that this loss was deeply significant. Ronald Reagan reached high office by promising to help people forget that Vietnam had ever happened, a promise he with the active collusion of a large majority of the population was by and large able to keep. Some people did learn something: high military and political functionaries learned that they could not fight a colonial war successfully with conscript troops and that the public would not tolerate too many casualties even among volunteers. Hence the Rumsfeld doctrine of "war lite." Serious public discussion of the defeat in South Asia, however, effectively ceased. What counts as "failure" is, to be sure, itself sometimes open to differing interpretation, depending in part on what is conceived to be the relevant goal. What might look like "failure" relative to the publicly announced aim of "installing democracy" might really be a "success" if the real project is to topple a client-dictator who has shown too much independence, as in Iraq. What will happen when the troops scuttle from Afghanistan is anyone's guess, but to learn anything from this episode will require resisting the strong political pressure that will exist to obfuscate the real reasons for the invasion and the real results of it. Obama's record of political weakness, lack of moral fiber, and sheer insouciance does not suggest that he will even try to initiate an honest public discussion of this kind.

II.

SPECTACLE

My friend Gérald Garutti recently invited me to attend a theatrical event for which he wrote the script and that he directed at the Vingtième Théâtre, a pleasant, small theater in a part of northeast Paris near Père Lachaisse Cemetery that is off the usual tourist and academic circuit. The opening of the channel tunnel and the shift of Eurostar's London terminus from Waterloo to Saint Pancras is one of the very few "developments" in the infrastructure during the past roughly twenty years that has actually improved the quality of my life, because I can now leave Cambridge in the morning, have lunch with Gérald, see the afternoon matinee, and return home at a reasonable hour. For the Saturday matinee on March 10 the Vingtième Théâtre is completely sold out, and the audience seems expectant and ready to pay close attention. The "spectacle" is entitled *"Haïm—à la lumière d'un violon"* and tells the story of Haïm Lipsky, born in Lodz in the 1920s, who overcame the severe disabilities imposed by poverty to become a violinist and survived Auschwitz because he was put into the camp orchestra. After the war he decided not to return to Poland, gave up music altogether, and emigrated to Israel, where he became an electrician. Half a dozen of his children and grandchildren, however, are now professional musicians. His grandson Naaman Sluchin, taking the part of the young Haïm, plays the violin (magnificently). The other classical musician in the cast, the pianist Dana Ciocarlie, also plays with brilliance and flexibility. Gérald, in addition to his practical activity as a director, is one of the world's leading experts on Brecht, and Brecht's "epic theatre"—as well, of course, as *"l'histoire du soldat"*—has clearly had a significant influence on the texture of the piece. Gérald's text is all sobriety and restraint, with not the slightest admixture of holocaust-kitsch, and Anouk Grinberg as narrator is a luminous presence throughout. The paratactic structure of the piece with its succession of extremely vivid but minimalistically sketched images appropriately deflects attention from unanswerable questions of causality and motivation and from pseudo-questions about meaning. A piece of music establishes its own internal relations of time that hold without necessarily tracking the ticking of any physical clock. In a way this "spectacle" is about the ways in which different kinds of time—lived time, remembered time, "historical" time, "objective" time, narrated time, dramatic time in the theater—intersect and also about how they diverge, how time speeds up, and how it slows down. Sluchin and Ciocarlie play together, giving themselves over to the forward drive of the music, then abandon their instruments and dance together very slowly to time of their own making. At the end of the performance, while the audience is clapping, Gérald goes over and takes a tiny, elderly man by the hand, leading him up onto the stage. It is Haïm Lipsky, who, implausibly, actually does exist, and shyly bows.

III.

POLITICS

After the performance Gérald and I go to the bistro opposite the
theater for a discussion with some members of the audience. A group
of women closer to his age than to mine seem to get very excited
when they hear I have just come down from Cambridge, and begin
to question me intently. I slightly panic because my French, which
had served me well all day, seems suddenly to have deserted me: I
cannot understand what they are asking me about. What is a *stroscan?*
Gérald helps me out. Last night, it turns out, there was a demonstration at the Cambridge Union against Dominique Strauss-Kahn,
who had been invited to speak. The assembled women are as pleased
as punch that the horrid little man has had a *"mauvais quart d'heure,"*
but are clearly disappointed that I cannot give them any further detailed information about exactly what happened. So instead of
Strauss-Kahn we talk about the Tory plans to privatize higher education and the National Health Service. The Tories are bright enough
to realize they cannot get away with a frontal attack on the principle
of universal provision of health services "free at point of delivery"
because it is so obviously in the interest of everyone who is not a
shareholder in a pharmaceutical company or an insurance firm, so
the plans seems to be to change the internal administrative structure of the health services so as gradually and imperceptibly to siphon away potentially highly profitable medical services to private
organizations on a variety of specious grounds, leaving a skeleton
public structure that is responsible only for less immediately profitable forms of provision. This public structure can then be expected
to collapse of its own weight, thereby seeming to validate self-
fulfilling claims about the inherent superiority of the private sphere
over the public. The universities, on the other hand, do not enjoy
the minimal protection provided by broad public support, so they
can be attacked directly with impunity. The whole discussion, however, seen from this bistro, seems merely bizarre, because no one
here can really imagine that one could *still*—after the events of
2007–2008—believe in the creed of neoliberalism. The world economic crisis is clearly the result of the Anglo-Saxon obsession with

deregulation; compared with that the imprudencies and sharp practice of a few million Greeks are utterly insignificant. How can the UK, regarded here as a model of the low cunning that often gives one material advantages, be so misguided as not to see that it is risking one of its few remaining world-class national resources, its university system, for the sake of conformity to an ideology that has just shown itself to be a colossal mistake?

IV.

NOVELS

In one of the bookshops of the Gare du Nord on my way back home to Cambridge I buy two novels. The first, *Un traitre*, by Domenique Jamet (Flammarion, 2008), is a novel "librement inspiré de faits réels." The main character, Jacques Deleau, is born in France at about the same time as Haïm in Lodz, and the exigencies of the Occupation allow him to discover that he has one notable skill—he is an exceedingly efficient "interrogator"—a skill that assures him a meteoric rise in the security section of the French police in 1942. At the end of his life, he looks back on it and tries to make sense of it by reducing it to a formula: $22 + 20 + 20 + 23 \ldots + 3$. That is, infancy and youth ($1920 - 1942 = 22$ years) + the period in hiding ($1945 - 1965 = 20$ years) + prison ($1965 - 1985 = 20$) + life after prison ($1985 - 2008 = 23$ years) + the three years of $1942 - 1945$. Alexi Jenni's *L'art français de la guerre* (Gallimard, 2011) is about learning to draw and also about the "Twenty Years' War." We are accustomed to think of the period between 1914 and 1945 as a kind of Thirty Years' War, and 1945 to 1975 constituted an era of uninterrupted economic growth that might be thought to form a natural unit. When real wages and productivity began flatlining in the late 1970s, maintaining the illusion of ever-growing prosperity more and more frequently required recourse to administering nonrepeatable jolts to the economy (such as by privatizing, that is, selling off, valuable national assets), to generating bubbles and to using gimmicks (mainly financial gimmicks). The gimmicks, however, seemed to work for such a long time—until 2007—that one lost the sense of the historical contingency and precariousness of their success. One might call the period between the mid-1970s and the beginning of the twenty-first century the "Thirty Years' Puffery." What, though, was the Twenty Years' War? Victorien Salagnon, the former soldier turned drawing-master who stands at the center of *L'art français de la guerre*, describes it succinctly as "France Libre, Indo, djebel," that is, the slice of time during which the French Resistance, construed as beginning in 1942, merged smoothly into the colonial wars that lasted until the withdrawal from Algeria in 1962. The traditional novel was an inferior literary form perhaps partly because of its predisposition to monodimensional narrative, relatively simple periodization, and homogenous successive or parallel time sequences. Pindar would have thought this intolerably naive.

16

Augustine on Love, Perspective, and Human Nature

—◦◦◦—

AUGUSTINE HAS GOT inappropriately short shrift in the standard histories of ethics. They often contain some vague references to his fusion of Christian and older Greco-Roman elements, sometimes there is mention of his contribution to the development of the doctrine of the Trinity, and almost always there is some discussion of his analysis of original sin. Important as these topics are, I think that one important aspect of the doctrine of original sin is usually overlooked and that there are at least two other views that Augustine develops and that are highly original and well worth further consideration. So in this chapter I talk about his doctrine of the variability of human nature, his views about love as constituting the human essence, and his reflections on the need to adopt a nonmonocular view of history and politics.

Philosophers have overwhelmingly assumed that there is such a thing as a fixed and unchanging "human nature" and that it made sense for ethics to begin by studying the invariant structures of that nature. As Aristotle says in his *nicomachean ethics*, just as fire burns everywhere in a similar way, in Greece and in Persia, so human nature is the same: we can study it without taking account of spatial, temporal, historical or eschatological variations, and this study can be the basis of an ethical theory that would have some universal validity (*EN* 1134b25–27). Augustine, however, does not believe that human essence or nature is invariant in this way. He believes Adam had an uncorrupted nature in the Garden of Paradise, but that this nature itself was changed for the worse by the sin he committed. He has bequeathed to all the rest of us this abased and transformed nature.

> *duo primi [homines] . . . a quibus admissum est tam grande peccatum, <u>ut in deterius <u>eo natura mutaretur humana,</u></u> etiam in posteros obligatione peccati et mortis necessitate transmissa. (de civitate dei* XIV 1)

["The two first humans by whom a sin so great was committed that by it human nature was changed for the worse, and a nature tied to sin and subject to the necessity of death was transmitted to later humans."]

Similarly, Augustine believes, the Incarnation also changes human nature in that it gives to humans possibilities that simply were not available to them before. The human nature of a Christian in a state of grace is radically different from that of a Christian in a state of mortal sin, which is again different from the human nature of the pagan. Then, in addition, there is the eschatological dimension to possible transformations of human nature: the members of the *Ecclesia Triumphans*—the departed saints now in heaven—are still human, but again different in nature. This belief in the variability of human nature is part of the reason why Augustine can accept what might seem to be rather large forms of ethical variety. Thus he noted that the patriarchs described in the Old Testament were chosen by and beloved of god, although many of them were polygamous, so this must have been ethically acceptable although in Augustine's time such polygamy would be deeply sinful.

The second of Augustine's original thoughts is his denigration of *ratio*, λόγος in favor of an understanding of human beings as constituted by configurations of desire and love (including, naturally, negative desires and forms of hatreds). Augustine does not deny that human beings are biological creatures endowed with the powers of speech and reason, but he seems to think that this is a shallow and superficial way to approach human life. To define man as "animal rationale" is in principle as misleading as defining him as a featherless biped or as the animal that laughs. His own preferred conceptual scheme is one that emphasizes "love"—in the most general possible sense of that term—as the most central constitutive feature of humanity. This does not mean that reason is unimportant, and it may well be, or rather, it surely is the case that, I could not have some of the more interesting, valuable, and highly developed forms of love if I did not also have reason, but admitting this does not in any way in itself constitute an argument for claiming that reason constitutes "the essence of man" in the traditional sense.

Remember that for Augustine it is not the case that all men desire "by nature" to know in any interesting or fundamental sense. That state is curiosity, potentially a sin; the fall from a state of perfect happiness in Paradise is caused by eating the fruit of the tree of knowledge. At the beginning of book XI of *confessiones* Augustine defends his attempt to inquire what god was doing before he created the heavens and the earth, and he gives some reason for thinking this is a legitimate. He specifically rejects the suggestion that god was preparing a place in hell for those who ask questions like this. What is interesting about the discussion is not that Augustine eventually decides that asking the question is legitimate, but that his default position is that it is potentially sinful. Even to take the objection that asking the question is sinful seriously at all, is to inhabit a different world from that of Plato and Aristotle. Finally even sense perception for Augustine, as one can see from even a cursory inspection of the later books of *de trinitate* is a process in which a voluntative or desirous *"intention"* (*animi intentio*) holds our mind in contact with some feature of the external world and without this desirous connection there would be no knowledge.

Human nature is variable because a human being is essentially a mutable configuration of loves and desires and his own identity is the particular constellation of specific libidinous and caritative components as well as the history of its change. Not only do the individual objects of love change historically, both in an individual's history and in the history of a human collectivity, but the forms and possibilities

of love themselves change. Human history is mostly about not
learning to love new things but learning to love differently, and the
most important part of history is the history of the epochs during
which different kinds of love become possible or impossible. Adam's
fall changes human nature, making certain forms of love impossible,
and the incarnation does not just provide humans with a new love
object, but potentially changes human nature by rendering a new
form of love possible. We can look forward to other changes in our
nature in an eschatological context.

Before Augustine there had been three full-blown traditional approaches to how to live our lives in the West, and he develops a
fourth. The first approach is that of an ethics centered on law, rules,
duty, obligations, and the whole apparatus of consistency and rationality that is associated with this. This view is instantiated for Augustine in the Old Testament, the domain of law, and we can see it
continuing in Kant. For Augustine, this whole tradition is a dead end,
rendered irrelevant by the incarnation. "Law" is the province of the
Old Dispensation, annulled and superseded by the New Regime of
freedom and grace through the incarnate Christ. The second approach to ethics is that of Greek thought, centered on happiness. It
actually exists in two slightly different variants, one oriented to the
satisfaction of desires, wants, and preferences, and the other oriented
to some notion of healthy or maximal functioning. So, roughly
speaking, you are happy if you get what you want or have your desires satisfied, or you are happy if you are functioning well. The third
approach, which is definitely a minority one, could be called stoic or
perhaps Gnostic and is centered on "acceptance." It emphasizes the
possible acquisition of some kind of enlightenment that gives us the
ability to continue to live and function, and to accept the impossibility of satisfying our desires and thus of attaining happiness in this
world. I take this to be the strand that later Freud developed. It is an
"ethics" based on "enlightened *acceptance*." This is not the same as
eudiamonia; Freud says that the point of psychoanalysis is to allow
the patient to overcome neurotic blockages and face the true horror
of human existence, that is, the absence of the possibility of happiness as usually construed.[1]

Augustine's thought is structured not around "happiness," "law/ reason/right," or enlightened acceptance, but around "love." This becomes clearest perhaps in the following passage (*de civitate dei* XIV 25).

De vera beatudine, quam temporalis vita non obtinet

Quamquam si diligentius adtendamus, nisi beatus non vivit ut vult, et nullus beatus nisi iustus. Sed etiam ipse iustus non vivet ut vult, nisi eo pervenerit, ubi mori falli offendi omnino non possit eique sit certum ita semper futurum. Hoc enim natura expetit, nec plene atque perfecte beata erit nisi adepta quod expetit. Nunc vero quis hominum potest ut vult vivere, quando ipsum vivere non est in potestate? Vivere enim vult, mori cogitur. Quo modo ergo vivit ut vult, qui non vivit quandiu vult? . . . Verum ecce vivat ut vult, quoniam sibi extorsit sibique imperavit non velle quod non potest, atque hoc velle quod potest (sicut ait Terentius:

Quoniam non potest id fieri quod vis.

Id velis quod possis):

num ideo beatus est, quia patienter miser est? Beata quippe vita si non amatur, non habetur. Porro si amatur et habetur, ceteris omnibus rebus excellentius necesse est ametur, quoniam propter hanc amandum est quidquid aliud amatur. Porro si tantum amatur, quantum amari digna est (non enim beatus est, a quo ipsa beata vita non amatur ut digna est) fieri non potest, ut eam, qui sic amat, non aeternam velit. Tunc igitur beata erit, quando aeterna erit.

["On the True Happiness that Life in Time Cannot Provide

If we pay attention more carefully, we shall see that no one lives as he wishes except the happy person, and no one but the just person is happy. But even the just person will not be living as he wishes, if he does not attain a state in which it is utterly impossible for him to die, to be deceived, or to be harmed, and is certain that this state will last forever. For nature seeks this, and life will not be fully and completely happy unless it attains what it seeks. However, what man is capable of living as he wishes when he does not have it in his power to [cause himself

to continue to] live? He wants to live, but is forced to die. In
what way is he living as he wishes, if he does not live as long as
he wishes? . . . Consider then the case of someone who [purport-
edly] lives as he wishes by virtue of tormenting himself and
commanding himself not to wish that which he cannot do but
to wish [only] that which is he can do (as Terence says:

Since that which you want cannot be
Wish for that which you can attain)

So is a man happy who is patiently miserable? If a [purport-
edly] happy life is not the object of love it certainly is not led by
the person whose life it is as a happy life. But if it *is* loved and
led, of necessity it is loved as being more excellent than all
other things, because whatever else may be loved is lovable because of [contributing to] this life. If it is loved as much as it
deserves to be loved (and no one is happy by whom that life is not
loved as it deserves to be loved), it cannot be that he who loves
that life in the proper way does not wish for it to be eternal. Thus
it will be a happy life."]

Augustine canvasses the other three approaches before settling on
his own, but philosophers are natural magpies and cannot help themselves from trying to appropriate the best of all that is good in other
views. So it is not a surprise that devotes of each of these four approaches tries to appropriate for his own view all the good things
associated with other approaches, and even to pinch terminology. So,
of course, law- and rights-based approaches try to show that one can
only be "truly" happy by following the law, although in most cases
this requires torturing the meaning of "happy" into unrecogniz-
ability. What is important then is not just to observe the vocabulary
used, but to see what is the central driving structure, what the
working parts are, and what is *Beiwerk*. They all, or at least most of
the more important ones, talk about happiness, acceptance, good
functioning, rationality, even rights. Augustine is no exception to this
rule. Furthermore, to reject a law-centered view is not necessarily to
deny that conceptions of "law" have *any* role to play in the understanding of human life or in giving us an orientation in the sphere of
action. It is merely to claim that they play a subordinate or secondary

role and are not foundational. After all, when Christianity claimed to superseded the Jewish Law, this was clearly not originally intended as an invitation to radical "antinomianism," if that meant that law had no standing *whatever*, that it never made any difference at all whether one contradicted oneself grossly, or that a good human life might well consist entirely in killing people indiscriminately. What it did mean was that law, and action in conformity with law, was not central, freestanding, able to be understood fully and finally in its own terms. Rather it had to be given a place, perhaps a not unimportant but still subordinate place, in a larger framework for thinking about human life. The real principle of understanding, validity, and motivation lay not in law (and its associated notions of reason) but elsewhere, and understanding this would not leave the substantive content of law itself unchanged, although how law, reason, a possible system of rights, and so on, were to be modified by understanding them as not self-grounding but as subordinate phenomena was a complicated issue and probably not one that could resolved at one stroke and by a simple formula. That framework is, for Augustine, constituted by the phenomenon of love.

Even by the usual standards of philosophy, though, the discussion in *de civitate dei* XIV 25 is so deeply weird as to suggest that a significant conceptual change is in train. Notice the phrase *"beata quippe vita si non amatur, non habetur."* The first peculiarity is the connection of *vita* with the verbs *amare* and *habere*. This seems to me already to break the mold of previous Greek philosophy and of the then existing discussion of "happiness." It is hard even to imagine an ancient Greek philosopher saying anything like, "X loves (or does not love) his life." The very question of "loving" or not "loving" "life/one's own life" is not one that is raised. And although "βίος" is used as object of any number of verbs, it is hard to imagine any Greek philosopher using anything quite so colorless as an equivalent of *habere* in connection with it *in this sense* of "having a life to live." The second bit of apparent perversity is that although the discussion of happiness in this passage up to this point had been conducted in the active voice *vivit, vult, potest* ("he or she lives, wishes/wants, is able to") now suddenly it is all reversed into the passive: *"amatur/ametur/ amari"* (seven occurrences of these passive forms in about three lines) and two occurrences of "*habetur.*" Some reasons for the peculiarity of the discussion will show themselves to those who read on, I hope, but for the moment suffice it to say that there is something odd and rather unclear being suggested about "agency" and love.

Finally I point out what might seem like a gratuitous addition or perhaps qualification, the claim that I am happy only if I love what is worthy of love in a way worthy of it *(ut digna est)*. This raises the question of what it means to say that something is worthy of love and how we are to decide that. It is also what allows Augustine to claim that whenever we want anything we really want it for the sake of eternal life.

Since "love" is such a hard category to keep in focus, I proceed *ex negativo* by first analyzing some mistakes that one can make about it. The first mistake is to reduce the phenomenon too quickly to categories derived from *eudaimonia*. "Love" does not have the same logic as either preference, or functioning, or the pursuit of success in attaining more or less fixed goals, and it is much more fundamental than any of these. The ability to love may be an essential component of happiness, but that does not mean that an ethics of love can be adequately grasped through the categories of happiness.

A conception of happiness based on the satisfaction of desires is not the same as one based on the idea of good functioning. "I need" is the central idea in accounts that emphasize good human functioning. "I need x" means if I do not get x I will not function well: "I need," however, has a different logic and cannot be reduced to "I want."[2] I want lots of things I do not need, and I may "need" things I do not want. Similarly "I love" cannot be reduced to "I want." Just as "I need" does not mean "I want *very intensely*," so "I love" does not mean "I desire *very intensely*." "I love" expresses a kind of openness to something and a fundamental attachment to it; I allow it to touch and affect me. But the fact that I am attached to something, and what touches it touches me, may be the origin of my having certain desires, but it is not constituted by any set of such desires, certainly not any that can be maximally satisfied in the way Greek philosophers imagined. Hatred in this view is also a species of love because it is a way of being attached to or potentially affected by something. Despite the air of paradox that might be thought to surround this claim, the observation that certain forms of hatred can exhibit the same focused fascination with an object as is found in certain kinds of love is one that has been made repeatedly. Perhaps one can make this more comprehensible by thinking that the opposite of love is not hatred but indifference.

The second mistake is Plato's in *Symposium*. Diotima was deeply wrong about love: it is not oriented toward moving ever upward from the concrete to the ever more abstract. Love is directed sometimes and basically to the stubbornly individual and particular, *not* to this particular as stand-in for something more general or universal, much less as stand-in for the universal form of the good. In particular love is characterized by some degree of unsubstitutability in its object. Even in the case of relatively low-level loves, the connection with a concrete particular is essential. If my cat dies, I do not want "another tabby." I loved *this* cat.

At some level, our loves, like our hates, are a-rational; the very concepts of reason (and unreason) have no purchase in the most primordial part of their domain. Λόγος does not go "all the way down."[3] Basic attachments and basic revulsions are beyond the reach of reason. This aboriginal latching on to the world without which nothing else would be possible is individual, contingent, and surd. In *de trinitate* Augustine explores parallels between the Trinity and the human world, finding such parallels in such unlikely places as human sensation, but one could perhaps add to his account that this primordial affective *Ur*-fastening on to the world that always takes place via some contingent detail, is like god's utterly unmotivated choice of Jacob over Esau, when both were still in the womb (*de civitate dei* XVI 35 *sine ullis bonis meritis eligitur minor maiore reprobate*). This was a divine primordial choice and had nothing to do with merit or rationality. The same is true of the primordial forms of love—it will always be something like a contingent fetish-grain around which our attachment to the world constructs itself,[4] without which it would not exist, and that no amount of retrospective ratiocination will either do away with or transform into something that is really transparent and fully rational—the fact is that god loved Jacob and hated Esau, *from the start* while they were both still in the womb, and there is nothing that can be done about that. So although god's love is, it seems, unrelated to merit, desert or worth, our love, according to the passage from *de civitate dei* cited earlier (XIV 25), is subject to some conditions about the worthiness of its object, but these, to the extent to which they exist, must at best be rather general and indeterminate and in no way annul the necessary individuality and rationally undetermined nature of the attachments created by love.

But if this is true of love, it is a fortiori also true of cognition. Our knowledge, too, builds out from the bits of it that fascinate us, and we can never fully extract ourselves from that situation. Of course, our loves and hates are not just cognition enabling; they can also be cognition distorting. This is no reason to deny their role in the *Urkonstitution* of our world.[5] Without love and the quirkiness, whimsy, and idiosyncrasy of its attachments there is no cognition, and not only can these never be fully left behind; they can have positive value. As Adorno wrote, *"Der Splitter in deinem Auge ist das beste Vergrößerungsglas"* ("the splinter in your eye is the best magnifying glass") (*Minima Moralia* §29). Even the ultimate object of love for Augustine, the Christian god, is not a mere abstraction like Plato's idea of the good, but a person, or a set of complex person-like interconnected processes, that is, the Trinity.

Just to ward off an obvious misinterpretation of the position being presented here, to say that in some primordial sense or some very basic domain, the concepts of "rational" and "irrational" have no clear application, it *not* to say that *all* human evaluation, liking, choice is irrational *in every respect*. That all love has an aspect of the a-rational about it is not to say that all love is in all respects completely irrational. The fact that my love is essentially constituted by an orientation to some feature of the world and that *both* the orientation and the feature have an irreducible property of contingency and are radically prior to or radically beyond *ratio*—one can see sense in both of these ways of describing it—does not mean that we cannot evaluate love in any way. Quite the contrary, trying to discover what is a "worthy (or unworthy) love of a worthy (or unworthy) object" is the central content of human life for Augustine. This requires us continually to negotiate the jagged edges of the world, where, as we might *retrospectively* say, contingency and reason meet, and also the smooth places where each almost imperceptibly merges with and goes over into the other.

Love, then, is always individualized in its object, but, paradoxically, *not* in its subject; hence perhaps the frequent use of the passive voice by Augustine in discussing it. It is not really the individual who is finally the unique bearer of love. For Augustine it is the church, a collective, that loves god, and a person loves god as part of the church. Love, I am suggesting, is like "objective spirit" for Hegel.[6] A good example is the English language, which exists only as a collective social entity activated by individuals. It is true that English would not exist if there had never been individual speakers who made use of it. But it is also true that the language preexists any individual speaker; every speaker finds it always already there. There is no path either from universal structures of rationality or from my individual consciousness or action to the language as a social phenomenon—a point that Herder and Hegel saw clearly, that Kant signally failed to grasp with catastrophic consequences for his philosophical views, and that the late Wittgenstein rediscovered in the 1930s and 1940s.

Only when the appropriate collective structures exist can an individual love. Protestants may think every individual can have a direct relation to god, perhaps one mediated by individual reading of scripture, but Catholics know that a church, a social institution, is required as a set of social structures to enable love of the proper kind to be generated, transmitted, exercised, and focused.[7] Love of course in *some* sense can be ascribed a main locus in a particular individual and for certain purposes this is sensible, just as English speech can. I love, just as I speak. However this is dependent on the preexistence of a whole network of social structures, and love, like speech, is an individual activation of some of those fundamentally collective structures.[8]

So Plato got it wrong in *Symposium*, which tells the story of an individual subject in the throes of love moving by a series of internal steps to a realization that the true object of love is something very abstract, the idea of the good; however, the subject of love is not an individual and the object not something abstract. The interesting parts of Augustine are those where he gets this right, and tries to explain how a collective, like the church, comes to love a highly individuated particular, the Trinitarian Christian god.

Augustine's third good idea is that one must always look at politics and history from two distinct perspectives at the same time: that of the city of god and that of the city of man. These two cities (and thus the two perspectives), he emphasizes again and again, are themselves constituted by forms of love (*de civitate dei* XIV 28). The city of god is composed of those whose main love is given focus by *"vera religio"*; the city of man by one or another form of individual or collective self-love. The two cities are inextricably interconnected the one with the other here on earth; their respective viewpoints cannot, however, be reduced the one to the other and their judgments diverge radically. The "virtues" that are necessary, and rightly praised and cherished in the city of man, have no standing whatever in the city of god. The reason for this is that for Augustine it is not the actual external disposition to behave that is important, but the inner source from which the action springs, and the only truly laudable virtuous action is that which arises from "true religion" *(vera religio)*— love of the right god in the right way.

> ### Quod non possint ibi verae esse virtutes, ubi non est vera religio
>
> *Proinde virtutes, quas habere sibi videtur . . . rettulerit nisi ad Deum, etiam ipsae vitia sunt potius quam virtutes. Nam licet a quibusdam tunc verae atque honestae putentur esse virtutes, cum referuntur ad se ipsas nec propter aliud expetuntur; etiam tunc inflatae et superbae sunt, ideo non virtutes, sed vitia iudicanda sunt.*

["That there can be no true virtues where there is no true religion. Unless [the virtuous person] refers the virtues he appears to have on his own back to god, they are vices rather than virtues. By some people it is thought that virtues can be true and honest when they refer only to themselves and are not sought for the sake of anything else. But then these purported virtues are puffed up and haughty, and so are to be judged to be not virtues but vices."] (*de civitate dei* XIX 25)

Note that this is not the view that one can sometimes find, which has its source in Plato, that virtues have no fixity, consistency, or stability as habits of behavior unless tied down to something else more substantial. For Plato tied down in structures of that constitute true knowledge, but one could imagine a modification of this view that would have it that they needed to be tried down either by religious faith or church discipline (or some combination of both). Augustine thinks that this is probably right; virtues are unlikely to be stable without some religious backing, but that is very definitely not the point here. These human dispositions may be stable enough on their own, but their stability is their rootedness in human self-love, desire for glory, and so on, so they are for Augustine stable forms of vice, albeit forms of vice that have the adventitious advantage that by cementing the *pax romana*, they allowed Christians the respite of momentary, if illusory, worldly peace.

All Roman virtues count for *nothing* for Augustine, because they are forms of striving for glory, self-affirmation, or autonomy and thus are forms of love of self (either of "self" in the narrower sense of the individual person or "my city" construed as myself writ, as it were, large, or finally myself as member of an imaginary cosmopolitan kingdom or republic encompassing all humanity). Since these "Roman virtues" did not arise from the right sources, were not activations of the correctly structured love of god, they were actually vices *("non virtutes sed vitia iudicanda sunt")*.

Regulus, the archetypical "virtuous Roman" in choosing to sacrifice himself for the good of the city of Rome, or choosing to be virtuous "for its own sake" *("virtutes cum referuntur ad se ipsas")* does "evil" in Augustine's view. If this seems harsh, recall that the Christian Augustine, who had been a Manichean and knew what he was rejecting, became an explicit anti-Manichean, that is, an opponent of the notion that there was a metaphysical dualism opposing "good" and "evil." Everything that exists is created by god and thus metaphysically "good." "Evil" is nothing but choice of a lesser good over a higher. So Regulus in one sense chose a higher good over a lower in that he chose the good of the city of Rome over his own welfare. That is the judgment from the perspective of the city of man. However in choosing the good of Rome *rather than* god, he did what can correctly be called evil. Of course, he had no real choice in this because he lived *before* the Incarnation so could have had no access to "true religion," but that, for Augustine, is irrelevant.

The two cities for Augustine are utterly different, yet inextricably connected. Each saved Christian is a member of the Church Militant and a citizen of the city of god, but also a *peregrinus*, a wandering foreigner, here below and in the city of man (XIX 26). The sinner and the non-Christian are full citizens of the city of man and would be a wandering foreigner in god's city. No one knows for certain which individuals belong to which one, but it is also true, as we have learned, that evil too, like love, is not a merely individual phenomenon. Rather it is in an important sense a property of structures, the work of an apparatus in which individual humans are embedded and from which they cannot extricate themselves, so we have to try to de-individualize this account, too. After all, just as the *"city"* of god is a "city," the "city" of man is a collective entity. If evil is a choice of lesser over greater good, then it clearly can be instantiated not just by individuals, but also by institutions, because they too can choose the lesser over the greater good. In fact institutions can be *set up in order to ensure* that they systematically choose the lesser over the greater good. The Roman Republic, structurally arranged to pit groups of aristocrats against each other in such a way as to maximize a certain kind of aggressive imperialism, was an instance of this known to Augustine.

Just as Augustine recognized that the lawless, violent polygamous world of the Old Testament patriarchs was not that of the *pax romana*, so we might need to recognize that our world is not in all respects his. We have our institutions of the city of man, devoted for better or worse to ensuring minimal forms of human peace and justice, the EU, the European Security Council, the UN, the Red Cross, but we also live in a landscape that has other occupants of a kind Augustine could not have imagined. What would he have made of the CIA, the National Front in France, Google, Microsoft and Amazon, and Murdoch's News Corp? International and other vehicles of systematic human spiritual, moral, and physical degradation? He had, of course, a conception of "demons" as disembodied praeterhuman agents who prowled the world doing evil—he calls them *"spiritus nocendi cupidissimos, a iustitia penitus alienos, superbia tumidos, invidentia lividos, fallacia callidos"* ("spirits most eager to do harm, utterly alien to justice, swollen up with pride, green with envy, skilled in deceit") (VIII 22)—and perhaps there is something of the demonic in these organizations. He also had the idea of the "pirates" and "armed band of brigands," and perhaps some of these groups are better understood in those terms (IV 4).[9]

Regulus, in the context of the earthly city, might deserve praise, but from the point of view of the city of god all his purported virtues were vices. When Stalin reportedly said that one death is a tragedy but a million a statistic, he was also probably making a point about a shift between perspectives, not saying that each of those million deaths was not itself an individual tragedy.[10] It was grouping and presenting these deaths cumulatively in this particular way, putting them in a certain framework or context that deprived them of their tragic character. Perhaps, if we succeed in avoiding ecological catastrophe, the members of the classless communes of the future shall love each of these communes as the unique individual entity it is, and be able to dispense with the bifurcation, duality, or even multiplicity of points of view, but for those of us still living in the present under the current historical dispensation, this is something we cannot avoid.

APPENDIX I:

A Theological Note

One might say that when Saint John the Evangelist writes, ὁ λόγος σάρξ ἐγένετο (=et verbum caro factum est=The Word was made flesh) this is only half the truth and it needs to be complemented with ὁ σάρξ ἐγένετο λόγος (Flesh became Word/Reason/Intelligibility, and so on, whatever "logos" actually means/meant). So the full two-part assertion would read: ὁ λόγος σάρξ ἐγένετο ὡς καὶ ὁ σάρξ ἐγένετο λόγος. I note the slippage between the Greek aorist and the Latin perfect and the potential further slippage involved in the lack of a proper perfect form of fieri so that factum est from a different verbal stem has to stand in, but will resist any further Heideggerian reflections on this. The Christian location of my addendum to the formula, the second half, is the doctrine of the "resurrection of the flesh." Here, too, I merely note that even a cursory consultation of Denziger-Schönmetzer's Enchiridion symbolorum definitionum et declarationum de rebus fidei et morum (I use the thirty-sixth edition, Herder, Freiburg, 1965) will reveal an uncertainty in the early formulae about what exactly it is that is "resurrected," as indicated by the shift between σαρκὸς ἀνάστασις (resurrectio carnis, even resurrectio huius carnis), ἀνάστασις νεκρῶν, ἀνάστασις ψυχῆς καὶ σώματος, resurgere cum *corporibus suis*, and eventually *resurrection mortuorum*. In any case, within Christianity the resurrection of the flesh is a hope for the future, whereas the assertion in John is past/timeless (aorist).

If σάρξ is also a kind of metaphysical stand-in for prerationalized impulses and primordial attachments to the world, then my addendum, then my thought is precisely not that σάρξ "is made" λόγος *by* some other person or thing who makes it that way as a potter makes a pot, so that σάρξ is radically transformed while λόγος remains itself. Recall Bernard Williams's example: My wife is on a sinking ship, and I am able to rescue only one person. If I rescue her *because* I have reasoned, "If I can rescue only one, rescuing *any one* is licit, so I may rescue my wife," I have had one thought too many. The reason I save her is not that I have rational warrant to pick any one and so "may" pick her to save, but because *it is her.*

Needless to say, I do not present the above speculations as in any way an interpretation of Augustine.

APPENDIX II:

A Note on Nonsubstitutability and Theodicy

There have been several different ways of approaching the problem of "theodicy," that is, attempts to "justify" the existence of evil, especially human suffering in a world that is assumed to be in every respect the creation of an omnipotent and omnibenevolent god. One way is to try to deny, despite appearances to the contrary, that evil (and suffering) are "really real" and to assert that in some way "if one understands them correctly" they shows themselves to be not fully real, mere illusions, only the superficial way things look to us, and so on. Earlier versions of this tend to be more visibly "metaphysical"—evil as a negation or absence has no metaphysical reality. This view confronts the difficulty that no amount of ratiocination will plausibly convince some people of the *relevant* unreality of the pain they themselves experience or the suffering they see being experienced by those who are closest to them. Later versions of theodicy often adopt a more economistic approach. It is not that pain, suffering, and evil do not "really" exist—to claim that flies in the face of all human experience—or that pain and suffering are really in some sense not "evil" (either they are actually "good" or they belong to the Stoic category of "indifferent things"). This pain exists and is a bad thing, but "if one understood the *full* picture" and had a complete view of the world, one would see that this instance of suffering was "necessary" because it was appropriately linked to other goods. Thus, the momentary pain at the dentist's is real pain, but is somehow "justified" by the good of avoiding much greater pain later. The economistic view generalizes this from the limited case of balancing my real pain today against my (potentially greater) pain tomorrow to a theory of the whole world in which in principle this child's pain today can be seen to be "counterbalanced"—if one saw the *full* picture— by enormous benefits to thousands of other in the future.

Kant, in his essay *Über die Unmöglichkeit einer philosophischen Theodizee*, makes two objections to this economistic form of theodicy. First, the "full picture" does not exist; at any rate it does not exist as anything humans as the finite beings we are could even potentially have access to, but an argument that appeals to a perspective that we could in principle never inhabit is not a philosophical argument at all, but at best a gesture of "faith." Kant's second objection, however, is, if possible, even more powerful. He claims that there is something morally reprehensible about even approaching the topic of individual human suffering in this way. Even to try to put *this* person's suffering into a "larger picture" in the context of which one can reason about it one way or the other is to have taken the first step on a morally reprehensible path, because it is to envisage the possibility that John's benefit can somehow compensate for, outweigh, counterbalance, or *offset* Jill's pain. This is not to take Jill's pain (and Jill) seriously.

Notes

Preface

   1. For further discussion of this, see my *"Republik, Markt, Demokratie"* which is reprinted as a "commentary" at the end of Jacques de Saint Victor, *Die Antipolitischen* (Hamburger Edition, 2015), 97–110.

1 Dystopia: The Elements

This text is a translation and revision of my response to two (unpublished) papers, one by Richard Raatzsch and the other by Jörg Schaub. These were presented at a seminar organized by Prof. Rahel Jaeggi at the Humboldt-University, Berlin, in autumn 2011.

   1. Some of the most influential papers of the earlier analytic movement can be found in *Readings in Philosophical Analysis*, H. Feigl and W. Sellars, eds. (New York: Appleton-Century-Croft, 1949); often reprinted, most recently in 2012.

   2. See Adolf Loos, "Ornament und Verbrechen" in his *Trotzdem* (Prachner, 1982), A Opel, ed., 78–89 [reprint of first edition 1931].

   3. *More: Utopia*, Logan, Adams, Miller, eds. (Cambridge: Cambridge University Press, 1995) (bilingual edition).

   4. Richard Raatzsch, "Geuss gegen die Herrschenden" (unpublished manuscript).

   5. Unpublished comment.

   6. I am aware that the form of "normative" political philosophy that has become canonical in the post-Rawlsian period itself stands in a potentially problematic relation to "analytic philosophy." It is not at all clear that many of the original proponents of analysis would have had any time whatever for "normative" theories. Post-Rawlsian standard form is also at best only *one* of the possible forms an "analytic" approach can take. As people used to say about the "really existing socialism" of Eastern Europe, it had the advantage over all possible other forms of socialism of actually existing.

   7. Nietzsche (in some moods), Dewey, Brecht.

8. See Q. Skinner, "The State," in *Political Innovation and Conceptual Change*, T. Ball, J. Farr, R. Hanson, eds. (Cambridge: Cambridge University Press, 1989).

2 Realism and the Relativity of Judgment

I would like to thank the members of the Department of International Relations at the University of Aberystwyth for the kind invitation to give the lecture on which this chapter is based and to the audience at the lecture for their very helpful comments. I would also like to thank John Dunn, Lorna Finlayson, Peter Garnsey, and Eva von Redeker for discussions and particularly Hilary Gaskin for her detailed suggestions for improvement of the manuscript. The editors of this journal, particularly Prof. Kenneth Booth, and the anonymous reviewers raised a very significant number of important points that aided me enormously in reworking the chapter and gave me much to think further about. *Editors' Note:* This article is based on the E. H. Carr Memorial Lecture, delivered by Professor Geuss at Aberystwyth University on October 30, 2014. The lecture series was inaugurated to honor the contribution to scholarship of E. H. Carr, who was the fourth Woodrow Wilson Professor in the Department of International Politics. During his time in the department (1936–1947) Carr wrote, among other works, his landmark volume *The Twenty Years' Crisis 1919–1939: An Introduction to the Study of International Relations* (London: Macmillan, 1939; second edition, 1946). The first Memorial Lecture was given in 1984 by Professor William T. R. Fox, Bryce Professor Emeritus of the History of International Relations at Columbia University.

1. By saying that Carr is "underappreciated" I obviously do not mean that no one appreciates the importance of his work. See John Haslam, *The Vices of Integrity: E. H. Carr 1892–1982* (London: Verso, 1999); Michael Cox, ed., *E. H. Carr: A Critical Appraisal* (Basingstoke: Palgrave, 2000). See also especially Ken Booth, "Security in Anarchy: Utopian Realism in Theory and Practice," *International Affairs (Royal Institute of International Affairs)* 67, no. 3 (July 1991): 527–545, which in many ways anticipates the position I try to outline here.

2. On the positive value of theoretical opportunism, see the comments on the "bricoleur" in the preface to Lévi-Strauss's *La pensée sauvage* (Paris: Plon, 1962).

3. E. H. Carr, *The Twenty Years' Crisis*, new edition with an introduction by Michael Cox (Basingstoke: Palgrave Macmillan, 2001).

4. Ibid., 3–39.

5. Friedrich Nietzsche, *Zur Genealogie der Moral*, in *Nietzsches Werke: Kritische Studien-Ausgabe*, Colli and Montinari, eds. (Berlin: de Gruyter, 1967), vol. 5: Bernard Williams, *Ethics and the Limits of Philosophy* (London: Fontana, 1985).

6. Kant feels obliged to have a theory of "evil" but has extreme difficulty accommodating one within his general theoretical position. One of his late works, *Religion innerhalb der Grenzen der bloßen Vernunft* in *Immanuel Kant. Werke in sechs Bänden*, Wilhelm Weischedel, ed. (Darmstadt: Wissenschaftliche Buchgesellschaft, 1963), 4:649–878 (originally published 1793), which contains a long discussion of the concept of "evil," was particularly influential in the first

half of the nineteenth century and I strongly suspect that one of the reasons for its popularity is that it brings out the inconcinnities, limitations, and implausibilities of Kantian moral thought in a particularly striking way. It gave the idealists a strong motivation to try to think about morality in a way that would avoid the visible deficiencies of Kantianism. For later discussion of the difference between "bad" and "evil," see Nietzsche *Zur Genealogie der Moral*, 5:247–289.

7. Plato, *Protagoras*.

8. The most interesting book on the history of preaching known to me is Robert Cruel's *Geschichte der deutschen Predigt in Mittelalter* (Detmold: Menersche Hofbuchhandlung, 1879). For a more recent view, see Werner Schütz, *Geschichte der christlichen Predigt* (Berlin: de Gruyter, 1972). Some theologians distinguish "preaching (a sermon)" from "giving a homily" in a variety of ways. Saint Stephen, of course, is stoned to death in Acts 7 after "preaching," and traditionally Saint Barnabas was supposed to have been stoned to death while preaching in Cyprus.

9. Gospel according to Luke 18:9–14.

10. Gospel according to Matthew 7:1–3. Among the stories about the Desert Fathers is one about Saint Moses the Black, who apparently refused even to give spiritual advice, much less to preach. See B. Ward, ed., *The Desert Fathers* (London: Penguin, 2003), 80. See also the famous anecdote about him in ibid., 85. See also John Wortley, ed., *The Anonymous Sayings of the Desert Fathers* (Cambridge: Cambridge University Press, 2013), 304n476: 'οὐ κατακρίνει αὐτὸν τῷ λογισμῷ. I also note the generally pejorative sense the term "λογισμός" has in many of these anecdotes and sayings.

11. The most sophisticated modern internal attack on the Christian practice of preaching was Kierkegaard's, and much of his philosophical work can be seen as the attempt to find a way to transmit Christian truth indirectly without preaching it. Given the nature of this claim, one would not expect to be able to find a single clear passage in which Kierkegaard states that he intends to communicate with his readers indirectly, but one can consult *The Point of View of My Work as an Author* (Princeton, NJ: Princeton University Press, 1941), translated by W. Lowrie.

12. The contemporary philosopher who has pursued this line most forcefully is probably Philippa Foot. See her *Natural Goodness* (Oxford: Oxford University Press, 2001).

13. Even Plato tacitly admits this, although he tries his best to squirm out of it and to obfuscate his admission as much as possible. See my *Outside Ethics* (Princeton, NJ: Princeton University Press, 2009), 78–111.

14. I have used this example before (in my *Politics and the Imagination* [Princeton, NJ: Princeton University Press, 2010], 34), but it is too enlightening to resist.

15. Otto Fürst von Bismarck, *Gedanken und Erinnerungen* (Stuttgart: Cotta, 1915), 1:198.

16. Carr, *The Twenty Years' Crisis*, 62–83.

17. Bernard Williams analyzes the importance of the "absolute conception" in his *Descartes: The Project of Pure Enquiry* (London: Penguin, 1978). I also have

some remarks in my *Philosophy and Real Politics* (Princeton, NJ: Princeton University Press, 2008), 1–17.

18. Plato, *Gorgias*, 511–513.

19. Nietzsche, *Zur Genealogie der Moral*, 5:365.

20. *Les murs ont la parole*, ed. Julien Besançon (Paris: Éditions Tchou, 1968), 69.

21. See M. Doyle, "Kant, Liberal Legacies, and Foreign Affairs," *Philosophy and Public Affairs* 1–2, no. 12: 205–235, 323–353.

22. E. H. Carr, *Dostoevsky (1821–1881), a New Biography* (London: Allen and Unwin, 1931). Carr's discussion of *The Idiot* (210–215) is especially relevant.

23. F. Rabelais, *ouevres complètes*, Mireille Huchon, ed. (Pleiades: Gallimard, 1994), 139–153.

24. Karl Popper, *The Open Society and Its Enemies* (London: Routledge, 1942), 2 vols. Note that this work was first published after *The Twenty Years' Crisis*.

25. Marx's main criticism is found in "Das Manifest der Kommunistischen Partei," in *Marx-Engels-Werke*, 6th ed. (Berlin: Dietz, 1972), 4:489–492, also in *Die Deutsche Ideologie Marx-Engels-Werke* (Berlin: Dietz, 1958), vol. 3, passim.

26. Gustav Landauer, *Revolution* (Berlin: Karin Kramer Verlag, 1974).

27. See also my "Wer das Sagen hat" in *Mittelweg 36* 20, no. 6 (2011): 3–12.

28. Carr, *The Twenty Years' Crisis*, 6–7.

29. Ibid., 10.

30. Ibid., 7.

31. Ibid., 10.

32. Friedrich Nietzsche, *Der Antichrist*, in *Nietzsches Werke: Kritische Studien-Ausgabe*, Colli and Montinari, eds. (Berlin: de Gruyter, 1967), 6:170.

33. Carr, *The Twenty Years' Crisis*, 65.

34. See works cited above in footnote 1.

3 Chaos and Ethics

1. The Hellenistic philosophers spoke of ἀταραξία as the goal of philosophy.

2. It has often been claimed that what fascinates us in art is the possibility of undoing for a moment that conjunction, and allowing ourselves to be surprised without going numb from fear: "*Denn das Schöne ist nichts / als des Schrecklichen Anfang, den wir grad noch ertragen / und wir bewundern es so, weil es gelassen verschmäht / uns zu zerstören*" (Rilke, *Duineser Elegien*, I, line 3f).

3. John Dewey, *The Quest for Certainty*.

4. Freud does not actually ever say exactly this. He says "*Sie werden sich überzeugen, daß viel damit gewonnen ist, wenn es uns gelingt, Ihr hysterisches Elend in gemeines Unglück zu verwandeln. Gegen das letztere werden Sie sich mit einem wieder genesenden Nervensystem besser zur Wehr setzen können*" (Breuer and Freud, *Studien über Hysterie* [Frankfurt am Main: Fischer, 1991]), and he says various things about the unattainability of happiness as a human goal (S. Freud, *Das Unbehagen in der Kultur* in *S. Freud Studienausgabe* [Frankfurt am Main: Fischer, 1974], vol. ix, 197–270). So this is what I hope is a "conservative extension" (to use philosophers' jargon) of his views.

5. I intentionally speak here of "the Platonist's dream' and not of "Plato's dream" because it is not at all clear that Plato thought the knowledge of the good, which he compared to a certain kind of vision, could actually be reduced to the kind of thing I am calling a "doctrine."

6. Plato, *Ap* 40c4, 41c8, *Phaedo* 67b7–c3.

7. See the advice of Iokasta *OT* 977–983: εἰκῆι κράτιστον ζῆν, ὅπως δύναιτό τις.

8. Plato, *Gorgias*, 511–513; also see *supra*.

9. Diogenes Laertius VI. 11: αὐτάρκη δὲ τὴν ἀρετὴν πρὸς εὐδαιμονίαν, μηδενὸς προσδεομένος, ὅτι μὴ Σωκρατικῆς ἰσχύος.

4 Russell Brand, Lady T, Pisher Bob, and Preacher John

I am particularly indebted to Dr. Lorna Finlayson, who gave me the original idea to write this chapter.

1. London: Century, 2014.

2. *Pisher* means annoying young fellow, irritating person, in Yiddish.

3. See below, Chapter 10.

4. Valérie Trierweiler, *Merci pour ce moment* (Paris: Les Arènes, 2014).

5. No entry for the word occurs in the index, and I encountered only one instance of its use, on page 270 where it is being contrasted with "draconian."

6. See Geuss, *Philosophy and real politics* (Princeton, NJ: Princeton University Press, 2010).

7. Brand's interpretation of Ganesh (p. 53) needs to be slightly revised: it is surely just as important to remove external obstacles as it is to remove internal ones. Perhaps he did not mean to deny this.

8. Gandhi, Graeber, Chomsky, all passim.

9. Éditions Maspero.

10. *Comité invisible* (Paris: La Fabrique Éditions, 2007).

5 The Idea of a Critical Theory, Forty Years On

1. See Robert Brenner, *The Boom and the Bubble* (London: Verso, 2001).

2. Thomas Friedman, *The World Is Flat* (New York: Farrar, Straus and Giroux, 2005).

6 István Hont (1947–2013)

These are comments prepared for presentation at the memorial service for István Hont held at Kings College, Cambridge, in August 2013. My thanks to Lorna Finlayson and Peter Garnsey for helpful comments on the first draft.

1. "Ich möchte die Frage nach dem Werthe der Erkenntniß behandeln wie ein kalter Engel, der die ganze Lumperei durchschaut. Ohne böse zu sein, aber ohne Gemüth" (19 [234]). This is a fragment from 1872–1873 *Friedrich Nietzsche: Sämtliche Werke. Kritische Studienausgabe*, Colli and Montinari, eds. (Berlin: de Gruyter, 1980), 7:493. Although this is a remark specifically about the "value

of cognition," it seems reasonable to adopt for the purposes described in a more general form.

2. "Inde consilium mihi pauca . . . tradere . . . sine ira et studio": *Ab excessu divi Augusti*, ed. Koestermann (Leipzig: Teubner, 1960), I.1.

3. Whether or not he actually succeeded in avoiding them in his history is, of course, another matter. Similarly, it is an open question whether this aspiration could in principle be realized (even if it is not by Tacitus), whether it is a dangerous or an innocent illusion, or whether, even if it is realizable, it might retain value as an ideal to be approached asymptotically.

4. *Friedrich Nietzsche: Sämtliche Werke. Kritische Studienausgabe*, 3:63; 7:668–669.

5. G. W. F. Hegel, *Grundlinien zur Philosophie des Rechts in Werke in zwanzig Baenden* (Frankfurt: Suhrkamp, 1970), 7:11–28. ("Vorrede.")

6. In this they differ from Homeric gods, who are invulnerable but have both the capacity for complete detachment and for active engagement. Walter Benjamin's "angel of history" is presented as essentially a passive spectator of what has happened: He stares in openmouthed horror at the past as its catastrophes pile up in front of him, a single mountainous mass of ruins that reaches to the skies, and he is propelled *backward* into the future by a wind that blows from a utopian past. An "angel" (from the Greek word for "announce" [ἀγγέλλειν]) is essentially a messenger. If they *do* intervene, it is as mere ministers of divine will, so without fully human forms of independent decision making. (The history of angels is very complex and these offhand remarks do not claim to be more than a crude first approximation of a full account.)

7. This has been repeatedly emphasized by John Dunn. See especially his *The Cunning of Unreason* (London: HarperCollins, 2000).

8. See Bernard Williams, *Ethics and the Limits of Philosophy* (London: Fontana, 1985), chap. 9.

7 *The Moral Legacy of Marxism*

I am particularly indebted to Richard Raatzsch for conversations about the topics discussed in this essay.

1. Gary Becker, *The Economic Approach to Human Behaviour* (Chicago: University of Chicago Press, 1976), one of the sacred texts of the neoliberals.

2. Neither the shift to heliocentrism nor Darwin's theory of evolution had as much of an effect on undermining religious belief as the development of what is called "historical consciousness" in the nineteenth century and the application of the associated methods of textual criticism to the Bible did.

3. The Faculty of Philosophy at Cambridge now offers a special M.Phil. program (funded by banks) for the study of how one can restore public trust in banks. This is a particularly ingenious ploy because how could anyone object to a "philosophical" study of such eminently important topics as trust, public institutions, debt?

4. So the mistake people make is to assume that because "in our society it is dog eat dog, in every possible society it must always be dog eat dog."

5. *Vide supra*, 22–43.

6. Obviously the discussion in this paragraph is highly compressed and simplified.

7. To avoid misunderstanding, I note that this is a mere report of the way I think many people would think. I do not mean to endorse any final distinction between "moral in the broad sense" and "descriptive"; this distinction actually seems to me a subordinate one that is contextual and depends on point of view.

8. Karl Marx, *Die moralisierende Kritik und die kritisierende Moral*, in *Deutsche Brüsseler Zeitung* 28 & 31 October, 11, 18, 25 November 1847. (In MEW, 4:331ff.)

9. See also R. Geuss, *A World without Why* (Princeton, NJ: Princeton University Press, 2014), 45–67.

10. Thus, the book is eminently suitable for use as a set text in university courses.

11. John Rawls, *Political Liberalism* (New York: Columbia University Press, 1993).

12. Tomasi di Lampedusa, *Der Leopard* (Munich: Piper, 1962), 33.

13. Lucherhand, 1968, esp. 58ff.

14. MEW, 23:90ff. Robinson, of course, grew up in England and has corresponding powers and abilities, which cannot be understood apart from that formation. Also MEW, 23:192–195 about the spiders and bees in competition with the human architect.

15. The whole notion of the "starting point" was an obsession for Hegel and philosophers who came after him, including Marx. Marx has a highly complex discussion of his method, where to begin, how to proceed, and so on. Suffice it here to say that he agreed with Hegel that there is not any "absolute" starting point, because there are no such thing as "foundations" in the traditional sense, but that he also distinguished clearly between the method one should use for doing research (the *"Forschungsmethode"* with its appropriate starting point) and the method one should use when, at the end of one's research one had the conclusions, no matter how tentative they were, and wished to present them in the best form (the *"Darstellungsmethode"* with its appropriate starting point).

16. Title of a book by Tom Nagel (Oxford: Oxford University Press, 1989).

17. S. Kierkegaard, *Concluding Unscientific Postscript*, trans. Hong and Hong (Princeton, NJ: Princeton University Press, 1992).

18. Like my own teacher, Sidney Morgenbesser.

19. Plato, *Republic*, 352D6–7.

20. What one might call the "North American" school of Hegel interpretation fails because it makes no attempt to formulate and interpret one of Hegel's basic claims, namely, that the descriptive and the normative (to put it in a vocabulary Hegel himself would not have used) are not, finally, distinct. It is fully understandable that interpreters would shy away from this claim because it does seem hard to maintain.

21. And, as Brecht has his Galileo say, "Woe to the land that needs heroes."

22. Marx could also hardly fail to wish to point out that even if a morality of this type was useful in helping a social formation like ours to maintain itself, it was not sufficient, and it would be a gross error to think one could succeed in

allowing this society to maintain itself *merely* by continuing to cultivate the same kind of habits.

23. A constant theme in Brecht, cf. *An die Nachgeborenen (Die Gedichte)* (Frankfurt: Suhrkamp, 1981), 722ff.

24. See also Trotsky in Trotsky and Dewey, *Their Morals and Ours* (London: Pathfinder, 1973), 21–22.

25. I recall once reading the memoirs of a clown who expressed his deep gratitude to his father, also a clown, who had taken him out into the woods one day and intentionally broken both his legs: if he was to be a successful clown, the author of the memoir needed to have an irregular and ludic walk.

26. On the concept of "need," see David Wiggins, "Claims of Need," in *Needs, Values, Truth* (Oxford: Blackwell, 1987); also Agnes Heller, *The Theory of Need in Marx* (London: Allison & Busby, 1974). Also Heller, Féher, and Markus, *Dictatorship over Needs* (London: Blackwell, 1983) and L. Hamilton *The Political Philosophy of Needs* (Cambridge: Cambridge University Press, 2003).

27. This point is made repeatedly in *Die Heilige Familie* (MEW, 2).

28. Friedrich Nietzsche, *Sämtliche Werke: Kritische Studienausgabe*, ed. Colli and Montinari (Berlin: de Gruyter, 1980), 6:74 *(Götzen-Dämmerung)*.

29. Colin Turnbull, *The Mountain People* (New York: Simon and Shuster, 1972), 280.

30. Montaigne, *"Du repentir"* and *"De l'expérience,"* in *Essais* (Paris: Flammarion, 1979), 3:20–33, 275–328.

31. See Kierkegaard, *Concluding Unscientific Postscript*, trans. Hong and Hong (Princeton, NJ: Princeton University Press, 1992).

32. F. Dostoyevsky, *Aufzeichnungen aus dem Kellerloch*, trans. S. Geier (Frankfurt am Main: Fischer, 2006).

33. After *"Das Gleichnis des Buddha vom brennenden Haus,"* in Brecht, *Die Gedichte* (Frankfurt: Suhrkamp, 1981), 664–665.

8 Economies: Good, Bad, Indifferent

I am particularly grateful to the members of the Cambridger Forschungskolloquium for discussion of this chapter. I have also greatly benefited from conversations with Lorna Finlayson about previous German versions of the chapter.

1. In an interview for the German television network ZDF in January 2009.

2. L. Hamilton, *The Political Philosophy of Needs* (Cambridge: Cambridge University Press, 2003).

3. Of course, one could add to this list the following: cultural needs, educational needs, emotional needs, and so on. Some would think it important to classify "psychological needs" as a distinct category, and there are, of course, in most advanced societies "legal requirements" that must be observed in social interaction. In all these cases it is difficult to know whether some purported "need" is really a need and is really of a distinct kind from other needs. For discussion of a fuller list, see A. Maslow, *Motivation and Personality* (New York: Addison-Wesley, 1970).

4. Recall Hans Castorp's astonishment in Thomas Mann's *Der Zauberberg* (set in 1907) that the men in the sanatorium *Berghof* do not wear hats outside.

5. See Edna Ullmann-Margalit and Sidney Morgenbesser, "Picking and Choosing," *Social Research*, 44, (1977), 757–785.

6. This point was made with all requisite clarity by David Wiggins in his "The Claim of Needs," in Wiggins, *Needs, Values, Truth* (Oxford: Blackwell, 1987), 1–57.

7. It is a commonplace in the literature that this is the origin of one strand of the modern concept of "toleration." See J. Dunn, *The Political Thought of John Locke* (Cambridge: Cambridge University Press, 1969).

8. Flavius Josephus, *De bello judaico* in *Opera* (Leipzig: Teubner, 1888), 2.224.

9. "'Et si l'on vous demandait la lune?' demanda Sartre à Fidel. Celui-ci réflechit un instant, regarda par la fenêtre ouverte vers le brouillard sur la lagune et lui répondit: 'S'ils me demandent la lune, c'est qu'ils en ont besoin et il faudrait la leur donner. Toutes les demandes qu'ils font, quelles qu'elles soient, ils ont le droit de les obtenir.' Sartre conclut: le seul humanisme possible est basé sur le besoin." L. Otero and S. Vassallo, "Sartre à Cuba: Le chemin se fait en marchant," *Rue Descartes* 1/47, (2005), 116–123.

10. G. Becker, *The Economic Approach to Human Behavior* (Chicago: University of Chicago Press, 1976).

11. See discussion of the liberal idea of anti-paternalism *infra*.

12. Karl Marx, *Marx-Engels-Werke* (Berlin: Dietz, 1968), Erg. Bd. 1, 541–542.

13. See Plato, *Apologia Socratis* (Oxford: Oxford University Press, 1995), esp. 37D–38B.

14. Recent relevant discussions of these issues include the papers in Harry Frankfurt, *The Importance of What We Care About* (Cambridge: Cambridge University Press, 1988); Bernard Williams, "Practical Necessity," in Williams, *Moral Luck* (Cambridge: Cambridge University Press, 1982), 124–131; Williams, *Shame and Necessity* (Berkeley: University of California Press, 2008).

15. See R. Wagner, *Rheingold*, act II.

16. Aristotle, *Ethica Nichomachea* (Oxford: Oxford University Press, 1894), book III.

17. Agnes Heller (with F. Féher and G. Markus), *Dictatorship over needs* (London: Blackwell, 1983).

18. The complexities of the virtue of thriftiness have been noted since antiquity. See Cicero *"magnum vectigal est parsimonia"* in his *Paradoxa Stoicorum* (London: Macmillan, 1953); also N. Machiavelli, *The Prince*, ed. R. Price (Cambridge: Cambridge University Press, 1988), chaps. XV–XVII.

19. Max Weber, *Gesammelte Aufsätze zur Religionssoziologie I*, (Tübingen: Mohr, 1920), 43–48.

20. For instance, this is one of the main points of Brecht's "Der gute Mensch von Szechuan," (Frankfurt: Suhrkamp, 1964).

21. Philippa Foot, *Natural Goodness* (Oxford: Oxford University Press, 2001).

22. See R. Raatzsch in his essay in the collection "On the Notion of Sustainability," in *Inquiry* 55 (4) (2012), 361–385.

23. Max Weber, *Wirtschaft und Gesellschaft* (Tübingen: Mohr, 1972), 44–45 et passim.

24. Again, using "Aristotle" and "Hume" as ideal-typical terms to represent types of theories, not necessarily identical with those of the two historical individuals who here lend their names to them.

25. But see also *supra* 361–385.

26. See M. Friedman, *Capitalism and Freedom* (Chicago: University of Chicago Press, 1962).

27. H. R. Haldeman, *The Ends of Power* (New York: Time Books, 1978), 122.

28. The veto was a classic instance of what Max Weber would have called an action based on a *Gesinnungsethik;* see his *Politik als Beruf* (Berlin: Duncker & Humblot, 1982, 52–67), that is, one intended to be expressive of a certain ethos regardless of the results. The public rationale for the veto was to protect the City of London. Regardless of whether one thought that was a good or a bad thing, it was clear that vetoing the agreement was not going to have the desired effect, because the other members of the European Union simply made the agreement Cameron vetoed *outside* the structures of the EU. This meant that the agreement was passed *and* Britain had excluded itself from any further discussion of financial arrangements that would deeply affect the city. So the veto had the reverse effect from that which was cited as its rationale. Nevertheless, it had a strong symbolic significance for Cameron's eurosceptic backbenchers.

29. See Raymond Geuss, *The Idea of a Critical Theory* (Cambridge: Cambridge University Press, 1981), esp. chap. 2.

30. My thanks to Martin Eichler for this point.

9 Can the Humanities Survive Neoliberalism?

1. For further discussion of the history of classification of disciples, see "Goals, origins, disciples," in my *A World without Why* (Princeton, NJ: Princeton University Press, 2014), 1–21.

2. G. W. F. Hegel, *Grundlinien zur Rechtsphilosophie* in *Werke in zwanzig Bänden*, Moldenhauer and Michel, eds. (Frankfurt: Suhrkamp, 1970), vol. 7, 21.

3. Plato, *Meno*, 93b–e.

4. Instruction and education would not, of course, be "private" matters in the society depicted in Plato's *Republic*.

5. Notice that this explains the seeming anomaly that the most socially exclusive and expensive secondary schools in Britain, such as Eton, Harrow, Charterhouse, and Rugby, have the technical name "*public* schools." In principle anyone could *apply* to Eton, although without money, minimal academic aptitude, and probably social connections one would probably not be admitted. They were "public" in the eighteenth century compared with the aristocratic habit of having individual tutors hired to give instruction at home. The philosopher Hobbes was such a private tutor for the whole of his life, and in central Europe this was a phase of life through which any number of people who eventually made significant contributions passed: Hölderlin, Hegel, too, for a

while. As various people pointed out, the combination of intellectual authority and social servility was not conducive to happiness.

6. G. W. F. Hegel, *Vorlesungen über die Ästhetik* in *Werke in zwanzig Bänden*, Moldenhauer and Michel, eds. (Frankfurt: Suhrkamp, 1970), vol. 13, 25. See also vol. 13, 50–52.

7. Gary Becker, *The Economic Approach to Human Behaviour* (Chicago: University of Chicago Press, 1976).

10 Identification and the Politics of Envy

1. Karl Marx, *Zur Kritik der Hegelschen Rechtsphilosophie MEW* (Berlin: Dietz, 1978), *Erg.* I, 534.

2. See Peter Garnsey, *Thinking about Property* (Cambridge: Cambridge University Press, 2007).

3. See Raymond Geuss, *Philosophy and Real Politics* (Princeton, NJ: Princeton University Press, 2008), 76–80.

4. See Helmut Schoeck, *Der Neid* (Freiburg: Alber, 1964).

5. *Rhetorica*, 1387b23.

6. For discussion of envy in general in ancient philosophy, see E. Milobenski, *Der Neid in der griechischen Philosophie* (Wiesbaden: Harrassowitz, 1964).

7. See David Konstan, "*Nemesis* and *Phthonos*," in *Gestures*, ed. Bakewell and Sickinger (Oxford: Oxbow Books, 2003), 74–87; also *Envy, Spite, and Jealousy*, ed. D. Konstan; also the essays in *Envy, Spite and Jealousy*, ed. Konstan and Rutter (Edinburgh: Edinburgh University Press, 2003); also Robert Kaster, *Emotion, Restraint, and Community in Ancient Rome* (Oxford: Oxford University Press, 2005), chap. 4.

8. Milobenski, *Der Neid in der griechischen Philosophie*.

9. Plutarch, *Vita Caesaris*, 54.

10. The Latin word *invidia* unfortunately seems to be used for both what the Greeks called "νέμεσις" and for what they called "φθόνος." See Kaster, *Emotion, Restraint, and Community*, chap. 4.

11. I note that positionality is something completely different from the comparative dimension of certain kinds of envy that was discussed above.

12. Rawls never really seems to understand the implications of giving the kind of centrality he does to Pareto optimality.

13. Medea is the classic case from the ancient world.

14. See Richard Raatzsch, "Wohlhabende, denkt nach!" (unpublished manuscript).

11 Identity, Property, and the Past

1. James Cuno, *Who Owns Antiquity? Museums and the Battle over Our Ancient Heritage* (Princeton, NJ: Princeton University Press, 2008), abbreviated *WO*.

2. Margaret M. Miles, *Art as Plunder: The Ancient Origins of Debate about Cultural Property* (New York: Cambridge University Press, 2008), abbreviated

AP. Additional books discussed in this chapter are Robin F. Rhodes, ed., *The Acquisition and Exhibition of Classical Antiquities, Professional, Legal, and Ethical Perspectives: A Symposium Held at the Snite Museum of Art, University of Notre Dame, February 24, 2007* (Notre Dame, IN: University of Notre Dame Press, 2007), abbreviated *AE;* Colin Renfrew, *Loot, Legitimacy and Ownership: the Ethical Crisis in Archaeology* (London: Duckworth, 2000), abbreviated *LL;* Peter Watson and Cecilia Todeschini, *The Medici Conspiracy: The Illicit Journey of Looted Antiquities—from Italy's Tomb Raiders to the World's Greatest Museums* (New York: BBS Public Affairs, 2007), abbreviated *MC*.

12 *The Future of Evil*

I should like to thank the members of the audience at the Zeno Lecture, which I gave at the University of Utrecht in April 2010, for several clarifying comments that helped me improve this chapter.

1. *Secunda secundae, quaestio C.*

2. See Hans Blumenberg, *Die Legitimität der Neuzeit* (Frankfurt: Suhrkamp, 1966).

3. *KSA* 5.152–178. All quotations are from *Friedrich Nietzsche Sämtliche Werke: Kritische Studien-Ausgabe*, Colli and Montinari, eds. (Berlin: de Gruyter, 1967), cited as *KSA*, by volume and page.

4. Ibid., 5.254–255, 261, 288–289.

5. Ibid., 5.263. I cite Theognis following *Delectus ex iambis et elegis graecis*, ed. M. T. West (OCT).

6. *KSA* 7.386.

7. The poems of Theognis have come to us in collections that seem to comprise various poems by various authors, and it is extremely unclear which of the poems in this collection are really by the sixth-century man from Megara, which are imitations by other people of poems by this sixth-century figure (that is, poems "in the manner of Theognis of Megara"), and that are completely independent poems by completely different people that simply happened for one reason or another to have been copied together into the collection. This sort of historical-philological detective work—"Is this poem *really* by Theognis? Has an imitator added something at the end? If so, where does the genuine 'material' end and the added imitation begin?"—was exactly the sort of thing the young Nietzsche was trained to do, and one of his early published works was an article for a scholarly journal about which bits of the Theognid corpus were genuine (that is, written by the original sixth-century man from Megara) and which were not. One can see the connection between this kind of enterprise and Nietzsche's later views about "genealogy." So we can be sure that Nietzsche had read and studied his body of poetry with the greatest philological care.

8. The other classic discussion of the way ethical terms change meaning in extreme circumstances is, of course, Thucydides's discussion of the events in Corcyra during the Peloponnesian War (III.82).

9. Theognis 53–58.

10. Theognis 1109–1112.

11. Theognis was keen to ensure that human marriages conformed to the principles of eugenics derived from our knowledge of how to breed the best "rams, asses, and horses"; see Theognis 183–192.

12. See also a slightly later literary representation in Aristophanes, *Nubes*, 41–55, of a similar case to the one envisaged here.

13. *KSA* 5.254–255.

14. *KSA* 6.98.

15. *KSA* 5.270–277.

16. *Quaestiones disputatae de malo* Quaestio VIII.

17. *Quaestiones disputatae de virtutibus.*

18. *Quaestiones disputatae de malo* Quaestio VIII.

13 Satire, Who Whom?

This was originally written as an exercise in French, then translated into German by Marie Döring and appeared in the journal *360°* under the macaronic title: "Non. Je ne suis pas Charlie: Über Satire und die Grenzen der Zumutbarkeit." I am very grateful to Döring for suggesting that I add some further material to her German text. This is a translation by Lorna Finlayson of Döring's German version.

1. Friedrich Nietzsche, *Kritische Studienausgabe*, Colli and Montinari, eds. (Berlin: de Gruyter, 1980), Band 8, S. 454.

14 The Radioactive Wolf, Pieing, and the Goddess Fashion

I am grateful to Manuel Dries, Lorna Finlayson, and Jörg Schaub for some exceedingly helpful comments on a previous draft of this chapter.

1. *"Dada heißt im Rumänischen Ja Ja, im Französischen Hotto- und Steckenpferd. Für Deutsche ist es ein Signum alberner Naivität und zeugungsfroher Verbundenheit mit dem Kinderwagen."* Hugo Ball, *Die Flucht aus der Zeit* (as cited in *Dada in Zürich* [abbreviated *DZ*], ed. Karl Riha [Ditzingen: Reclam, 1994], 14).

2. Ibid., 30.

3. "Addio, steigt mir, bitte, den Rücken runter, auf Wiedersehn ein ander Mal!" (*DZ* 30).

4. Tristan Tzara, *Sept manifestes DADA* (Société Nouvelle des Éditions Pauvert, 1979), 41.

5. *DZ* 12.

6. On the modern as the "ephemeral," see Baudelaire, *Peintre de la vie moderne* (in his *Écrits sur l'art* [Paris: Gallimard, 1971], 2:133–193).

7. *"Während wir in Zürich, Spiegelgasse 1, das Kabarett hatten, wohnte uns gegenüber in derselben Spielgelgasse, Nr. 6, wenn ich nicht irre, Herr Ulianow-Lenin . . . Ist der Dadaismus wohl als Zeichen und Geste das Gegenspiel zum Bolschewismus? Stellt er der Destruktion und vollendeten Berechnung die völlig donchichottische, zweckwidrige und unfaßbare Seite der Welt gegenüber?* (*DZ* 25).

8. Plautus, Asinaria 495; see also Sigmund Freud, "Das Unbehagen in der Kultur" in *S. Freud Studienausgabe* (Frankfurt am Main: Fischer, 1974), vol. ix, 240.

9. *King Lear*, Act I, scene 4.

10. Walter Benjamin, *Illuminationen* (Frankfurt: Suhrkamp, 1977), 136–169.

11. Ibid., 184.

12. *DZ* 20–21.

13. *DZ*.

14. Ibid., 14–15; for a discussion of the contemporary political use and significance of puppets, see David Graeber, *Direct Action* (Edinburgh: AK Press, 2009).

15. *DZ* 33.

16. Ibid., 29.

17. See Joel Bakan, *The Corporation* (New York: Random House, 2003).

18. G. E. Lessing, *"Zerstreute Anmerkungen über das Epigramm und einige der vornehmsten Epigrammatisten"* in *Werke* (Vienna: Verlag von Sigmund Bensinger, n.d.) edited by Heinrich Laube, vol. v, 42–99.

19. See John Berger, *Ways of Seeing* (London: Penguin, 1972).

20. Alexander Nehamas, *Only a Promise of Happiness* (Princeton, NJ: Princeton University Press, 2007).

21. *"Préface"* by Yvon Belaval to Sade's *La philosophie dans le boudoir* (Paris: Gallimard, 1976), 7–8.

22. Thomas Friedman, *The World Is Flat* (New York: Farrar, Straus and Giroux, 2005).

23. Daniel Bell, *The End of Ideology* (Cambridge, MA: Harvard University Press, 1962); Francis Fujiyama, *The End of History* (New York: Free Press, 1992).

24. Herbert Marcuse, *One-Dimensional Man* (Boston: Beacon Press, 1965).

25. *DZ* 29.

15 What Time Is It?

1. "The gods smiled on the side that won [the party of Caesar], but Cato still preferred the defeated side [that of the Republic]" (Lucan I. 135).

16 Augustine on Love, Perspective, and Human Nature

1. Freud, "Das Unbehagen in der Kultur" in *S. Freud Studienausgabe* (Frankfurt am Main: Fischer, 1974), vol. ix, 197–270.

2. David Wiggins, *Needs, Values, Truth* (Oxford: Blackwell, 1987), 1–57. R. Geuss, *The Idea of a Critical Theory* (Cambridge: Cambridge University Press, 1981), 46–8; R. Geuss, *Outside Ethics* (Princeton, NJ: Princeton University Press, 2005), 145–146.

3. See Appendix I.

4. Oddly enough, the person who seems to me to have seen this most clearly is Stendahl, in *Sur l'amour*.

5. The only book I know that pays any attention to this is Negt and Kluge's *Geschichte und Eigensinn* (Frankfurt: Zweitausendeins, 1981).

6. I note that Augustine gets *no entry* in the three volumes of Hegel's *History of Philosophy* in which such luminaries as Alexander of Hales and Julian of Toledo get a page or two each.

7. The church, of course, is prior to and much older than the scriptures, having existed for decades before even the earliest of the Gospels was written down, and the Gospels have their standing as the recognized central texts of Christianity by virtue of a long collective decision process by the church that did not get started until a century after Christ's death and was not completed until two centuries (at least) later. The only reason anyone reads "the Gospel according to Matthew" rather than the thirty or so other "gospels" that we know were circulating in the first and second century, is that church councils "authorized" *this* version. So rather than the church being based on scripture, it is rather that scripture—what counts as canonical—is based on the church and its decisions.

8. I note that what is said here about the need for collective structures like the church to give love its correct focus and form, might also *mutatis mutandis* be said about political parties or other social formations.

9. *Remota itaque iustitia quid sunt regna nisi magna latrocinia? . . . Eleganter enim et veraciter Alexandro illi Magno quidam comprehensus pirata respondit. Nam cum idem rex hominem interrogaret, quid ei videretur ut mare haberet infestum, ille libera contumacia: Quod tibi, inquit, ut orbem terrarum; sed quia id ego exiguo navigio facio, latro vocor; quia tu magna classe, imperator.* ["Thus, if justice is taken away, what are kingdoms other than huge bands of robbers? For the pirate gave an elegant and correct response to Alexander the Great, when he was captured. Alexander asked him what he thought he was doing by making the sea unsafe. He replied with the outspokenness a free man uses: The same thing you think you are doing when you make the whole world unsafe. But because I do it with one little ship, I am called a bandit, whereas when you do it with a huge fleet, they call you emperor."]

10. See Appendix II.

Index

abstract/abstraction, 5, 7, 20, 27, 32, 100–111, 115, 137, 154, 164–166, 170, 178, 180, 183, 193, 199, 206, 269–271
Abu Ghraib, 132, 223, 233
acceptance, 10, 43, 264, 266; arts of, 54–56, 59
Adorno, T. W., 21, 22, 23, 79, 142–143, 146–147, 251, 270
Agricola (work by Tacitus), 220
analytic philosophy, 1–24, 83
anthropology, 14–15, 54, 100, 170, 211
anti-paternalism, 156–157, 160
anti-philosopher, 228, 239
Archilochus, 220–221
argumentum hystericum, 265
Aristophanes, 78, 222
Aristotle, 57, 138, 141, 145, 165, 171–176, 178–179, 224, 261–263
Arkesilaos of Cyrene, 254–255
art, 3, 80, 92, 148, 150–151, 184–203, 219–220, 223, 226–252
Art as Plunder (book by Margaret Miles), 184–189
L'art français de la guerre (novel by Alexi Jenni), 259
Augustine, Saint, 221, 261–274

bad. *See* good and bad
Ball, Hugo, 226–228, 242
Becker, Gary, 160
Benjamin, Walter, 199, 232, 242
Bismarck, Otto von, 38
Black Camisole (painting by Chantal Joffe), 246–251

Blair, Tony, 34–38, 225
"Blair, Tony" (species of fallacious argument), 224–225
Bolsheviks/Bolshevism, 74, 228–229, 242
Brand, Russell, 64–78
Brecht, Bertold, 137, 255, 257
Büchner, Georg, 239–240

Cabaret Voltaire, 226–228, 239
Cameron, David, 145, 225
capitalism, 24, 81, 84–85, 98–99, 109–111, 116, 168, 170, 250
Carr, E. H., 25–50
Castro, Fidel, 125, 127
Cato, 177–179, 194, 255
Cervantes, 222–223
chaos, 51–58
Charlie Hebdo, 218
Christ, 30, 71, 264
Christianity, 27, 29–33, 3842, 44, 58, 91–92, 96, 105, 114–115, 123, 176, 189, 205, 206, 209–215, 226, 235, 261–277
Christian preaching, 29–33
church, 147, 151, 187, 271; Catholic, 92, 151, 204, 222, 224, 262, 271, 273; Christian, 149
CIA, 92, 224, 274
Cicero, 185
de civitate dei (work by Augustine), 221, 265–267, 269–270
comforting, 12, 23, 63, 83, 86–88, 99–100, 161, 210–211, 242
communism, 4, 163–167, 169–170, 182

confessiones (work by Augustine), 263

consolation, 30, 59, 83, 87–88, 90, 155

context, 15, 19, 23, 27–29, 33–45, 48–49, 60–61, 67, 69, 72, 76, 79, 83, 94, 96–96, 99–100, 102–105, 110, 112, 121–127, 133–133, 146, 153, 174, 177, 189, 192, 195, 196–198, 201, 222, 233, 236, 244–246, 254, 264, 275

Le contrat social (book by Jean-Jacques Rousseau), 78

control, arts of, 52, 54–55

cosmopolitanism, 270, 190–194, 273

criticism/critique, 4, 10–14, 18–19, 22–24, 39, 45–47, 79–84115, 145, 170, 181, 193, 219, 222, 255

Cuno, James, 184, 189–203

curiosity, 205, 263

Dada Is Dead (painting by Adrian Ghenie), 226–246

Dadaism, 226–246, 250

Dante, 204, 242

Dantons Tod (play by Georg Büchner), 239–240

"Degenerate Art," 92–93, 230, 246

demand, 4, 27, 42–43, 45, 60, 74, 83, 123, 125–128, 131, 138–145, 170

democracy, 15, 24–25, 43–44, 87–88, 99–100, 140, 150, 189, 194, 255–256

demons, 227, 275

desert. *See* merit

desires, 41–44, 46–49, 50, 54, 59, 61, 63, 71, 89, 104, 112–114, 118–122, 125–131, 139, 141–146, 154, 156–157, 160–161, 169, 173, 180, 210, 223, 255, 263–264, 268–269

Dewey, John, 52–55

Diogenes the Cynic, 193

distance, 2, 11, 59, 127, 145, 242, 255

Dix, Otto, 228–232

doctrine, 57–63

Dostoyevsky, Feodor, 44, 114

dystopia, 1–24, 184, 226

economic approach to human behavior, the, 91

economy, 47, 64, 66–70, 80–83, 98–101, 110, 113, 116, 117–146

egalitarianism, 71, 82, 166–171, 182

envy, 163–183, 206

eschatology, 226, 261, 264

ethica nicomachea (work by Aristotle), 261–262

ethics, 4, 17, 18–19, 27, 51–63, 99–116, 154, 204–206, 261–262, 264, 268; history of, 261

ethnology, 14–15, 20, 211

evaluation, 2, 4, 6–7, 11–13, 16, 19, 24, 28, 31–33, 37, 42, 48, 50, 69, 73, 96, 98, 100–102, 109, 112, 133–134, 137–139, 152–153, 159, 187, 204–205, 209, 212, 214, 223, 242, 249, 251, 270

evil, 27, 32–38, 205, 273, 276

explanation, 5–7, 16, 30, 33–39, 87, 169, 179, 201

Fanon, Franz, 76, 81

fashion, 246–252

fear, 3, 42, 54, 57–59, 61, 92, 169, 173–174, 181

Feuerbach, Ludwig, 83

Foucault, Michel, 21, 81

Frankfurt School, 81

freedom, 3, 25, 59, 70–71, 96, 141, 154, 161–163, 177, 185, 212–214, 218, 223–225, 251, 264

free speech, 218–225

free will, 32–33, 206, 213

Freud, Sigmund, 55, 264

Friedman, Thomas, 250

function/functioning, 11–12, 24, 28, 32–33, 36, 71, 86, 97, 100, 102, 110–111, 120, 122, 130, 146, 222–223, 228–229, 264, 266

45% erwerbsfähig (painting by Otto Dix), 230–232, 241

Gallerie Burchard, 228–230, 238

Gandhi, Mahatma, 75

Garutti, Gérald, 256–258

Genealogy of Morality, The (work by Friedrich Nietzsche), 203–217

Geschichte und Klassenbewußtsein (book by Georg Lukács), 101

Gildersleeve, Basil, 253–255

gluttony (*gula*), 205

good, 3–4, 11, 18, 27, 31–35, 41–42, 94–98, 101, 106, 108, 113–115, 117–119, 132–133, 135, 137–139, 142, 154, 157–158, 172–175, 177–180, 199, 205; the, 27, 33–34, 57, 210, 269–271, 273; the human, 45

good and bad, 32, 205–210, 212–218
good and evil, 32–33, 212–218
Google, 17, 274
grace, 33, 262
Grüne Heinrich, Der (novel by Keller), 159
Guantanamo Bay, 132, 224
guilt, 210, 212
Gurnemanz, 159

Haïm- à la lumiére d'un violon (play by
   Gérald Garutti), 257
happiness, 55, 61, 190, 263–268
Hayek, Friedrich, 82, 182
Hegel, G. W. F., 7, 50, 79, 83, 101, 106,
   150–151, 271
Heidegger, Martin, 275
Herder, 271
Hesiod, 15
history, 11–12, 23, 33, 36, 45–47, 49–50,
   54, 56, 72–73, 77, 79–82, 85–90, 99–105,
   113–115, 120, 128, 141, 143, 145–149,
   153, 159, 170–171, 184, 187, 189–190,
   192, 197–198, 200–201, 203, 205–217,
   219, 222, 228, 231–232, 236, 240,
   242–244, 246, 248, 250, 254–275, 277
Hobbes, Thomas, 22
Höch, Hannah, 228, 241
Hollande, François, 69
Hont, István, 85–90
hope, 59–63
Horace, 222
Huelsenbeck, Richard, 227, 235, 241, 252
Humanities, the, 148–162
human nature, 261–264
human rights, 15
Hume, David, 139, 141, 142, 145

ideal language, 8–9
Idea of a Critical Theory, The (book by
   Raymond Geuss), 79–84
identification, 176–183
identity, 135, 184–203, 263
ideology, 82, 156–157, 200, 221, 250
ignorance, 73, 256
illusion, 24, 61–62, 193, 212
impossible, the, 42–50, 264
Incarnation, the, 262, 264
incentives, 68–70, 82, 127
individual, the, 263, 269–271
individualism, 66, 77, 101–104, 161, 200
inequality, 66, 82–83

Inferno (part of poem by Dante), 204
inquiry, 10, 16, 62
L'insurrection qui vient (anonymous
   pamphlet), 78
interests, 13, 39, 49, 52, 93, 145, 157–159
intervention, 12, 16, 17, 19–20, 80–81, 93
intuitions, moral, 55, 72, 100–101

Jamet, Domenique, 259
Jealousy of Trade (book by István Hont), 85
Jenni, Alexi, 259–260
Joffe, Chantal, 246–252
John the Evangelist, Saint, 275–276
Julius Caesar, 177–179, 188
justice, 4, 16, 24, 27, 31, 70–72, 101
justification, 18–19, 21, 76–77, 104, 276
Juvenal, 222

Kant, Immanuel/Kantian, 6, 27, 40, 42,
   44, 58, 61, 73, 82, 96, 99, 105, 114, 137,
   235–237, 264, 271, 277
Keynsianism, 135–136, 155
Kierkegaard, Søren, 106, 113, 114
knowledge, 12, 24, 33–34, 40–41, 57–58,
   60, 68, 73, 88, 103–103, 115, 138, 156, 173,
   188, 196–198, 207, 244, 263, 270, 272
*Kunstwerk im Zeitalter seiner technischen
   Reproduzierbarkeit* (work by Walter
   Benjamin), 199

Lady T, 66, 69, 76–77
Landauer, Gustav, 46–48
law, 80, 88, 111, 124, 150, 186, 188, 190,
   192, 200, 207, 219, 242, 264–267
learning, 158–159
de legibus (tract by Cicero), 78
Lenin, V. I., 106, 228, 239
Leviathan (book by Hobbes), 78
liberal democracy, x, 24, 87, 99–101
liberalism, 3, 91
life, 47, 120, 129, 142, 147, 267–268;
   comfortable, 63, 116; eternal, 41, 268;
   everyday, 1, 16; form of, 24; good/
   valuable, 57–58, 66, 116, 154, 215;
   human, 13, 16–18, 26, 40, 52, 55–56, 59,
   61, 63, 65, 67, 69, 75, 91, 107, 114, 117,
   120, 127, 129, 145–146, 161, 170, 182,
   190–191, 210, 215, 251, 263–267, 270;
   meaningful, 65; modern, 8; philosophical, 129; social, 122–124; traditional
   form of, 132, 134–135

Lipsky, Haim, 257–259
love, 101, 107, 228, 239, 261–271
Lukács, Georg, 101
Luther, Martin, 130
Lykambes, 220–221

malfunctioning. *See* function/
   functioning
Malraux, André, 199
Mani/Manicheanism, 130, 273
Marcuse, Herbert, 81
market, 68, 132, 143–144, 154–157,
   161–162, 167, 182, 187, 190, 192–197,
   200, 203; free, 143–144, 154–156, 161,
   187, 190, 192–193, 196–197, 200
Martial, 222
Marx, Karl, 21, 45–46, 71, 75, 97,
   101–116, 159–160, 163–171, 242
Marxism, 91–116, 236
masks, 238–241
meaning, 2, 21–23, 230–236, 246, 257
merit, 66–70, 140, 181–182, 269–270
Merkel, Angela, 117, 131, 134
Metelli, 218–219, 221, 222
method, 1–5, 56–57, 86–89, 101
Microsoft, 224, 243, 274
Miles, Margaret, 184
Mill, J. S., 223
Minima moralia (work by T. W. Adorno),
   270
Montaigne, 114
morality, 31–33, 94–116, 203–217
moralizing/moralism, 25–39, 69, 94–98,
   115, 149
moral judgments, 26–27, 31, 94–98, 134
moral legacy, 94–116
More, Thomas, 3–4
Murdoch, Rupert, 180, 243
Musée sans murs (book by André
   Malraux), 199
museums, 184–203, 245, 250, 188

Naevius, 218–219, 221
Napoleon, 188
narcotics, 65, 73, 78, 137
nation/nationalism, 44, 189–201, 203,
   253–254, 259
necessity, 11, 17, 31–32, 40, 55, 61, 64–65,
   67, 69, 76, 82, 87, 102, 106, 109,
   113–114, 117–128, 130–135, 137–138,
   141–142, 144, 166, 170, 172, 178, 181,

195, 198–199, 211–212, 245, 251, 257,
   262, 265–266
needs, 1, 46–50, 101, 112–116, 117–132,
   139–147, 150, 268–269
neo-liberalism, 84, 142–145, 148–162,
   258–259
NHS (National Health Service), 75, 78,
   89, 166, 258
Nickelodeon (painting by Adrian Ghenie),
   237–242
Nietzsche, Friedrich, 21, 25, 48, 83,
   86–87, 104, 205–217, 222–223, 239
1984 (book by George Orwell), 4, 20,
   184
normative turn (in political philosophy),
   17, 101, 114
normativity, 17, 108, 111, 114–116

Old Testament, 262, 264, 274
One-Dimensional Man (book by Herbert
   Marcuse), 81
optimism, 33–34
ordinary language, 8–9
Orwell, George, 4, 20, 184
ownership, 72, 134–135, 151–152, 165,
   184–189

Pareto optimality, 179
Parsifal, 159
Parthenon, the, 189, 200, 244
participant observer, 15–17
Paul, Saint, 73
pedophilia, 205, 207
pharisaism, 29
philosopher, tasks of, 2
philosopher-king, 27
Picasso, Pablo, 248
Pindar, 253
Pisher Bob, 70–72, 77
Plato/Platonism, 27, 28, 38, 40–41, 42,
   44, 47–48, 56–63, 73, 150–151, 165,
   169, 184, 235, 263, 269, 271, 272
political philosophy, 10–11, 17–22, 70,
   99–116
politics (real), 11–13, 2–50, 88–90, 125,
   168–169, 271–277
positivist/positivism, 8, 91, 142, 146
possible. *See* impossible
power, 13, 39, 49, 58–59, 80, 180–181,
   219–220, 236, 265–266
praxis, 19, 88–90, 96, 104, 106

Preacher John, 70, 71, 73–74, 77
preferences. *See* desires
program, 5, 6, 92; different from a
    philosophy, 7
Prussian Archangel (Preussischer Erzengel)
    (work of art in Gallerie Burchard,
    1920), 236–237, 238
public, 148–154
Pyrine, Monsieur, 228, 239
Pythagoreans, the, 151
Pythian, Fourth (poem by Pindar),
    253–254

Quintilian, 220

Raatzsch, Richard, 12–19, 24, 138
Rabelais, François, 45, 78
Rand, Ayn, 83
ratio, 262
rationality, 58–59, 61, 103, 130–144, 179,
    195, 225, 264, 266, 269, 271
Rawls, John, 14, 15, 17, 21, 81–84, 99–101,
    115
Rawlsianism, 12
Ray, Man, 232
Reagan, Ronald, 82–83, 256
realism, 12–14, 21, 25–50
reason, 7, 13, 18, 21, 25, 56–57, 100–101,
    104, 109, 112–115, 190, 263, 265, 267,
    269, 270, 275
reasonable, the, 5, 13, 22, 39, 49, 69, 76,
    80, 100–102, 104, 143, 181
Rechtsphilosophie (i.e., *Grundlinien der
    Philosophie des Rechts*, work by G. W. F.
    Hegel), 150
Regulus, 273–274
relativity/relativism, 28–50
religion, 3, 54, 77, 80, 137, 148, 185–187,
    189, 204, 272–272
Republic, Roman. *See* Rome
Republic, The (dialogue by Plato), 165,
    169
research, 152–153
revolution, 8, 64–65, 74–78, 88, 168–169,
    228–229
rhetoric, 3, 149, 218
Rhetorica (work by Aristotle), 171,
    174–175
rights, 14–15, 24, 72, 88, 154, 161,
    163–166, 187–188, 190, 200, 254,
    265–267

Rome, 86, 89, 107, 124, 150, 177, 184–188,
    194, 218–221, 261–262, 273–274
rules, 19, 44, 53–54, 57, 62, 88, 94,
    108–109, 111–113, 135, 169, 186, 189,
    201, 234–235, 251, 264
Rumsfeld, Donald, 225, 256

Saddam Hussein, 34–38, 224–225
Sartre, Jean-Paul, 76, 81, 125, 127, 145
satire, 218–225
Schaub, Jörg, 20–21
science, 1, 52–53, 55, 148, 153, 160
simony, 204–206
sin, 33–34, 113, 210–211, 261–263
skepticism, 23, 88, 156, 201, 204,
    227–228
La société du spectacle (book by Guy
    Debord), 81
Socrates, 21, 57–63, 129–130, 151, 184
Stalin, Joseph, 275
state, the, 81, 100, 143, 151, 155–156, 168,
    180, 190–191, 200–202
Strauss-Kahn, Domenique, 258
Summa theologiae (work by Thomas
    Aquinas), 204
sustainability, 138–139
Swift, Jonathan, 222
Symposium (dialogue by Plato), 269, 271

Tabitha, 224
Tacitus, 86–87, 220
Tatlin, Vladimir, 228–229
Thatcher, Margaret, 82–83, 134, 155
Themistocles, 150
theodicy, 87, 276
Theognis, 206–209
Theogony (poem by Hesiod). *See* Hesiod
theology, 3, 23, 30, 33–35, 235, 275
theories, 1–2, 5–7, 10, 16–17, 19–21,
    88–93, 96, 109–112, 149, 152–153
Theory of Justice (book by John Rawls),
    81–84, 99–101
Thomas Aquinas, 204, 215
titles, 244–246
totality, 7, 21, 101–102
Traître, Un (novel by Domenique Jamet),
    259
tranquility, 51–56, 61–63
transcendence, 21, 45
de trinitate (work by Augustine), 263, 269
Trotsky, Leon, 53

Tzara, Tristan (pseudonym of Sami
    Rosenstock), 227–228, 233–237

*Über die Unmöglichkeit einer philosophischen
    Theodizee* (tract by Kant), 277
universities, 148–158, 258
utopia, 3–5, 22
Utopia (book by Thomas More), 4
utopian impulses, x
utopianism, 25, 26, 28, 42–50, 155, 166,
    169, 226

value/value-judgment, 26, 49, 66–67, 82,
    93, 95, 204
Verres, Gaius, 185, 189

vice, 204, 272–273
virtue, 204, 272–273
Voltaire, 221

Wagner, Richard, 159
wants. *See* desires
Weber, Max, 26, 134, 140
Who Owns Antiquity? (book by James
    Cuno), 184, 189–203
Wilhelm Meister, 159
Williams, Bernard, x, 25, 253, 276
witch doctor, 14–15
Wittgenstein, Ludwig, 18, 19, 20, 21, 271
work, 68–69, 77, 135, 143, 164
Wotan, 130, 141